MW01254444

Why EMP Protection?

(EMP = Electromagnetic Pulse)

- Get "free" electricity for 20 years — both before and after an EMP event.

- Increase in property values and property taxes because of influx of security-minded individuals, families communities and companies.

- Can be 100% financed and/or you can buy County investment bonds.

- EMP protection for security, waterfront escape cottages, homes, and buildings with solar rooftops.

- Get lifestyle insurance, similar in concept to flood or hurricane damage, but far, far better on Investment Returns.

- Helps generate new products & services, thereby creating millions of new jobs.

- A great opportunity to pay down the $18 trillion national debt through job creations.

What does this mean?

A better lifestyle for you, your family and your community!

Treatise Abstract

This book is a consolidation and update of our four other books on EMP protection plus substantial, newly-added how-to-do-its, most of which are not yet on the Internet, and ways and means.

To make a long overdue, national EMP protection happen, applied *Bottom-up Management* is executed at the county level. Yes, the fed and states have their respective contributing missions and goals, too.

Major protection advances are presented from shielding, bonding, grounding, surge suppression. filtering and site test and certification. Then, they are applied at family, residential, commercial, industrial and electric-utility levels. Vehicle protection and long-range (over 400 miles) vitals replenishments methodology are developed.

Presented are comprehensive and secure workable protection programs with options and rationale, new products and services, financing, ways and means, that generate millions of new jobs over the next decades.

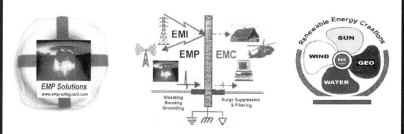

Summary of this Treatise

EMP Protection Plans & Options do not yet exist for America. Although the Internet is replete with Electromagnetic Pulse (EMP) articles, media, videos, etc. and its cataclysmic outcome is well known, no national EMP protection plan is yet available. Since the abdication of the Government's EMP fiduciary responsibility of protection plans continue, the EMP Survivalist and Preppers have already prepared for their own limited survival. Limited, because they are usually without electricity, have post-EMP burned-out electronics, and nearly everything doesn't work.

Survival with some degree of recovered lifestyle, greatly increases with (1) EMP preparation size in groups (circle-the wagon concept) instead of limited to a single family with no one else to share the loads, costs and survival, (2) long-distance provisioning for vitals replenishments, and (3) protected operational solar rooftops for electricity for lighting, water pumps, fans, communications, etc.

Central to our EMP protection plan is county-level government because of its resources to construct EMP protection on homes and buildings, utilities, communications, and selected infrastructure. Also, a big need to raise awareness to train HOA (Home Owners Association) members and residents about real-estate development of EMP protected cottages. Most units can have an adjacent-connected structure for vehicle EMP shielding, a golf cart, and space for a vegetable garden.

The major plan, is orchestrated at the state level and executed at the county level in two phases. Phase I, lasting two years, is the building of eight EMP protected villages in different parts of the country (one or two can be constructed with fed funds if the location is adjacent to a DoD or DoE field laboratory). A museum and training theater at each location allows visitors from other counties to become knowledgeable and trained. This activity develops the prototypes or templates for nationwide EMP protection, and raises awareness with brochures, planning documents, webinars, radio and TV talk shows.

Phase II, lasts for about eight years and implements EMP protection for a thousand or more counties (out of a total 3,142 US counties) utilizing lessons learned during Phase I. Financing is mostly from the sale of local county and some corporate bonds (no fed subsidies needed). Perhaps half of the homeowners will have a small EMP protected escape cottage averaging $50k/site. (Remember, each site gets "free" electricity). This investment (also serving as an escape, weekend entertainment center) costs about $3 trillion for national participation. This also generates new products and services and produces about 43 million job-years or average 5.4 million jobs per year for eight years – a truly win-win-win situation.

Disclaimer

Estimates and projections contained herein are prepared by EMP Solutions, LLC and Renewable Energy Creations, (SREC) and are based on information currently available (Feb, 2015) and that developed by SREC. The latter involves many visits and discussions, many engineering and economic calculations, subjective value judgments and analysis. While believed sound, no representation or assurance is made as to their accuracy or attainability.

The author tried to contact engineers and others in the EMC (electromagnetic compatibility) community. Few of these professionals provide information contained in this handbook. It is believed the reason may be that EMP protection details are classified because of restrictions placed on Department of Defense and other related activities performed by EMC contractors. This book has been written without the benefit of any kind of access to classified information.

Further, recognize that the protection of a home, building, or solar-PV installation is a function of many (roughly 30) variables. Thus, it is nearly impossible to generalize performance and predict accurate future outcome. While several product photos are shown, courtesy of a named company or other source, this does not mean that that product is manufactured for EMP application. Rather, it is representative of the product, with some modification, that may be used for EMP protection of homes, buildings and their solar installations. Thus, it is concluded that this book is a protection catalyst for an EMP attack that is deemed inevitable. As the Boy Scout motto says, "Be Prepared." So, do your own due diligence.

Finally, recognize while severe geomagnetic storms and cyber attacks on the power grid could be dysfunctional beyond anything U.S. residents have ever faced, they fall far short of the cataclysmic impact of an effective nuclear EMP attack.

About 60% of the 197 images (illustrations) used in this book are developed by the author, especially tables, spreadsheets, drawings, sketches, diagrams, charts, and graphs. However, some photos pose a problem. For example, *Tine ye*, an Internet inverse image search engine site allows the user to search for sources of photos from their 2.5 billion inventory. On the Swiss chalet with solar rooftop, for example, they produced 106 hits – making it impossible to identify the real and original source for credit. Thus, some source photos are unknown and cannot be credited.

—————————————————————————————————

Printed in the United States of America
Library of Congress PCN: (in process)
Library of Congress Cataloging-in-Publication Date:
Library of Congress Card Number: (in process)
ISBN-13: 978-1508839675
ISBN-10: 1508839670

Acknowledgments from the Publisher

This book, *EMP Protection Plans & Options,* is based on civil morality, capitalistic growth objectives, and scientific and engineering principles. This book is dedicated to the Glory of God – the only Author of Truth. Truth is difficult to practice by mankind due to our limited vantage point, selfish attitudes, and frequently biased presentations of facts.

The humble Greek philosopher, Diogenes of Sinope, walked throughout Athens carrying a lantern in daylight, searching for, but not finding, an honest man.

This book falls short of providing all relevant and meaningful facts about EMP protection. Yet, with the author's wealth of experience in the EMC (Electromagnetic Compatibility) arena (authoring 16 books in this and the EMP field) – the practices of electromagnetic shielding, bonding, grounding, and cable/ connector surge suppression and filtering for EMI control are brought to bear to help EMP protect our civilization and modern infrastructure from this threat.

The publisher will contribute most of the profits from the sale of this book to charity including *Grace Presbyterian Church* of Lake Suzy, FL USA, the *Wounded Warrior* Project, and *Son-Light Power,* a small solar installation company that, for free, brings both solar electricity and the Bible to schools, clinics and churches in impoverished locations in Central America and Africa.

Contents

If we have made no errors, we have made no decisions

How to Use This Book

First a prologue statement: About 20% of this book will inspire most readers to new and creative accomplishment depending on your management-doer level and your topic(s) of responsibility. The rest of the book completes the mission *(EMP Protection Plans & Options)* to be optimized. So, read, learn, plan, apply, act, measure results, and prosper. If you don't win by at least $10,000 plus significantly help and benefit fellow man, ask for your money back.

There are several features and subjects about this book the reader should know in order to maximize the benefits in his areas of concern, interest, and responsibility.

• This book covers topics from overall benefit of a specific national EMP protection plan orchestrated at the county level, cost and how to finance, down to the openings per inch best for a thin-film, solar panel screen, EMP-protection material. So there is a wide spread of material herein for nearly anyone having a part time or full time connection or is tasked to do some facet of EMP protection with mitigation of lifestyle loss.

• About 4% of the total images (photos, drawings, sketches, spreadsheets, tables, charts, diagrams, graphs) are repeated in more than one chapter. The reason is that the subject, (usually a table) is both referred to as well as used in two or more chapter topics. Otherwise, making the reader go back to its earlier first display is wasteful of the reader's time and tends to disrupt his chain of thought fingering through pages. Therefore, seeing an image more than once does not mean accidental repetition of the original material.

• When a topic gets quite technical, or uses numbers and several math symbols or too involved for most readers, we plant a man with a digging shovel in the left margin (dig deeper now). This means the paragraph(s) may be somewhat difficult for the lay to follow and can be skipped unless one wants to dig deeper. Regrettably, USA ranks 23rd in global nations on math and science.

• This book has, perhaps, 5 to 20 times (i.e., 197 illustrations) as many images as most books of this ilk that the reader is familiar with. This tends to slow down reading. But if "a picture is equal to a thousand words", this book just grew from 275 pages to over 800 pages. And. you will finish up much more knowledgeable and replete with ideas, especially when most illustrative tables are unique (first time ever presented, except maybe in another recent book by the author).

• Many of the things discussed herein are not yet covered in other sources because (1) the author has created or suggested solution options, (2) they may be classified, or (3) the author has spent most of his professional years working on solutions or technically forecasting physical realizability with a high batting average.

• About the "he" or "she" (him or her) thing in writing and speaking, it is a waste of time and distraction from the points being made. Correct English years ago was "he" or "him" which is understood to mean either sex, as applicable. The author follows the correct English. Another, even worse offense, is speaking of a single person and in the next sentence saying. "Instead **they** suggested....." Who is they? Nearly all the major American newspapers and other publications are guilty of this bad English. Just ask a foreigner who has another language as his major.

• The words, "political correct" are an invention of the devil and are not used in this book. These words are far worse than cursing or swearing, since they are attempting to give morality, honesty or trustworthiness to an intention designed to do otherwise. Rather, "To thine own self be true. And, it must follow, as the night the day, thou canst not then be false to any man." (Shakespeare). Trust is earned – not granted.

Lessons learned: Focus on problem solutions – not problem aggrandizement. Practice "positive accountability" = the art of making things happen – not why they didn't.

• Warning and caution regarding the first EMP event. It has been nearly 70 years since an Atomic bomb was dropped on Nagasaki and Hiroshima, Japan, rapidly ending WWII. The cold war with Russia ended after 40 years of a standoff that, if an EMP event had happened, would have been cataclysmic - making 9/11 or Pearl Harbor like a cakewalk. But, with hundreds of nuclear weapons missing and thousands available following the USSR breakup plus other uncertain developments plus the growing of radicals from lone-wolf types to no-go zones participants, it is only time. What is your family, neighborhood, community, county, state or country doing to practice the wisdom in the boy-scout motto which is "be prepared" in regards to this threat?

The Bottom Line

Knowing that many readers may be impatient or in a hurry, this book offers seven take aways at the end of the day:

(1)- On anti-missile-laser defense, go into production and placement as earlier planned, but held up by the present administration..

(2)- Replacing the present admin with leadership will do most to achieve the mission objectives. Lessons learned: modify the constitution or whatever so that future presidential candidates must first have had five years of successful experience as a corporate officer of a large company with international sales.

(3)- Employ *Bottom-up Management*, where the rubber meets the road, for seeking and achieving missions & goals. Get leadership and employ positive accountability.

(4)- Focus on post-EMP lifestyle, since nearly everything else is lost. A high score goes to suburban/rural Communities of EMP protected cottages with solar rooftops, each around a small lake with an "electronic security fence" The unit cost and lifestyle loss are relatively low. They are second inexpensive and nearby homes with "free" pre- and post-EMP electricity and weekend entertainment.

(5)- About 150, 4,000 ft. mat-covered, dirt runways, on the outskirts of towns and cities (not having airports) to provide timely vitals replenishments by Globemaster III cargo aircraft, or equivalent.

(6)- For commercial and industrial buildings, under about five stories, their solar rooftops and the rest of applicable infrastructure, use the EMP protection materials and techniques described herein.

(7)- For motor vehicles, apply the recommended practices for government standards; manufacturer wiring and microprocessor protection, test & certification; and EMP protection of vehicle parking structures.

(8)- Hardening the electric grid with the latest version of the earlier Shield Act. This was not addressed in this book as there are other larger and more qualified companies involved.

Chapter 1

Solar Flares, HEMP, Cyber & HPM Events

Chapter Overview

This chapter addresses three sources of electromagnetic radiation that can disrupt or destroy electronics activities on the ground in areas from less than one square mile (2.6 sq. km) up to 10 million sq miles (26 M sq. km.) or more. The least is HPM for high power microwave used primarily for military combat applications.

The second, far more powerful source, is known as Solar Flares, which are radiations from the sun during active periods of sun spots. Solar Flares produce Geo-Magnetic Storms (GMS) that can disrupt the electric grid, knocking out electricity that, in the worst case, can destroy substation transformers over extended areas, unless they are protected. However, GMS will not destroy electronic devices and electrical/ electronic systems unless they are directly connected to long conductors such as a long electrical transmission lines, telephone or fuel pipelines.

The third electromagnetic radiation threat, by far the most damaging, is HEMP that stands for High altitude Electromagnetic Pulse (shortened to EMP for brevity in articles, books and discussions). A nuclear bomb burst above about 20 miles (32 km) in altitude can impact most of the East or West coast of USA affecting 90 million people. They do not feel the impact and there is no physical damage to infrastructure. But, people are instantly thrown back to the 1870 dark ages with no electricity, no running water nor sewage disposal; no communications, radio and TV and many damaged vehicles.

Relatively new are cyber terrorism and direct attacks on electric grid substations, discussed herein.

This chapter focuses on defining the threat amplitude and victim susceptibility so the amount of EMP protection is defined for later solution-oriented chapters.

Note: The reader already familiar with Solar Flares may wish to skip this section of Chapter 1. The reader who is also familiar with the Electromagnetic Pulse, EMP, may also wish to move directly to Chapter 2, *The EMP Threat and Countermeasures* or directly to Chapter 3, on an *Overview of the National EMP Protection Plan..*

1.1- Solar Flares and Geo-Magnetic Storms

In the early stages of the work of the United States EMP Commission, the chairman of the Commission realized that nuclear EMP causes some of the same problems as geomagnetic storms which are caused by solar activity.

1.1.1- Impact on the Electric Grid

Nuclear EMP (discussed in the next section) is actually a multi-pulse consisting of 3 components. These are called E1, E2 and E3. The E1 pulse is the *radioflash* pulse that is so destructive to electronics. The E3 component of nuclear EMP, however, is a much slower pulse, lasting several seconds to a few minutes that is caused by movement of the Earth's magnetic field. Geomagnetic storms (GMS) have a similar effect to nuclear E3.

However, both solar-induced GMS and nuclear E3 only affect infrastructure having long lines. This includes the electric power grid and wired telecommunications lines. The most susceptible component here is the power-grid transformers at the ends of long-power lines. (long-wired telephone lines today are largely replaced by unaffected fiber-optic lines). Transformers are made to handle AC (alternating current at 50 or 60 Hz.), something that they do quite well.

Geomagnetically induced currents, however, (whether from a nuclear detonation or a GMS) are nearly DC (direct current such as a battery produces). These direct currents play havoc with a power grid designed for AC, and especially with the transformers. Transformers will overheat with a relatively small amount of direct current. A number of power grid transformers have failed and become unrepairable as a result of GMS. The GMS of late October and early November of 2003 quickly destroyed 14 transformers in the power grid of South Africa.

To protect the electric grid from a GMS, special surge suppression is needed at the point(s) of failure at the power generation, step-up. and step-down transformers at substations.

While both EMP and a severe GMS, may take out the electric grid in a designated area, a GMS would not immediately disrupt transportation and would result in essentially all electronics and electrical devices still in working condition. If the food and water grocery stores, pharmacies and gasoline stations, have back-up generators, then life is severely curtailed but not as depicted here with an unprotected nuclear EMP incident.

The illustration below presents an overview of the general impact of a nuclear EMP incident vs. a GMS, although, unless protected, the GMS can destroy a substation transformer servicing a long transmission line. As mentioned above, a GMS has a very-low frequency radiation (in other words, a long wavelength, nearly a

Fig. 7.11 - General identification of EMP and Solar Flare threats and survivors

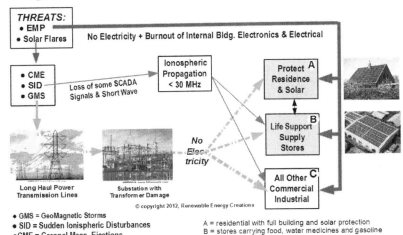

DC signal, coupling mostly into very long, high-voltage power transmission lines. Since a building may have wires not longer than 500 feet (0.1 miles), a GMS couples into a building with a level of (0.1mi/100mi) = 0.1% of the level of a long power line. For a private home with 50 foot (0.01 miles) long wires, a GMS couples into homes and internal devices with less than 0.01mi/100mi = 0.01% of the level of long transmission lines.

Thus, a small portable electric or electronic device, not connected to the grid, would pick up only a minuscule voltage from a GMS and therefore would not be damaged.

There are about 2,000 large transformers in the USA rated 345 kV or above, about 18,000 generating plants rated 20 MW or above, and about 14,000 large (10+ transmission lines each) substations in the United States. Until very recently, no large transformers had been produced in the U.S. for decades. Worldwide production capacity for these units, which are built to order and take 12 to 18 months to manufacture, is under 100 per year, with most going to China and India. It takes three years from when the order is placed for a large transformer, for it to finally be delivered on site.

The U.S. replaces about 20 of its large transformers every year. So a loss of even 10% or 20% of the large transformers in the U.S. would take several years of worldwide production to make good, with no assurance that foreign manufacturers would give the U.S. priority over orders for other customers already in the pipeline. The two U.S. plants that have recently started production could not produce those transformers if the power grid were down;

[According to a study by Metatech Corporation, a storm with a strength comparative to that of 1921 would destroy more than 300 transformers and 130 million people would be without power (a cost totaling several trillion dollars.)] A massive geomagnetic storm could knock out electric power in large sections of the grid for months. This statement should be contrasted with a single EMP incident above 50 miles altitude which, in addition to destroying many transformers in the electrical grid, destroys the electronic contents of millions of buildings and may leave millions of vehicles dysfunctional in their tracks.

By receiving geomagnetic storm alerts and warnings (for example, by the Space Weather prediction Center; via Space Weather satellites as SOHO or ACE), power companies can minimize damage to power transmission equipment by momentarily disconnecting transformers or by inducing temporary blackouts. Preventative measures also exist, including preventing the inflow of geomagnetically induced currents into the grid through the neutral-to-ground connection.

1.1.2- GPS Impact on Satellites & Gas/Oil Pipelines Navigation Systems

Systems such as GPS and, LORAN are adversely affected when solar activity disrupts their signal propagation. GPS signals are affected when solar activity causes sudden variations in the density of the ionosphere, causing the GPS signals to scintillate (like a twinkling star).

Satellite Hardware Damage

GMS and increased solar ultraviolet mission heat Earth's upper atmosphere, causing it to expand. The heated air rises, and the density at the orbit of satellites up to about 1,000 km (621mi) increases significantly. This results in increased drag on satellites in space, causing them to slow and change orbit slightly. At low Earth orbits, they slowly fall, and eventually burn up in the Earth's atmosphere.

Skylab is an example of a spacecraft reentering Earth's atmosphere prematurely in 1979 as a result of higher-than-expected solar activity. During the great GMS of March 1989, four of the Navy's navigational satellites had to be taken out of service for up to a week, the US Space Command had to post new orbital elements for over 1,000 objects affected, and the Solar Maximum Mission satellite fell out of orbit in December the same year. The vulnerability of the satellites depends on their position as well. The South Atlantic Anomaly is a perilous place for a satellite to pass through.

As technology has allowed spacecraft components to become smaller, their miniaturized systems have become increasingly vulnerable to the more energetic solar particles. These particles can cause physical damage to microchips and can change software commands in satellite-borne computers.

Gas and Oil Pipelines

Rapidly fluctuating geomagnetic fields can produce induced currents in pipelines. This can cause multiple problems for pipeline engineers. Flow meters in the pipeline can transmit erroneous flow information, and the corrosion rate of the pipeline is dramatically increased. If engineers incorrectly attempt to balance the current during a geomagnetic storm, corrosion rates may increase even more. Once again, pipeline managers thus receive space weather alerts and warnings to allow them to implement defensive measures.

1.1.3- References #1:

[1] "A Perfect Storm of Planetary Proportions" IEEE *Spectrum*. 2012-02. Retrieved 2012-02-13.

[2} Natuurwetenschap & Techniek Magazine, June 2009

[3]
http://192.211.16.13/curricular/ENERGY/0708/articles/solar/SolarForecast07SkyTel.pdf
Solar Forecast: Storm AHEAD

[4] Severe Space Weather Events: Understanding Societal and Economic Impacts

[5] Metatech Corporation Study

[6] Severe Space Weather Events: Understanding Societal and Economic Impacts: a Workshop
Report. Wash. D.C.: National Academies, 2008 web Nov. 2011. Pages 78, 105, & 106

[7] "Massive solar flare 'could paralyse Earth in 2013'". The Daily Mail. September 21, 2010.

1.2- Cyber Terrorism of the Electric Grid

What is Cyber Terrorism?

Cyberterrorism is the use of the Internet-based attacks in terrorist activities, including acts of deliberate, large-scale disruption of computer networks, especially of personal computers attached to the Internet, by the means of tools such as computer viruses. (Wikipedia).

(Ed. DW Note: A computer connected to the *Internet* is not a necessary condition. Laptop computers (and some others) have wireless transception capabilities. Thus, unless operated in a shielded or other EMP protested area, computers can pick up troubling radiations from without. The cyber radiation software could also contain a time or event-delayed activation from a sleep mode. For example, unless otherwise protected, a blackout event-cascading command might be given on New-Years eve at 11:59 P.M., or whatever for later activation.

WASHINGTON – The head of the NSA issued a blunt warning, 20 November 2014 Thursday to lawmakers: China can shut down the United States.

The grim assessment came from Admiral Michael Rogers, the director of the National Security Agency and commander of the U.S Cyber Command.

Rogers said he believed China along with "one or two" other countries had the capability to successfully launch a cyber-attack that could shut down the electric grid in parts of the United States. Rogers reiterated that if the U.S. remains on the defensive, it would be a "losing strategy."

Speaking to the House Intelligence Committee, the NSA director said the cyber threat was "so real," and that agreeing to an international code, a sort of "laws of law" in the cyber realm is urgent. The possibility of such cyber attacks by U.S. adversaries has been widely known, but never confirmed publicly by the nation's top cyber official.

At a House hearing, Rogers says U.S. adversaries are performing electronic "reconnaissance," on a regular basis so that they can be in a position to attack the industrial control systems that run everything from chemical facilities to water treatment plants.

Outside experts say the U.S. Cyber Command also has that capability, which in theory should amount to mutual deterrence.

Dec. 19, 2014, (Reuters) – U.S. President   vowed on Friday to respond to a devastating cyber attack on Sony Pictures that he blamed on North Korea, and scolded the Hollywood studio for caving in to what he described as a foreign dictator imposing censorship in America.

Obama said the cyber attack caused a lot of damage to Sony but that the company should not have let itself be intimidated into halting the public release of "The Interview," a lampoon portraying the assassination of North Korean leader Kim Jong Un.

"We will respond," Obama told an end-of-year news conference. "We'll respond proportionally, and we'll respond in a place and time and manner that we choose."

1.3.- Electromagnetic Pulse (EMP)

EMP in a surface level nuclear explosion was observed in the very first nuclear test in July, 1945. In fact, it had been predicted just before that first nuclear test by the physicist Enrico Fermi.

The official technical history of the project that produced that first nuclear explosion states, "All signal lines were completely shielded, in many cases doubly shielded. In spite of this many records were lost because of spurious pickup at the time of the explosion that paralyzed the recording equipment."

\EMP continued to be a problem during the nuclear tests of all nuclear-capable countries. In Great Britain, nuclear EMP during the early years of testing was called "radioflash." In many ways, radioflash is a much more descriptive term and better understood by non-technical people since nuclear EMP is an extremely intense flash of radio energy over a broad range of frequencies.

To compare the EMP radioflash with the energy density of a flash of visible light, a flash of light of the same energy density would be more than 6,000 times the typical total energy density of sunlight at noon on a bright sunny day.

Nuclear explosions at ground level produce an EMP that is much different than nuclear explosions at high altitude. The EMP of a near-surface level nuclear explosion is generally dangerous only within the area that experiences intense blast effects (e.g: Nagasaki and Hiroshima, Japan, just before the end of WWII). An exception to this is that wires extending outward from the blast area can conduct the EMP induced in the wires for many miles outside of the blast zone.

The real danger with nuclear EMP comes from the effects of high-altitude EMP. A high-altitude nuclear explosion produces an electromagnetic pulse that is generated in the mid-stratosphere in what is called the source region (since it is the source of the EMP). The source region is a part of the mid-stratosphere that is 20 to 40 kilometers up (about 12 to 24 miles above sea level).

The first openly published report of the effects of high-altitude EMP came in the report of the helium-balloon launched Hardtack-Yucca test which occurred on April 28, 1958. The technical report of that test reported results that were completely unexpected and too large and too fast to be measured accurately.

In 1962, the widely-reported Starfish Prime nuclear test burned out the fuses of 300 streetlights in Honolulu at the instant of the nuclear explosion 897 miles away. Starfish Prime also set off numerous burglar alarms and knocked out a telephone company microwave link that provided service to the island of Kauai.

Later in 1962, the Soviet Union (which had also experienced lots of problems with the EMP phenomenon) tested 3 nuclear weapons in space over Kazakhstan, which was then a Soviet Republic. The Soviets attached instruments to some of the Kazakhstan infrastructure to measure the induced EMP level. They were particularly interested in the effects of a 350-mile long overhead telephone line.

That telephone line was divided into sub-lines of 24 to 48 miles in length, with each sub-line connected by repeaters and protected by fuses and gas-filled, over-voltage protectors. During the Soviet high-altitude nuclear test of October 22, 1962, all of the over voltage protectors fired and all of the fuses blew across the entire length of the 350-mile long telephone line.

In addition, the nuclear EMP shut down a 600-mile long underground electric power cable and caused a major fire at the power plant in Karaganda, Kazakhstan.

On overhead power lines, the Soviet scientists reported major problems with the insulators that support the high-voltage transmission lines. A report written for Oak Ridge National Laboratory states, "Power line insulators were damaged, resulting in a short circuit on the line and some lines detaching from the poles and falling to the ground."

The exact cause of the extremely high level of EMP from a high-altitude nuclear explosion remained a mystery until 1963 when Los Alamos physicist Conrad Longmire was given the EMP results of the Kingfish and Bluegill Triple Prime nuclear tests of October, 1962. Longmire immediately deduced what was causing the high intensity and other characteristics of high-altitude EMP.

At first, other physicist were skeptical of Longmire's new theory, but after working through the problem for themselves, they became convinced that Longmire was right.

From 1963 through 2001, work continued intensely within the defense sector of the United States to develop methods for protecting against high-altitude EMP. Other countries, even many without nuclear weapons, began protecting much of their military sector against EMP. Some countries even began protecting some of their civilian infrastructure.

In the United States, however, essentially nothing was being done about EMP in the civilian sector. By 1999, however, many people were beginning to become increasingly concerned about EMP in the civilian infrastructure as electronics became increasingly deeply embedded in the infrastructure of the United States and the newer electronics were even more sensitive to the effects of EMP.

Between 1999 and 2001, concerns about the vulnerability of the United States to EMP were starting to be addressed at hearings before the U.S. Congress. In 2001, Congress established the Commission to Assess the Threat to the United States from Electromagnetic Pulse (EMP) Attack. This Commission is more commonly known as just *The EMP Commission.*

The EMP Commission remained active from 2001 until 2008. It released a number of important reports. Some of them remain classified. A basic unclassified report was issued in 2004, and another more important and more detailed report was issued in

2008. The 2008 report was called the *Critical National Report.* This was a very detailed report on many aspects of the infrastructures of the United States upon which the residents of the United States depend for a multitude of functions critical to the maintenance of their lives and their well being.

All of the critical infrastructures in industrialized countries depend most critically on electricity. Very gradually during the 20th century, electricity evolved from a convenience to a necessity for human life. This evolution from convenience to necessity occurred so gradually that few people even noticed. Our pre-electric infrastructure is nearly all gone. Also, nearly all of the knowledge needed to operate a pre-electric infrastructure has been lost. Basic living in a 19th century infrastructure is something that most of us would have to learn starting from the fundamentals of how to grow and process our own food to how to properly dispose of all of our own waste. Even the daily water supply for nearly all of us requires electric pumps, which are usually also controlled by electronic circuitry that is very sensitive to EMP.

Since the EMP Commission was dissolved in 2008, other serious concerns about EMP have arisen. One of these concerns was about the dependence of nuclear power plants upon external sources of electricity for pumping cooling water in the event of an emergency shutdown. This problem was identified well before the Fukushima Daiichi nuclear catastrophe in the aftermath of the 2011 earthquake and tsunami, but the Fukushima accident highlighted the vulnerability of nuclear power plants to EMP.

There are 104 nuclear power plants in the United States that could suffer the same fate as the Fukushima reactors, and it would all happen at the same time with a large-scale EMP event. Because of this possibility, the United States Nuclear Regulatory Commission is considering a requirement to extend the on-site diesel fuel requirement for nuclear power plants to include at least a two-year fuel supply at each reactor for the backup diesel generators. This requirement should be extended to include a requirement for EMP protection of the standby generator control and transfer circuits.

1.4- U.S. Government EMP Preparations

The U.S. Department of Defense (DoD), portions of the Pentagon, the Intelligence Agencies and other selected government office buildings and site locations have had their infrastructure EMP hardened. Tens of billions of dollars have been so spent to insure the government can still function in the event of a nuclear event. This also applies to most U.S. Navy warships. *With few exceptions, clearly, no such preparedness exists for any civilian sector.*

Threat Assessments Summary

EMP is an instantaneous, intense energy field that can overload or disrupt at a distance numerous electrical systems and high technology microcircuits, which are especially sensitive to power surges. A large scale EMP effect can be produced by a single nuclear explosion detonated high in the atmosphere. A similar, but far smaller-scale EMP effect can be created using non-nuclear devices with powerful batteries or reactive chemicals. This method is called *High Power Microwave* (HPM). Several nations, including reported sponsors of terrorism, may currently have a capability to use EMP as a weapon for cyber-warfare or cyber-terrorism to disrupt communications and other parts of the U.S. critical infrastructure. Also, some equipment and weapons used by the U.S. military may be vulnerable to the effects of EMP.

The threat of an EMP attack against the United States is hard to assess, but some observers indicate that it is growing along with worldwide access to newer technologies and the proliferation of nuclear weapons. In the past, the threat of mutually assured destruction provided a lasting deterrent against the exchange of multiple high-yield nuclear warheads. However, now even a single, low-yield nuclear explosion high above the United States, or over a battlefield, can produce a large-scale EMP effect that could result in a widespread loss of electronics, but no direct fatalities, and may not necessarily evoke a large nuclear retaliatory strike by the U.S. military. This, coupled with published articles discussing the vulnerability of U.S. critical infrastructure control systems, and some U.S. military battlefield systems to the effects of EMP, may create a new incentive for other countries to rapidly develop or acquire a nuclear capability.

Policy issues raised by this threat include (1) what is the United States doing to protect civilian critical infrastructure systems against the threat of EMP, (2) could the U.S. military be affected if an EMP attack is directed against the U.S. Civilian infrastructure, (3) are other nations now encouraged by U.S. vulnerabilities to develop or acquire nuclear weapons, and (4) how likely are terrorist organizations to launch a smaller-scale EMP attack against the United States?

Policy Analysis

Private Sector Vulnerability

What is the United States doing to protect critical infrastructure systems against the threat of electromagnetic pulse? What is the appropriate response from the United States to a nuclear EMP attack, where there may be widespread damage to electronics, but relatively little, or possibly no loss of life as a direct result? How could the United States determine which nation launched a EMP attack? After experiencing a EMP effect, the United States may retain its capability to use strategic weapons for nuclear retaliation, but will the U.S. industrial base and critical infrastructure be crippled and incapable of supporting a sustained military campaign? During such time, would the United States be capable of making an effective response should other nations chose to make military advances in other parts of the world?

Some assert that little has been done by the private sector to protect against the threat from electromagnetic pulse, and that commercial electronic systems in the United States could be severely damaged by either EMP or smaller-scale HPM. Officials of several U.S. power stations and public utilities have stated that their electrical systems currently have no protection against electromagnetic pulse. However, electric power and telephone utilities have been known to fail as a result of solar storms which cause effects similar to, but less severe than EMP from a nuclear blast. Commercial electronic surge arresters used for lightning strikes reportedly do not clamp fast enough to protect against the instantaneous effects

26

of the electromagnetic pulse, and some also may not have great enough current carrying capacity.

Military Vulnerability

The effects of large-scale EMP have been studied over several years by the Defense Atomic Support Agency, the Defense Nuclear Agency, and the Defense Special Weapons Agency, and is currently being studied by the Defense Threat Reduction Agency. However, the application of the results of these studies has been uneven across military weapons and communications systems. Some analysts state that U.S. strategic military systems (intercontinental ballistic missiles and long-range bombers) may have strong protection against EMP, while most U.S. weapons systems used for the battlefield do not, and that this uneven protection is undoubtedly known to our potential adversaries.

Some analysts reportedly state that limited testing has shown that modern commercial equipment may be surprisingly resistant to the effects of electromagnetic pulse, and in addition to the SCAMP system, some military systems using commercial equipment are retrofitted to increase resistance to EMP. However, there is disagreement among observers about whether test procedures used by the U.S. military may have been flawed, leading to erroneous conclusions about the effects of electromagnetic pulse on commercial electronics.

The U.S. military has adopted a policy where possibly vulnerable commercial electronic equipment is now used extensively in support of complex U.S. weapons systems. For example, a large percentage of U.S. military communications during Operation Iraqi Freedom was reportedly carried by commercial satellites, and much military administrative information is currently routed through the civilian Internet. Many commercial communications satellites, particularly those in low earth orbit, reportedly may degrade or cease to function shortly after a high altitude nuclear explosion. However, some observers believe that possible EMP and HPM vulnerabilities of military information systems are outweighed by the benefits gained through access to innovative technology and increased communications flexibility that come from using state-of-the-art electronics and from maintaining connections to the civilian Internet and satellite systems.

New Incentive to Develop a Nuclear Capability

A single nuclear device exploded at an appropriate altitude above the continental United States could possibly affect U.S. industrial capacity, economic stability, and military effectiveness. Does knowledge of this vulnerability, combined with the proliferation of nuclear technology, provide a newer incentive for potential adversaries to develop or acquire a nuclear weapons capability? Will countries now view the development and acquisition of nuclear weapons, even a small arsenal, as a strategy for cyber-warfare?

During the Cold War, an EMP attack was viewed as the first step of a nuclear exchange involving many warheads, but the threat of mutually assured destruction provided a lasting deterrent. Today, the proliferation of nuclear technology makes the threat of EMP more difficult to assess. Would the leader of a rogue state be motivated to use a small nuclear arsenal to launch a crippling EMP strike against the United States, with no resulting fatalities, if it believed the U.S. would likely not retaliate with a nuclear salvo that would destroy thousands, or millions of innocent people? Would a EMP strike over a disputed area during a regional conflict be seen as a way to defeat the communications links and network centric warfare capability of the U.S. military, and gain maximum battlefield advantage from an existing supply of smaller nuclear warheads?

Terrorist Use of HPM

A smaller-scale HPM weapon requires a relatively simple design, and can be built using electrical materials and chemical explosives that are easy to obtain. It is estimated that a limited-range suitcase-sized HPM weapon could be constructed for much less than

$2,000, and is within the capability of almost any nation, and perhaps many terrorist organizations.

Recently, DoD recruited a scientist to create two small HPM weapons for testing using only commercially available electrical components, such as ordinary spark plugs and coils. One device was developed that could be broken down into two parcels so it could be shipped by regular mail, for example, from one terrorist to another. The second HPM device was constructed to fit inside a small vehicle. Aside from specially-trained dogs, experts reportedly say there are no scientific methods that currently allow easy detection of an explosive device hidden in a vehicle or inside a suitcase before it can explode.

It is difficult to assess the threat of a terrorist organization possibly using a smaller-scale HPM weapon against the United States critical infrastructure. It could be argued that an HPM bomb by itself, may not be attractive to terrorists, because its smaller explosion would not be violent enough, and the visible effect would not be as dramatic as a larger, conventional bomb. Also, constructing an HPM device is still somewhat more technically complex than constructing a conventional bomb. However, observers have reported that the leadership of terrorist organizations may increasingly become aware of the growing advantages from an attack launched against U.S. critical information systems. In addition, the use by a terrorist group of a new weapon directed at U.S. information systems would attract widespread media attention, and may motivate other rival groups to follow along a new pathway.

Additionally, the explosives used in a smaller, or suitcase-sized HPM device could simultaneously be used to disperse radioactive materials, making it a so-called "dirty bomb". This combination would offer a possible two-for-one effect, where the dispersed radioactive materials could generate immediate near-panic, while the HPM-damaged computers might not be noticed until days later. This potential double effect could improve the attractiveness of using an HPM device as a terrorist weapon.

Champ, Robo Planes, Black Dart

Drones of the type used in Afghanistan with high explosives to take out terrorist and special targets can be equipped, instead, with HPM to burn-out enemy electronics on the ground. They radiate shorts bursts of microwave energy and their effective range is limited (classified) to, perhaps, one mile.

Since an adversary can use similar "robo planes", they must be disabled by ground-based or air platforms capable of knocking out the robo planes (burns out their electronics) with similar bursts of microwaves. Project Black Dart and others address these issues. However, they are beyond the scope of this book.

Objections

EMP and HPM energy weapons primarily damage electronic systems, with little or no direct effect on humans, however, these effects may also be difficult to limit or control. EMP or HPM energy fields, as they instantly spread outward, may also affect nearby hospital equipment or personal medical devices, such as heart pacemakers, and may damage critical electronic systems throughout other parts of the surrounding civilian infrastructure. For this reason, some international organizations may object to the development and use of EMP or HPM as weapons.

Legislative Activity

In 1997, the House National Security Committee held a hearing on the Threat Posed by Electromagnetic Pulse (EMP) to U.S. Military Systems and Civil Infrastructure, and in 1999, the House Military Research and Development Subcommittee held a hearing on the potential threats to United States civilian and military systems from an electromagnetic pulse attack.

A Commission to Assess the Threat from High Altitude Electromagnetic Pulse was established by Congress in FY2001 after several experts expressed concern that the U.S. critical infrastructure and military were vulnerable to EMP attack. Seven of the Commission members were appointed by the Secretary of Defense and two by the Director of the Federal Emergency Management Agency. On July 22, 2004, the Commission presented a report to the House Armed Services Committee, stating that EMP is capable of a causing catastrophe for the nation. However, the report, which focuses mainly on the effects of EMP and not necessarily on HPM, also states that such a catastrophe can be prevented by following recommendations made by the Commission.

Testimony during the presentation raised questions, such as: (1) how would the United States respond to a limited EMP attack against the U.S. homeland or against U.S. forces, where there is loss of technology, but no loss of life; (2) does the current lack of U.S. preparedness invite adversaries to plan and attempt an EMP attack; and (3) are the long-term effects of a successful EMP attack, leading to possible widespread starvation and population reduction, potentially more devastating to the U.S. homeland than an attack by surface nuclear weapons?

References 2:

1. Michael Sirak, "U.S. vulnerable to EMP Attack,"Janes's Defense Weekly, July 26, 2004.

2. Daniel G. DuPont, "Panel Says Society At Great Risk From Electromagnetic Pulse Attack,"Inside the Pentagon, July 15, 2004, p.1.

3. U.S. Congress, House Armed Services Committee, Committee Hearing on Com-mission to Assess the Threat to the United States from Electromagnetic Pulse Attack, July 22, 2004.

4. Stanley Jakarta, statement before the House Military Research and Development Subcommittee, hearing on EMP Threats to the U.S. Military and Civilian Infra-structure, Oct. 7, 1999.

Lowell Wood, Statement before the House Military Research and Development Subcommittee, hearing on EMP Threats to the U.S.

5.Military and Civilian Infrastructure, Oct. 7, 1999; Jack Spencer, "America's Vulnerability to a Different Nuclear Threat: An Electromagnetic Pulse," The Heritage Foundation Backgrounder, No.1372, May 26, 2000, p.6.; and Carlo Kopp, "The Electromagnetic Bomb: A Weapon of Electrical Mass Destruction," Air and Space Power,1993, [http://www.airpower.maxwell.af.mil/airchronicles/ kopp/ apjemp.html].

6. A nuclear explosion produces gamma rays, which interact with air molecules in a process called the Compton effect. Electrons are scattered at high energies which ionizes the atmosphere, generating a powerful electrical field. This EMP effect is strongest at altitudes above 30,000m, and lasts so briefly that current cannot start flowing through a human body to cause harm to people. [http://www.physics.northwestern.edu/classes/2001Fall/Phyx1352/19/emp.htm].

7. The Federation of American Scientists, "Nuclear Weapons EMP Effects," [http://www.fas.org/nuke/intro/nuke/emp.htm].

8. A Flux Compression Generator consists of explosives packed inside a cylinder, all of which is contained within a cylindrical copper coil structure. The explosive is detonated from rear to front, causing the tube to flare in a wave that touches the copper coil, which produces a moving short circuit. This compresses the magnetic field and creates an electromagnetic pulse that is emitted from the front end, which is then directed by a special focusing antenna. [http://www.physics.northwestern.edu/classes/2001Fall/Phyx1352/19/emp.htm].

9. Dr. Robert C. Harney, Naval Postgraduate School, Apr. 12, 2004, personal communication.

10. Victorino Matus, "Dropping the E-bomb," The Weekly Standard, Feb. 2, 2003.

11. William Graham, Electromagnetic Pulse Threats to U.S. Military and Civilian Infrastructure, hearing before the Military Research and Development Subcommittee, House Armed Services Committee, Oct. 7, 1999; and Carlo Kopp, "The Electromagnetic Bomb: A Weapon of Electrical Mass Destruction," Air and Space Power, 1993, at [http://www.airpower.maxwell.af.mil/airchronicles/kopp/apjemp.html].

12. [http://www.physics.northwestern.edu/classes/2001Fall/Phyx135-2/19/emp.htm].

13. Experts may disagree on whether the damaging effects of HPM actually diminish following the familiar inverse-square-of-the-distance rule. Michael Abrams, "The Dawn of the E-Bomb," IEEE Spectrum, Nov. 2003, [http://www.spectrum.ieee.org/WEBONLY/publicfeature/nov03/1103ebom.html].

Some experts state that the severity of HEMP effect depends largely on the bomb design, so a specially-designed low yield bomb may pose a larger HEMP threat than a high yield bomb. Lowell Wood, statement before the House Research and Develop-ment Subcommittee, hearing on EMP Threats to the U.S. Military and Civilian Infra-structure, Oct. 7, 1999.

14. Victorino Matus, "Dropping the E-bomb," The Weekly Standard, Feb. 2, 2003.

15. The Federation of American Scientists, "Nuclear Weapons EMP Effects," [http://www.fas.org/nuke/intro/nuke/emp.htm], and Report of the Commission to

Assess the Threat to the United States from Electromagnetic Pulse (EM₁ Attack, Vol.1: Executive Report 2004, p.5.

16. Kenneth R. Timmerman, "U.S. Threatened with EMP Attack," Insight on the News, May 28, 2001.

17. Lowell Wood, statement before the House Research and Development Subcommittee, hearing on EMP Threats to the U.S. Military and Civilian Infrastructure, Oct. 7, 1999.

18. Electrical systems connected to any wire or line that can act as an antenna may   be   disrupted. [http://www.physics.northwestern.edu/classes/2001Fall/Phyx135-2/19/emp.htm]. Army Training Manual 5-692-2, April 15, 2001, "Maintenance of Mechanical and Electrical Equipment at Command, Control, Communications, Computers, Intelligence, Surveillance, and Reconnaissance (C4ISR) Facilities, HEMP Protection Systems," Chapter 27, [http://www.usace.army.mil/publications/armytm/tm5-692-2/chap27VOL-2.pdf].

19. Lowell Wood, statement before the House Research and Development Subcommittee, hearing on EMP Threats to the U.S. Military and Civilian Infrastructure, Oct. 7, 1999.

20. Associated Press, "Experts Cite Electromagnetic Pulse as Terrorist Threat,"Las Vegas Review-Journal, Oct. 3, 2001.

21. Michael Abrams, "The Dawn of the E-Bomb,"IEEE Spectrum Online, Nov. 2003, [http://www.spectrum.ieee.org/WEBONLY/publicfeature/nov03/1103ebom.html].

Will Dunham, "U.S. May Debut Secret Microwave Weapon versus Iraq," Reuters, Feb. 2, 2003, [http://www.globalsecurity.org/org/news/2003/030202-ebomb01.htm].

1.5- U.S. Government EMP Specifications and Standards

Department of Defense MIL-STD-188-125-1 establishes minimum requirements and design objectives for high-altitude electro-magnetic pulse (EMP) hardening of fixed ground-based facilities that perform critical, time-urgent command, control, communications, computer, and intelligence (C4I) missions. The standard prescribes minimum performance requirements for low-risk protection from mission-aborting damage or upset due to HEMP environments. It also addresses minimum testing require-ments for demonstrating that prescribed performance has been

ℑ ... d and for verifying that the installed protection subsystem
... the operationally required hardness for the completed

Covered fixed ground-based facility types include subscriber terminals and data processing centers, transmitting and receiving communications stations, and relay facilities. Use of the standard for EMP protection of other ground-based communications-electronics facilities that require EMP hardening is also encouraged. The standard applies to both new construction and retrofit of existing facilities. Only local portions of facility interconnects are addressed. The standard implicitly assumes that survivable long-haul communications paths, fiber optic links, or other hardened interconnects between facilities will be provided as required for mission accomplishment. Uniform application of MIL-STD-188-125-1 requirements ensures balanced EMP hardening for all critical facilities in a network. *(It does not follow that these and other DoD specifications are properly applicable to the commercial world).*

MIL-STD-188-125-1 provides over 100 pages of detailed information on protecting ground-based facilities and equipment from the effects of high altitude EMP. In March 1999, the latest version of the US Department of Defense, MIL-STD-199-125-2 Interface Standard was issued. It is entitled, "High-Altitude, Electromagnetic Pulse (EMP) Protection for Ground Base C41 Facilities Performing Critical Time-urgent Missions, Part 2, Transportable Systems, AMSC N/A Area TCSS." The Forward states:

1.-This military standard is approved for use by all Departments and Agencies of the Department of Defense (DoD).

2.-Originally, Military Standard 188 (MIL-STD-188) covered technical standards for tactical and long-haul communications, but later evolved through revisions (MIL-STD-188A, MIL-STD-188B) into a document applicable to tactical communications only (MIL-STD-188C).

3. The Defense Information Systems Agency (DISA) published DISA circulars (DISAC) promulgating standards and engineering criteria applicable to the long-haul Defense Communication System and to the technical support of the National Military Command System.

4. As a result of a Joint Chiefs of Staff action, standards for all military communications are now being published in a MIL-STD-188 series of documents. The MIL-STD-188 series is subdivided into a MIL-STD-188-100 series, covering common standards for tactical and long-haul communications; a MIL-STD-188-200 series, covering standards for tactical communications only; and a MIL-STD-188-300 series, covering standards for long-haul communications only. Emphasis is being placed on developing common standards for tactical and long-haul communications, published in the MIL-STD-188-100 series.

5. This two-part document contains technical requirements and design objectives for EMP protection of ground-based systems and facilities that are nodes in EMP-hardened networks for performing critical and time-urgent command, control, communications, computer, and intelligence (C4I) missions. Part 1 of the document addresses EMP hardening for fixed facilities; this Part 2 addresses transportable systems. The requirements are stringent, in order to avoid both damage and functional upsets that prevent mission accomplishment within operationally prescribed timelines. The standards apply uniformly to all systems and facilities in the end-to-end chain, since disruption of a single node may result in network failure.

6. Performance, acceptance test, and verification test requirements are contained in the body of the standard. EMP-unique acceptance and verification test techniques are provided in their Appendices A, B, C, and D.

7. Implementation of MIL-STD-188-125-1 is supported by MIL-HDBK-423, "EMP Protection for Fixed and Transportable, Ground-Based Facilities. Among the EMP hardening tools and techniques are surge suppressors, shielding, and filtering and their grounding. These are discussed and applied in Chapter 6,

In summary, current High Altitude Electromagnetic Pulse (EMP)) Standards:

MIL-STD-188-125-1: *High Altitude Electromagnetic Pulse (EMP) Protection for Ground-Based C4I Facilities Performing Critical, Time Urgent Missions, Part 1, Fixed Facilities.*

MIL-STD-188-125-2: *High Altitude Electromagnetic Pulse (EMP) Protection for Ground-Based C4I Facilities Performing Critical, Time Urgent Missions, Part 2, Transportable Systems.*

MIL-HDBK-419: *Grounding, Bonding, and Shielding for Electronic Equipment and Facilities.*

MIL-HDBK-423: *High Altitude Electromagnetic Pulse (EMP) Protection for Fixed and Transportable Ground-Based Facilities, Vol. 1: Fixed Facilities.*

MIL-HDBK-423: High Altitude Electromagnetic Pulse (EMP) Protection for Fixed and Transportable Ground-Based Facilities, Vol. 2: Transportable Facilities.

References 3:

1. Broad, William J. "Nuclear Pulse (I): Awakening to the Chaos Factor," Science. 29 May 1981. Vol. 212, pp. 1009-1012

2. Broad, William J. "Nuclear Pulse (II): Ensuring Delivery of the Doomsday Signal," Science. 5 June 1981. Vol. 212 pp. 1116-1120

3. Broad, William J. "Nuclear Pulse (III): Playing a Wild Card," Science. 12 June 1981. Vol. 212. pp. 1248-1251

4. Bainbridge, K.T., Trinity (Report LA-6300-H), Los Alamos Scientific Laboratory. May 1976. Page 53.

5. Baum, Carl E., From the Electromagnetic Pulse to High-Power Electromagnetics. Proceedings of the IEEE, Vol.80, No. 6, pp. 789-817. June 1992.

6. Baum, Carl E., Reminiscences of High-Power Electromagnetics, IEEE Transactions on Electromagnetic Compatibility. Vol. 49, No. 2. pp. 211-218. May 2007.

7. Vittitoe, Charles N.,Did High-Altitude EMP Cause the Hawaiian Streetlight Incident?. Sandia National Laboratories. June 1989.

8. Longmire, Conrad L., "Fifty Odd Years of EMP", NBC Report, Fall/Winter, 2004. pp. 47-51. U.S. Army Nuclear and Chemical Agency.

9. Dyal, P., Air Force Weapons Laboratory. Report ADA995428. Operation Dominic. Fish Bowl Series. Debris Expansion Experiment. 10 December 1965. Page 15.

10. Rabinowitz, Mario (1987) Effect of the Fast Nuclear Electromagnetic Pulse on the Electric Power Grid Nationwide: A Different View. IEEE Transactions on Power Delivery, PWRD-2. pp. 1199-1222.

11. Longmire, Conrad L. Theoretical Notes - Note 353 - March 1985 - EMP on Honolulu from the Starfish Event. Mission Research Corporation.

12. Stephen Younger, et al. Scientific Collaborations Between Los Alamos and Arzamas-16 Using Explosive-Driven Flux Compression Generators. Los Alamos Science, No. 24, pp. 48-71, 1996.

13. Kompaneets, Aleksandr S., "Radio Emission from an Atomic Explosion". Journal of Experimental and Theoretical Physics, Vol. 35. December, 1958 (Russian-language publication)

14. Gilinsky, Victor. The Kompaneets Model for Radio Emission from a Nuclear Explosion. The Rand Corporation. August, 1964.

15. United States Central Intelligence Agency. National Intelligence Estimate. Number 11-2A-63. "The Soviet Atomic Energy Program." Page 44.

16. Defense Atomic Support Agency. ITR-1660(SAN) (Re-designated ADA369152). Operation Hardtack, Preliminary Report. 23 September 1959. (Also see the Chapter 10 pages on Yucca EMP measurements).

17. Armed Forces Special Weapons Project. Report ITR-1655 (Re-designated ADA322231). Operation of Balloon Carrier for Very-High-Altitude Nuclear Detonation. 25 July 1958.

18. Operation Hardtack High-Altitude Test Film, includes films of the Hardtack-Yucca balloon-launched 1.7 kiloton nuclear test, as well as the Redstone missile launched Hardtack-Teak and Hardtack-Orange 3.8 megaton high-altitude tests.

19. Defense Nuclear Agency. Report DNA 6038F. Operation Hardtack 1958

Although EMP does not directly destroy human life and infrastructure appearance, its range, time, and subtlety reach may be far more damaging than a ground-burst nuclear weapon.

Chapter 2
The EMP Threat and Countermeasures

Chapter Overview

This chapter addresses and quantifies the EMP threat and victim susceptibility levels. The threat levels are defined in some MIL-STDs and the susceptibility levels by International EMI test specifications and compliances. These, in part, determine the degree of shielding, surge suppression and other protection devices needed.

Post-EMP event remaining lifestyle becomes a principal measure of the degree of success in providing EMP protection at the family, neighborhood, community, town, county and state levels. While survivalists and Preppers in general are accomplished on the subjects of water, food medications, barter items, guns and ammo, exceptions acknowledged, they fail for no EMP protected solar rooftop electricity and scores of other lifestyle measures discussed herein.

The geographical EMP impact area or radius is very important for the ability to get (roughly inversely proportional to radius) timely replenishments of food, medications, fuel, tools, consumable items, repairs, working vehicles. etc.

Defense against a terrorist launched nuclear bomb, is in part dependent upon the deployment of anti-missile, missiles, that are too slow to "catch up" to the offending missile. Contrast this to anti-missile lasers for both land, ship and aircraft, where they are nearly instantaneous in destroying an offending on-coming missile.

2.0- Symbol Reminder

When the symbol of a man digging deeper is shown in the margin, the message is that the associated paragraph(s) to the right is getting more technical and the lay reader may wish to skip.

2.1- EMP Radiation Levels and their Meaning

The objective of this section is to determine the numerical amount of EMP protection that is needed to avoid victim dysfunction or destruction. This is then translated into specific shielding materials providing sufficient protection to avoid any internal victim device damage or upset. Thus, two things are needed: (1) The EMP radiation levels and (2) the victim susceptibility levels. Then, the protection needed is the product of the two levels; or in units of dB (decibels) the sum of the two.

Fig. 2.1 shows how the peak EMP on the ground varies with the weapon yield and burst altitude. Note that the yield here is the prompt gamma ray output measured in kilotons. This varies from 0.1-0.5% of the total weapon yield, depending on weapon design. The 1.4 megaton total yield 1962, Starfish test had an output of 0.1%, hence 1.4 kiloton of prompt gamma rays.

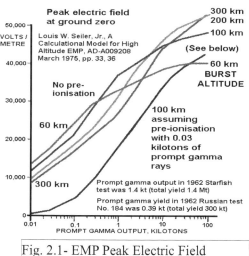

Fig. 2.1- EMP Peak Electric Field

The blue 'pre-ionization' curve in Fig. 2.1 applies where gamma and X-rays from the weapon's primary stage ionizes the atmosphere, making it electrically conductive before the main pulse from the thermonuclear stage. The pre-ionization can literally short out part of the final EMP. Note: Fig. 2.1 also shows that the ground-based, electric-field strength approximates 50 kV/m, a value used in MIL-STDs and in the next section, for calculating the 80-dB shielding effectiveness requirement for EMP protection.

39

First, the radiation levels are taken from Fig. 2.1. and are shown in Fig. 2.2 (below). The threat EMP pulse in the time domain (X-axis is time) has an amplitude of 50 kV/m (50,000 V/m), a rise time of 5 nsec and a pulse duration at the half amplitude of 150 nsec. This is shown in the insert at the left in Fig. 2.2 and represents the default test specifications for EMP testing and compliance.

Figure 2.2 also depicts the frequency-domain (X-axis is frequency) manifestation of the time-domain pulse just mentioned by the

Fig. 2.2- Shielding effectiveness requirements used for calculating EMP protection

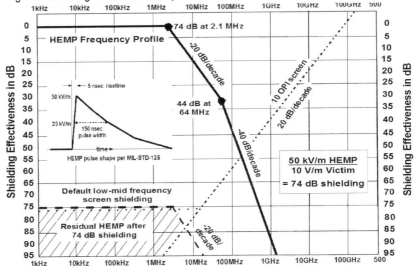

Fourier transform process. It is presumed here (default situation) that all electrical and electronic devices comply with European Union (CE mark) or other test compliance of radiation susceptibility limits of 10 V/m (for example, the European Union specifies in EN61000-4-3 that equipment subject to Level 3 requirements shall not have a radiated   susceptibility to a field strength 10 V/m over the frequency range (80 MHz to 1 GHz).

The Y-axis in the figure now becomes the reference for which the EMP civil standard pulse must be shielded by (SE = shielding efficiency):

$$SE_{dB} = 20Log_{10}(50,000 \text{ V/m}/10 \text{ V/m}) = 74 \text{ dB} \qquad (2.1)$$

A safety margin of 6 dB is added to produce an EMP shielding need of 80 dB below 2.2 MHz (for the civilian reference EMP waveform, this is what is known as the first Fourier corner frequency). However, above 2.2 MHz, the shielding need decreases as shown in Fig. (2.2). To get the actual shielding needed, subtract the Y-Axis value shown from 80 dB. When this is done the default shielding effectiveness of electronic devices, systems and installations becomes that of Table 2.1.

Table 2.1 – Shielding Effectiveness Needed
to EMP protect Building Victim Contents*

Frequency	SE Needed
≤100 kHz	80 dB
1 MHz	80 dB
3 MHz	77 dB
10 MHz	65 dB
30 MHz	52 dB
100 MHz	30 dB
300 MHz	10 dB
≥ 1 GHz	0 dB

*Remember, Table 2.1 assumes that the devices being shielded against EMP are not susceptible to radiations of 10 V/m, the general default value used. A 6-dB safety margin is added

Remember that the reason the above is so important is that an EMP protected installation cannot be EMP pulse tested out in the open without burning out all other electronics in the area. So, a discrete modulated frequency, listed above, is used so that no other EMI problems are generated during the test.

2.2- The Electric Power Grid:

The biggest and most damaging single target for both a strong Geomagnetic Storm, and, especially, an EMP event, is the USA electric power grid. For any readers not familiar with the grid, the following is an abstract taken from Wikipedia.

An electrical grid (also referred to as an electricity grid or electric grid) is an interconnected network for delivering electricity from suppliers to consumers. It consists of generating stations that produce electrical power, high-voltage transmission lines that carry power from distant sources to demand centers, and distribution lines that connect individual customers.

Power stations may be located near a fuel source, at a dam site, and make take advantage of renewable energy sources, and are often located away from heavily populated areas. They are usually quite large to take advantage of the economies of scale. The generated electric power is stepped up to a higher voltage at which it connects to the transmission network.

Fig. 2.3 – Sketch of the Electric Power Generation, Transmission, Distribution

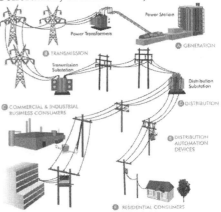

The transmission network will move the power long distances, sometimes across international boundaries, until it reaches its wholesale customer (usually the company that owns the local distribution network).

On arrival at a substation, the power will be stepped down from a transmission level voltage to a distribution level voltage. As it exits the substation, it enters the distribution wiring. Finally, upon arrival at the service location, the power is stepped down again from the distribution voltage to the required service voltage(s).

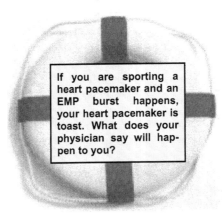

If you are sporting a heart pacemaker and an EMP burst happens, your heart pacemaker is toast. What does your physician say will happen to you?

2.2.1- Economic & Financial Market Loss from EMP Burst

Fig. 2.4, is a loss diagram under six categories resulting from an

EMP event. It is seen that the loss of electricity alone greatly impacts nearly everything in the 21st century, USA lifestyle. Thus, scan the 40 items listed in Fig 2.4 and the reader will agree. Thus, what options may exist to mitigate this incredibly damaging situation? Here are a few possibilities.

Not mentioned and not addressed earlier is the resulting potential catastrophic eco-nomic and finan-cial loss from an EMP burst. On April 23, 2013, the stock market "lost" about $200 billion dollars for a few minutes on a Twitter-hacked

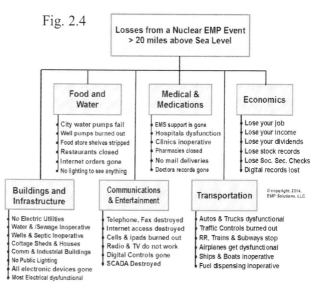

Fig. 2.4

Losses from a Nuclear EMP Event
> 20 miles above Sea Level

Food and Water
- City water pumps fail
- Well pumps burned out
- Food store shelves stripped
- Restaurants closed
- Internet orders gone
- No lighting to see anything

Medical & Medications
- EMS support is gone
- Hospitals dysfunction
- Clinics inoperative
- Pharmacies closed
- No mail deliveries
- Doctors records gone

Economics
- Lose your job
- Lose your income
- Lose your dividends
- Lose stock records
- Lose Soc. Sec. Checks
- Digital records lost

Buildings and Infrastructure
- No Electric Utilities
- Water & /Sewage Inoperative
- Wells & Septic Inoperative
- Cottage Sheds & Houses
- Comm & Industrial Buildings
- No Public Lighting
- All electronic devices gone
- Most Electrical dysfunctional

Communications & Entertainment
- Telephone, Fax destroyed
- Internet access destroyed
- Cells & ipads burned out
- Radio & TV do not work
- Digital Controls gone
- SCADA Destroyed

Transportation
- Autos & Trucks dysfunctional
- Traffic Controls burned out
- RR, Trains & Subways stop
- Airplanes get dysfunctional
- Ships & Boats inoperative
- Fuel dispensing inoperative

© copyright. 2014,
EMP Solutions, LLC

rumor of a White House explosion, before correcting. This resulted from many software account trigger, sell-order programs having a loss mitigation, safety "protection action."

What if there had been an EMP burst instead, in which the electric grid went down along with all RAM and backup memory becoming dysfunctional. Even flash memory was burnt out by being connected to a mother board. All the stock brokerage houses, banks, insurance companies, retirement funds, annuity records and the like back-up memory were lost. Are your equity records safe in the hands of EMP protected institutions? Can you prove your loss to the institutions who have also become dysfunctional ? Your life savings!

"Protect the USA Electric Grid should be the highest priority in America. As a result of this, the predecessor to the Shield Act was introduced by Congressman Trent Franks and Newt Gingrich, first in 2011. Here is the updated 2013 Version"

2.2.2- The SHIELD Act

(Secure High-voltage Infrastructure for Electricity from Lethal Damage Act)

The summary below was written by Congressman Trent Franks.

Why We Need it:

In 2008, the bipartisan Electromagnetic Pulse Commission testified before Congress that: Contemporary U.S. society is not structured, nor does it have the means, to provide for the needs of nearly 300 million Americans without electricity;

> • The current strategy for recovery from a failure of the electric grid leaves us ill-prepared to respond effectively to a man-made or naturally occurring EMP event that would potentially result in damage to vast numbers of components nearly simultaneously over an unprecedented geographic scale;

> • Should the electrical power system be lost for any substantial period of time the consequences are likely to be catastrophic to society, including potential casualties in excess of 60% of the population, according to the Chairman of the EMP Commission;

> • Negative impacts on the electric infrastructure are potentially catastrophic in an EMP event unless practical steps are taken to provide protection for critical elements of the electric system; Finally, most experts predict the occurrence of severe geomagnetic storms is inevitable, it is only a matter of when.

What it Does:

> • The SHIELD Act, which amends section 215 of the Federal Power Act, encourages cooperation between industry and government in the development, promulgation, and implementation of standards and processes that are necessary to address the current shortcomings and vulnerabilities of the electric grid from a major EMP event;

• The SHIELD Act incorporates most of the EMP-related language of HR 5026 from the 111th Congress, which passed overwhelmingly through the House, but was stalled in the Senate during the Lame Duck due mostly to additional language regarding cyber-security threats.

• However, the SHIELD Act omits language regarding cyber-security threats, (which can be better addressed in a separate bill), and then goes beyond HR 5026 by further requiring an automated protection plan and hardware-based solutions, without which the legislation would be toothless to truly address EMP threats.

• The SHIELD Act also requires that standards be developed within 6 months, as opposed to 1 year, of enactment, ensuring a faster timeline of protection.

HR.4298: Grid Reliability and Infrastructure Defense Act or the GRID Act - Amends the Federal Power Act to authorize the Federal Energy Regulatory Commission (FERC), with or without notice, hearing, or report, to issue orders for emergency measures to protect the reliability of either the bulk-power system or the defense critical electric infrastructure whenever the President issues a written directive or determination identifying an imminent grid security threat.

\2.2.3- An Additive Role for Electric Utilities?

Partly, because of the above, the role of the electric utilities will change gradually. They will continue to serve all solar grid-connected installations, especially at night and during overcast days or days of rain or snow.

The electric car is slowly becoming a reality and starting to sell in numbers by early 2011. By 2020, it is estimated by the Boston Consulting Group that 14 million electric cars (fully electric, electric with range extenders, and hybrids) will be sold world wide that year. Assuming the USA produces 20% of this market, 3 million electric vehicles are produced in 2020. For a linear build up from 2011, the number of electric cars, extenders and hybrids is

15M on the road. (M = million; B = billion)_

The 15M electric cars will be driving a total of roughly 100B miles/year. (this alone will save about 100B/20 (mpg) = 5B gallons or 5B/42 (gal/barrel) = 119M barrels. With a barrel of oil $\approx$ $85/bbl, the equivalent oil saved = $10B/year. However, this is destined to grow many times this amount in the post 2020 era.

One mile driven in an electric car creates a Lithium-ion battery discharge of about 350 Watt-hours. At a median electricity of 14.4 cents/kWh (Solatel median in Chap 9), this is equivalent to a cost of $0.05/mile. A normal 40 mile daily round-trip distance to/from work + 50 miles for miscellaneous driving per weekend = 250 miles/week = 88 kWh/week = 379 kWh/month = cost of $55/month. Thus, electric utility emphasis shifts slowly to charging electric cars and leveling off somewhat on home, commercial and industrial electricity consumption.

This also drastically reduces our dependency on foreign oil which would have cost about $150/month (20 miles/gallon assumed). This is considerably more than the electric charge for all Solatel state groups in Chap. 9). It also will be slowly freeing USA from being held hostage to foreign oil. Or, since more fuel is now being produced domestically, it requires less imports. Additionally, since battery capacity and longevity are slowly improving, electric cars may slowly replace fuel-dependent cars as their technology matures.

Electric Vehicle Charging Station

Fast 5 min. charge, $1
Station #3R-104, VA
Authorized: VA 89B

(1) Gas, plentiful in USA, is taking over heating homes from oil heat, releasing oil for conversion to gasoline for vehicle consumption.

Ed. Note: At year end 2014, the price for gasoline in SW Florida has dropped from a high of $3.65/gallon in 2013 to $2.35/gallon, a

36% reduction. This has happened for two reasons.

(1)- Gas, the most plentiful in USA is taking over heating homes from oil heat, releasing oil for conversion to gasoline for vehicle consumption, and

(2)- OPEC is now engaged in a price war with US shale oil producers. This has major repercussions for dozens of countries, from the United States to Russia to Iran. But, on 12 December 2014, prices went into serious free-fall. The reason? OPEC — a cartel of oil producers that includes Saudi Arabia, Iran, Iraq, and Venezuela — had a big meeting in Vienna on November 27. Before the gathering, there was speculation that OPEC countries might cut back on their own oil production in order to prop up prices. But in the end, the cartel couldn't agree on how to respond and did nothing. Oil prices promptly nosedived, with the price of Brent crude now hovering around $70 per barrel.

For the above reasons, the electric vehicle fuel concept of electric utility add on discussed above could end up becoming delayed for a few years.

2.3- Scenarios of Post-EMP Lifestyles

2.3.1- The Pros and Cons of the EMP Survivalists

In searching the Internet under the keywords, "EMP Protection", more than half of the listings are from EMP Survivalists. They are selling freeze-dried, 25-year, shelf-life food, Faraday cages (shielded shoe boxes or other metal-foil lined containers) to protect their portable radios, electronics, backpacks for different applications, Kindel or Nook e-books, and much more. The survivalist mission is basic survival, especially since they see that there is no support coming from the fed.

After a disaster, survival is often thought of as a bridge between lifestyle before an act of nature or man-made event strikes and when restoration of previous lifestyle is achieved. For most weather disasters this may be a few weeks. For hurricane Sandy in

2012, this may have taken from days to years depending on where you live. The default elapse time for an EMP Survivalist is about one year – relatively short by some standards.

Just how does the Survivalist score rate when compared to other EMP-protection options. Figure 2.5 compares three elements of

Fig. 2.5 – Standard of Living after an EMP, assuming the entire local gathering is also EMP protected.

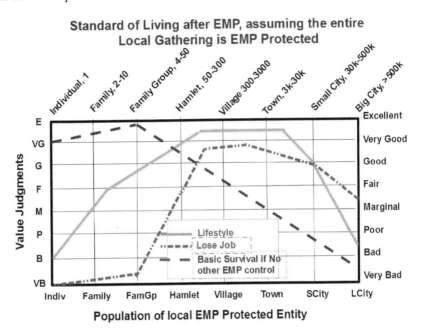

topic comparisons.

The Surviving group size from an individual to a large city is displayed as the horizontal axis. A value judgment is shown for the vertical axis. It ranges from excellent to very bad. Of course, some value judgments are in the eyes of the beholder (like lifestyle, per se), while others are absolute, like losing your job.

Fig. 2.5 shows that basic surviving (blue dashed line) is scored very good compared to no other EMP protection. It scores particularly bad in the big city since there is a plethora of starving people ready to break into the homes of anyone storing food. That's why survivalists prefer to move to the country when an EMP event happens. However, there is no electricity; so, lifestyle scores bad if no groups are involved.

Fig. 2.5 also shows that one major disadvantage of the EMP survivalists is that he loses his job after an event since nothing else is working anyway. However, if a village or town were EMP protected, and almost all employment is geared toward filling local needs, job retention may approximate 90% after an event. In fact it could theoretically exceed 100% if the town is also a manufacturer or it develops products or services in demand from unprotected neighboring areas struck by the same EMP event.

2.4- Geographical Areas of EMP Impact

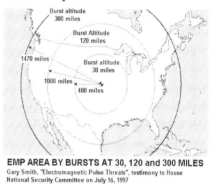

EMP AREA BY BURSTS AT 30, 120 and 300 MILES
Gary Smith, "Electromagnetic Pulse Threats", testimony to House National Security Committee on July 16, 1997

Fig. 2.6 – EMP, an upper atmospheric explosion. (In the daytime, there would be nothing but a brief flash.)

Fig. 2.7 – EMP coverage area at 30, 120 and 300 miles (Gary Smith, EMP Pulse Threats)

One perceived worst-case scenario of a EMP incident is: If a nuclear adversary of any type with a scud-like missile with nuclear warhead and the ability to explode it high above an American city were to do so, it would have a massive effect in all directions. Almost immediately all communications systems in line-of-sight would be disrupted completely (may be burnt out). In that case, there would be no radio, no television, no telephone and no Internet. Indeed, no electricity except certain protected buildings and certain classified government sites. Installations somewhat beyond the explosion's line-of-sight may be disrupted, but not burned out due to diffraction.

While, the following paragraph is somewhat repetitive of an explanation given in the previous chapter, it bears repeating; this time in the language of a *"High altitude EMP"* described by Dr. George W. Ullrich, Deputy Director, Defense Special Weapons Agency:

"A nuclear weapon detonated at high altitude releases some of its energy in the form of gamma rays. These gamma rays collide with air molecules and produce what are called Compton electrons. The Compton electrons, in turn, interact with the earth's magnetic field, producing an intense electromagnetic pulse that propagates downward to the earth's surface. The initial gamma rays and resultant EMP move with the speed of light. The effects encompass an area along the line of sight from the detonation to the earth's horizon. Any system within view of the detonation will experience some level of EMP. For example, if a high-yield weapon were to be detonated 400 kilometers (250 miles) above the United States, nearly the entire contiguous 48 states would be within the line-of-sight.

"The frequency range of the pulse is enormously wide -- from below one hertz to one gigahertz. Peak electric fields can reach tens of thousands of volts per meter. All types of modern electronics are potentially at risk, from Boston to Los Angeles; from Chicago to New Orleans."

2.5- Systems & Equipment Impacted & EMP/EMI Protection

Supervisory Control and Data Acquisition (SCADA) systems are electronic control systems that control electrical transmission and distribution, water management and oil and gas pipelines across the United States. Together with digital control systems (DCS) and programmable logic controllers (PLC) they find extensive use in these equipments and systems.

The U.S. power industry invests about $1.4 billion annually in new SCADA equipment, 50 times the reinvestment rate in transformers for transmission. Between 25 and 30 percent of the protection and control equipment is upgraded or replaced annually, with each new component generally being more susceptible to EMP damage than its predecessor because of the low-level of energy required for its operation (and a proportionately lower level of energy required for its destruction) and a greater bandwidth.

2.5.1- EMP Protected Solar Rooftops, Solar Farms & Communities

Solar electricity has been used by NASA in spacecraft for 45 years. Over the years it has been gradually increased in use for civil applications via solar rooftops and by electric utilities at solar farms.

Today there exists in USA over 500,000 solar rooftop homes and businesses (0.4% of homes and apartments) and 7 GW of solar farms (enough electricity for 1,700,000 homes). USA growth in this sector is expected to be about 30% per year for the next few years.

In recent years there developed *Community Solar Projects* or *Community Solar Gardens* in order to take advantage of cost reductions with community-size developments vs. private homes.

What do all the above solar installations (maybe a few exceptions) have in common? They are all **EMP unprotected.** What a huge potential loss in spite of their near "free" electricity. This is partly what this book is all about - How to EMP protect or convert buildings with/without solar rooftops and farms.

2.6- EMP Countermeasures

There are two meanings of countermeasures here: (1) active countermeasure, in which an anti-missile missile or anti-missile laser can lock on and dysfunction or destroy a terrorist missile in flight, and (2) passive countermeasures in which a location, region or nation is EMP protected so that a high altitude EMP burst has limited effect upon human lifestyle and the infrastructure within its radio horizon. The purpose of this book and its many chapters is the latter. The former will now be briefly discussed.

An anti-missile missile (AMM) defense, exceptions acknowledged, will not work. The reason is that the terrorist launch-to-detonation distance may be as short as 20 miles (32 km) and there exists no AMM within distance to overtake and destroy the Terrorist missile. For example, suppose the terrorist missile is launched from a small container ship off the Outer Banks coast. The missile trajectory is straight up and detonated at 20 miles height. This has a radio horizon of 490 miles, so that Maine, Ohio and Georgia are all impacted corresponding to 90 million inhabitants. Any likely AMM site will be much further away and cannot overtake the terrorist missile. If not quite the scenario, the terrorist missile might off-load a burst of chaff or use other countermeasures to twart its' interdiction and destruction.

What then is the defense?

Take a look at an anti-missile laser (AML). If not a submerged launch site, like from a submarine (sensed differently), the launch burst is detected by a satellite, and location handed over to a radar that is tracking the terrorist missile. Since the AML associated radar has acquired the missile, it immediately lays down a powerful laser beam on the missile at the speed of light. The missile is destroyed thermally, by jamming, or destroying its on board microprocessors.

Here are two AML platform sites announced over a year ago.

Laser Gun mounted on US Navy Ship, acts as Anti-Missile destroying weapon. Benefits: Intense laser radiation immediately hits target at speed of light Microprocessors on missile, burn out – dysfunctioning missile. Other laser radiating actions may detonate missile fuel. Cost of irradiation kill is tiny fraction of anti-missile missile. Navy ship dispatched to Eastern Mediterranean, Oct 2013.

Boeing's Laser mounted on nose of aircraft can lock on, irradiate, track and in X seconds, destroy a missile up to a distance of Y miles

(X and Y are classified)

Chapter 3
National EMP Protection Options
(this is a summary chapter of the plan)

Chapter Overview

This Chapter bears the title of the book, *A National EMP Protection Plan*. The chapter is an overview of the book, with the remaining chapters telling the reader how to do it or providing supporting information to facilitate the EMP protection process.

The broad EMP protection plan has two phases:

Phase I, lasting for two years, prepares and widely disseminates all awareness media on EMP protection, and how-to-do-its. It also builds and tests for compliance eight judiciously-located, EMP protected villages to ensure physical realizability with detailed construction plans, vendor source materials and trained installers. The phase uses the four-tier concept to build the EMP protected prototypes in counties of high-income, medium-income, low-income and EMP Survivalists installations.

Phase II is the fulfillment to many or most USA families living in detached homes, or apartment structures with solar rooftops and the village infrastructure including utilities, hospitals and clinics, food stores, pharmaceuticals, hardware, vehicle fuel, at least one hotel, undertaker, etc. Phase II lasts for eight years and develops many new products and services and generates nationally 43-million job years (average of 5.4 million jobs per year).

The two phases illustrate in a summary format how EMP protected cottage sheds, homes, buildings, industrial parks, solar rooftops, and community solar projects are later constructed and tested for compliance. This will introduce and facilitate a better introduction and understanding -- later other chapters that provide the details.

3.0- Prelude

Ask the person on the street if he has heard of EMP and maybe two in ten will say, "Yes". Ask if he has heard of the Electromagnetic Pulse and maybe the answer is about the same, or 20% of the USA nation. Ask them about five years ago and maybe a somewhat higher percent had said yes. How can this be?

Five years ago William Forstchen, had his book published, "One Second After", the first novel on EMP. It had a forward by Newt Gingrich. It was on the New York Times bestseller list; and 2,000,000 copies were sold. National Geographic produced well aired EMP videos, *Doomsday Preppers*, with both myths and some Hollywood-style alterations. So, EMP did get some air time. There has also been other National Geographic releases. Fox TV has run several sessions on EMP emphasizing protection of the electric grid.

Then came the demise of Cap-and-Trade, Fast and Furious, the Ft. Hood shootings, Benghazi, Boston Bomber, Navy Yard killings, border crossings, health care, Ferguson and a score of related national distractions so that EMP was moved to the back page eclipsed by other world tensions. Iran said before the United Nations, "Iran will wipe Israel off the face of the earth." Netanyahu of Israel replied before the United Nations, "....To prevent Iran from fulfilling its threat, Israel may need to preempt Iran." What does this mean? Will this mean the first "limited civil" EMP event or a more likely an HPM? Whatever, America is unprepared.

The Internet now has about 100 websites on EMP protection, mostly small item Faraday-cage, shielded envelopes and containers. Seeking creative solutions with lifestyle retentions instead of how cataclysmic EMP will be, our company has published four books on EMP protection and now this one, a culmination of them - *A National EMP Protection Plan*.

Meanwhile the Congressional hearings on "What should be the USA position on EMP? came and went with one big conclusion,

EMP is "Not if, but when." Then, the "Shield Act" was introduced in congress by Trent Franks, and has gone through updates, but never passed by a vote by the senate. It is perceived by many that the government has abdicated its fiduciary responsibility. This gave further impetus to the EMP survivalists and Preppers to do their low lifestyle thing for their own families. And, since then, the world in general, and the mid-East in particular, have become a latent tinder box, more likely to explode. Where do we go from here?

Ed. Note: With a new senate to convene in January 2015, on December 2, 2015, the House of Representatives passed H.R. 3410, *Critical Infrastructure Protection Act.* This basically updates and broadens the Shield Act. Assuming the senate approves and the president signs the Act into law in January 2015, the *Dept. of Homeland Security* is given the responsibility for its implementation.

Symbol 🪓 Reader Reminder of the meaning

3.1- EMP Awareness Needs, Means and Media

Many things of a globular and national concern are best aired by responsible presentations on national TV talk shows, with reruns or after hour programming and on the Internet. For starters, run public forums, slide shows, and videos. Perhaps, the most rapid to prepare are slide shows since some already exist and they are easy to put together or modify with animations and narrations.

Another option, to get awareness going almost immediately, since they are available, are our books by EMP Solutions and five others available at Amazon and elsewhere. By most recent date listing, they are:

• *A National EMP Protection Plan,* by Don White, EMP Solutions, LLC, Jan. 2015
• *EMP Protecting Housing & Solar*, aka *EMP Protecting Cottage*

Sheds, Homes, Buildings and Infrastructure with Solar Rooftops, by Don White, EMP Solutions, 2014

- *EMP – Protect Family, Homes and Community, 3rd Edition,* by Don White and Jerry Emanuelson, EMP Solutions & Renewable Energy Creations, 2013
- *A Nation Forsaken,* by F, Michael Maloof, 2013
- *Electric Armageddon: Civil-Military Preparedness for an Electromagnetic Pulse Catastrophe,* by Dr. Peter Vincent Pry, 2013
- *Contrasting EMP Survivals – A Tale of Two Towns,* a novel or sequel to *One Second After,* by Don White, EMP Solutions & Renewable Energy Creations, 2013
- *Disaster Preparedness for EMP Attacks and Solar Storms,* by Arthur T. Bradley, PhD., 2012
- *Nuclear EMP Threats – What Next?,* by Don White. Renewable Energy Creations, LLC, 2012
- *EMP Survival,* by Larry and Cheryl Poole, self published. 2011
- *Solar Flare Survival,* (Protect Yourself and Your Electronics with Faraday Cages) , by Marc Remillard, 2011
- *One Second After,* by William T. Forstchen, 2009

A series of EMP awareness and protection booklets or pamphlets should be put together for different uses and users, especially the consumer, so that they cover different applications and providers. Some would contain a DVD video placed in the back of the book. Some are simple, such as "Your options of what to do if an EMP strikes." The above book by the Pooles covers several topics for basic survival with limited lifestyle.

3.2- Planning at Federal, State & County Levels

The next page shows one organization structure for Phase I, two-year program, to achieve an effective mission objective of EMP protection optimization while playing "catch-up" as we may be at the eleventh hour of the first EMP event. Reason for concerns now:

(1) America has no EMP protection plan in action – neither

preparation nor planning is known to be underway.

(2) Netanyahu has already put the United Nations on notice that Israel may preempt Iran's threat to wipe Israel off the face of the earth.

(3) There exist rogue nations and terrorists who believe they are capable now of launching an EMP event over USA.

(4) There are many ways to launch an EMP event and terrorists already in USA and elsewhere may be waiting for the right moment.

Examine the US *Government EMP organization chart* shown on the next page at each of the three levels: federal, state and county. As explained in Chapter 5 and later chapters, *Bottom-up Management,* placing the county on the forefront, is the best pragmatic orchestration vehicle to make EMP protection viable and happen in a more timely manner.

First, a few words about the Fig. 3.1 org chart. In each of the three levels, the major resources available at that level are listed under the corresponding government level box. The listings to the right of each box are some of the major EMP protection responsibilities or the entities having those responsibilities.

3.2.1 Fed Government EMP Protection Role

More than 90% of the Fed roll resources come from the Executive Branch, such as, DoD, Dept. of Defense, field laboratories, and the DHS, Dept. of Homeland Security, under the new HR 3410 act to be voted in January 2015.

The primary early Fed responsibilities in Phase I are in raising awareness and construction and testing. Awareness in many parts is to inform all Americans of what EMP protection is all about. The media range from the printed word to the Internet, to books to symposium, conferences and TV talk shows.

The other major responsibility of the Fed. Gov. shown in Fig. 3.1, is to construct two EMP protected villages outside two of the DOD field laboratories (Army, Navy and/or Air Force). This is because in after hours, the government lab employees wear their civil hat and live at home until the next work morning. These two villages become part of the eight locations mentioned elsewhere that fulfill

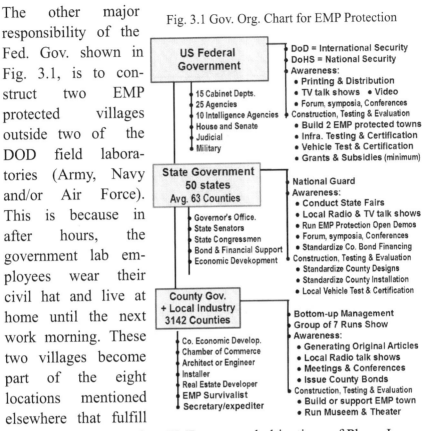

Fig. 3.1 Gov. Org. Chart for EMP Protection

US Federal Government
- 15 Cabinet Depts.
- 25 Agencies
- 10 Intelligence Agencies
- House and Senate
- Judicial
- Military

- DoD = International Security
- DoHS = National Security
- Awareness:
  - Printing & Distribution
  - TV talk shows • Video
  - Forum, symposia, Conferences
- Construction, Testing & Evaluation
  - Build 2 EMP protected towns
  - Infra. Testing & Certification
  - Vehicle Test & Certification
  - Grants & Subsidies (minimum)

State Government 50 states Avg. 63 Counties
- Governor's Office.
- State Senators
- State Congressmen
- Bond & Financial Support
- Economic Devekopment

- National Guard
- Awareness:
  - Conduct State Fairs
  - Local Radio & TV talk shows
  - Run EMP Protection Open Demos
  - Forum, symposia, Conferences
- Standardize Co. Bond Financing
- Construction, Testing & Evaluation
  - Standardize County Designs
  - Standardize County Installation
  - Local Vehicle Test & Certification

County Gov. + Local Industry 3142 Counties
- Co. Economic Develop.
- Chamber of Commerce
- Architect or Engineer
- Installer
- Real Estate Developer
- EMP Survivalist
- Secretary/expediter

- Bottom-up Management
- Group of 7 Runs Show
- Awareness:
  - Generating Original Articles
  - Local Radio talk shows
  - Meetings & Conferences
  - Issue County Bonds
- Construction, Testing & Evaluation
  - Build or support EMP town
  - Run Museem & Theater

the prototype or template EMP protected objectives of Phase I.

Because of the special equipment and skills, the feds will also provide the early testing and certification of all EMP protected towns in Phase I as they also train a number of industry installers to take over this responsibility for Phase II, Implementation.

Another special Fed undertaking, listed in Fig. 3.1, involves the slow handover of vehicle testing to the auto manufacturers who are also present at some symposia and conferences along with their EMP protection retrofit kits. Vehicle EMP protection is vital as transportation is greatly curtailed after an EMP event and roads and highways are blocked with dysfunctional vehicles. Clogged roads hinder distribution and replenishments of food, medications and other vitals. Most fuel stations are also dysfunctional, adding to the chaos. From this, transportation solutions are generated and detailed in Chapter 15 and 16.

Not shown is the new responsibilities of DoHS in executing HR 3410, assuming it is signed into law in 2015. This may develop some turf problems between DHS and Bottom-up Management discussed in Chapter 5, that will need to be promptly addressed.

Finally, the org chart in Fig. 3.1 speaks to grants and subsidies. Grants are especially important as they often bring to life unsolicited proposals from more creative sources in industry. Subsidies, on the other hand, should be unnecessary as most financing originates from County bonds as explained later on.

3.2.2- The State Government EMP Protection Role

The second government level shown in Fig. 3.1 org chart is the state level. Note, that it has a huge span of supervision with the average state having 63 counties. This is where state representatives from the counties can help. Since there is no planned financing from any fed subsidy, and nearly all is coming from the issuance of county bonds, the state works with each county and associate investment broker house of problems in arranging for and selling county bonds. As explained in later chapters, these bonds are used to finance both the retrofit of existing homes as well as the new cottage-shed communities and community solar gardens described in later chapters.

Some money will be returned to the county as property values will increase. Concerned residents and concerned business leaders and businesses will prefer to relocate to an EMP protected community and drive up property values, rather than live elsewhere where they will bear the full weight of social disruption in an EMP aftermath.

There will be several state fairs run to enhance EMP protection awareness. Some will be run like symposia or conferences in which scores of exhibitors will show their products and services. Some timely papers, both lay and technical, will also be presented for more details about EMP threat and how to protect. Also, here is where relevant trade journals can share the load with state government awareness types, such as State Economic Development Offices.

Where smaller talk shows tend to be non-national, usually spanning one or two states, the states assist in contacting and arranging both radio and TV talk shows as part of their awareness efforts.

The states also conduct frequent open-house shows of any EMP-protected villages constructed. If not the case, videos will be made to show the public what it is all about and what to expect. The Internet exposure will be a good gap filler. Many guest speakers will also be solicited and invited to participate.

3.2.3- The County Level EMP Protection Group

As explained in Chapter 5 on Bottom-up Management, for each county there exists a planning group of seven professionals (one from the county Economic Development Office, Chamber of Commerce, architect or engineer, solar-rooftop manufacturer supplier, solar installer, real-estate developer, and financial intermediary) for Phase I. Each group has a full-time Secretary, who also acts as an expediter. Their duties are many fold.

For counties containing the eight selected prototype/template EMP-protected villages or towns to be built, other adjacent or nearby counties share some of the load. For example, they run a museum and open-air state fair for many other counties, including visitors from some adjoining states. This offers live exhibitions and on-going convention meetings and demonstrations in preparation for Phase II, on implementing.

The above Fig.3.1 organization chart at the county level shows a large portion of their efforts are directed to both awareness and construction. Of course, since only 0.3% of the counties are directly involved in EMP related construction and protecting their counties, the remaining 99+% are running local video shows, meetings and conferences on how EMP protection is done. The highlights of many are the bus tours to the actual construction – the county village where drive and walk through visit tours are run nearly every day. The associated museum and theater are always packed as this is the site of one of the eight. Phase I EMP protected villages.

Finally, remember the county is the level at which financing is done via issuing of county bonds sold directly by the counties and associated stock brokerages. The federal government has no tax-paying subsidies, needed or otherwise, as capitalism is at work in which the civil citizenry invests in the County bonds to make it all work.

3.3- The Concept of a Four-Tier EMP Protection Plan

Lifestyle (L) value judgments following an EMP incident and corresponding cost (C) for EMP protection are the two principal elements to consider, plan for and score actual EMP protection performance (PP). Therefore, PP = L/C quotient. (This is similar to the well-known economic benefit-cost ratio). Without having a PP term there is no performance algorithm by which to rate different plans., With PP scores, proposed changes in plans can be quickly contrasted and compared among the prototype/template, EMP-protected villages or towns.

Lifestyle is rarely addressed in EMP protection literature. Does it not matter? Yet, EMP survivalist will lead a very different lifestyle vs. those in a whole village or town that is mostly or completely EMP protected. For example, following an EMP event, the EMP survivalists individual (or family) loses his job, loses access to shopping stores, hospitals, undertaker, etc. that have all become dysfunctional (see earlier Fig. 2.4) . Contrast this to an EMP-protected municipality in which there is little loss - almost nothing is lost except uncertainty of when the EMP-protected replenishment vehicles, airstrip or railroad siding may be revisited with more replenishments. Even here, a warehouse can store survivalists freeze-dried and selected canned food, principal medications, etc. These matters lead to the reason why different tiers of EMP protection are addressed as one strategy of several.

This section portrays four tiers of EMP protection to be initiated in order to get things started. Except for EMP survivalists, who have started their planning and implementing years ago, the top three tiers may initially be regarded as Phase-I, pilot programs, from which a substantial

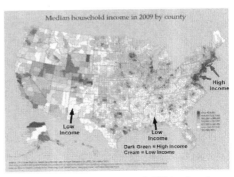

Fig.3.2 – County map of USA showing household income divided into five groups

pragmatic learning experience develops. They are started at the same time and have been selected by location and economy as discussed later. Each tier advisory group has a part-time representative of the other two tiers plus the Group of seven experts described in the previous section. All learn from the progress, failures, and wisdom of each other. Also, as discussed later, financing comes from issuing county and corporate bonds.

To get started, the 3,142 counties in the U.S. are divided into four quartiles of median household income: (1) Tier-1, highest quartile (25% of total US households earn more than $69,000), (2) Tier-2, median quartiles earn between $22,000 and $69,000 with $39,000 being their geometric midpoint), and (3) Tier-3, 25% of the total US county households earn less than $22,000 per year.

The above data are obtained from the Census Bureau. The U.S. map, Fig. 3.2, shows the household income by darkness of color for each county. The dark colorations are Tier-1 counties and light or no coloration are Tier-3 counties.

The master plan also provides for north and south locations and three geographical regions in the US in the four-tier EMP protections. This allows for coastal USA exposures and central regions to gain climatic and other information from each others' locations.

Fig. 3.3: 4-Tier EMP Protection Concept

The diagram, Fig. 3.3, illustrates the four tiers of EMP protection. Their assigned names (for ID here only) are located at the outer periphery of the four-sides of the square. Just inside the square, the corresponding household income range is listed. As mentioned, Tier-1 counties can afford greater EMP protection and Tier-3 less. Of course, there is allowance for exceptions, not discussed here. One example is that many counties will have poorer sections among the wealthier section locations within a single county. Fig. 3.3 also has a three-line summary, closest to the center square, to suggest what is covered in their respective tiers. A few details of these remarks are described in the next session.

3.4- How the EMP Protection Plan is Configured

The following discussion addresses some information about each of the four tiers of Fig. 3.3.

Tier-1, High Income Homes, Commercial and Other Buildings

There are 91 million homes in USA and 39 million apartments (130 million households) to shelter its 324 million population (year 2014). For Phase-1, two-year pilot program, a town of roughly 10,000 population is selected for the first tier. With an average household size of 2.6 people, this corresponds to 10,000/2.6 = 3,850 homesteads. Of these, 2,700 are detached homes and 1,150 are apartments. Therefore, at the end of Phase-1, about 2 locations x 3,850 = 7.7 thousand Tier-1 homes will be EMP protected.

Since average new home and new commercial building construction is assumed to be about 2.5% per year, Tier-1 site, 0.025 x 3,850 = 96 new Tier-1 homes per year will be added per site. This is first mentioned now to inform the reader that EMP protection for new home construction is estimated to cost about 65% of that for a retrofit home, since EMP protection is more easily and economically achieved on a new home during construction. Also, the EMP bottom floor shielding problem is overcome as discussed in Chapter 8.

Home EMP protection in Tier-1 involves a 100% shielding of the outside skin (including the floor, roof and all sides), the details are provided in Chapter 8. The shielding sections are bonded and grounded to earth and any lead-in power lines and others (telephone, data) are filtered or surge suppressed as also presented in later chapters.

Since the low end of home size in the high income counties is roughly 4,000 sq. ft. under air, the power required for a solar rooftop is about 9 kW. This is sufficient to handle air conditioning, and hot water loads in addition to the electrical appliances, lighting, computer and peripherals, radio and TV, etc. Of course, the solar rooftop is also shielded and processed as explained in Chapter 9.

Along with the solar rooftop is both a battery bank of about 30, 12-volt, deep-cycle

Fig. 3.4 – Identification of Principal Resources for survival and living needs.

Buildings and Topics	Hi-Income Counties	Median Counties	Lo-Income Counties
Shopping Malls	X	X	
Wal-Mart	X	X	
Vehicles	X	X	
Food Stores	X	X	X
EMS Services	X	X	
Pharmacies	X	X	X
Adjacent Farms	X	X	X
Water Utilities	X		
Gas Stations	X	X	
Airport-Trains	X	X	
Manufacturing	X		
Hospitals	X		
Clinics	X	X	X
Weapons-Ammo	X		
Boats-Ships*	X	X	
Marinas*	X		
Commerc. Office	X	X	
Home Depot,-Lowes	X		
Ace Hardware	X	X	X
Hotels/Motels	X		
Schools-College	X	X	
Funeral Services	X	X	
Churches	X	X	
Restaurants	X		
Theaters	X		
Arenas			

batteries. They provide an energy capacity of about 45 kwh (kilowatt hours), nominally sufficient to handle all night time use and a few overcast days when solar electricity is nearly unproductive. As explained later, the number of batteries is adjusted for greater latitudes and climates having more overcast days.

The cost for a high income county, EMP protected home with protected solar rooftop will range from about $50,000 to over $100,000 for large homes over 10,000 sq. ft. Ignoring inflation, this will reduce by about 30-40% in 10 years by Moore's Law for electronics and quantity production cost reduction. (Moore's Law is the engineering dictum that, among other things, describes the cost reduction of semiconductor products over time.)

The Fig. 3.3 wording speaks of "Larger retail replenishing stores." This term is illustrated in the table of Fig. 3.4. Focus on Column B (Tier 1) for the present. Scan down the list of facilities that will have been EMP hardened. It is noted that nearly everything has been protected so that the affluent town as a whole is nearly unaware of an EMP incident. The reason that the word "nearly" is used is that communication and transportation by delivery vehicles, delivering replenishment food, medications and other supplies is essential to survival. This requires that some modes of communication such as satellite and fiber optics are functional. Also, all Tier-1 communities have at least a 4,000 foot, metal-mat covered earth runway to help ensure vitals replenishment.

Tier 2 - Median Household Homes, Commercial & Other Buildings

This second tier, median income counties, Column C, Fig. 3.4, has at least one room in a home selected for shielding plus a limited EMP protected solar rooftop of about 3-4 kW. Unlike the entire home in Tier-1, Tier-2 homes are shielded on the *inside* of the room to protect it from all the exposed wiring in the walls (that act as EMP radiation pick up antennas), ceiling lights and duplex outlets that would otherwise severely compromise shielding effectiveness performance. The wiring from the protected solar rooftop goes directly to a small electrical panel *inside* the set-aside

65

room – not to the main electrical control panel used to service the house distribution from the electric grid.

The cost for a median income county, EMP-protected room in a home with 3 kW protected solar rooftop (plus supporting solar battery bank and generator) will range from about $15,000 to $35,000 for the larger end of homes approximating 3,500 sq. ft.

Fig. 3.4 shows that some of the commercial buildings and services are not protected since the county budget is less and other than the main survival retail outlets (for example: Walmart, Home Depot, Walgreen Pharmacy, etc.) the smaller provisioning stores are not included. Naturally, this has a set of very definitive rules as where the dividing line exists, and constitutes potential political, emotional, and economic problems mentioned elsewhere, but the solutions are beyond the scope of this book.

As an alternative, many people may wish to go with a community of EMP protected, cottage-sheds with solar rooftop homes as described in detail in Chapters 8-12.

Tier 3 - Low Income Homes, Commercial and Other Buildings

This is a continuation of the previous two EMP protected homes in Tier-1 and Tier-2 and provisioning retail stores and other services. Some suggested details are given in Column D of Fig. 3.4.

The selected room for shielding is smaller than for that for Tier-2. Perhaps the smallest bedroom or a pantry or a walk-in clothes closet will work out where the room is shielded and made into basically a large Faraday cage (Faraday and shielded are the same meaning). The solar rooftop consists of three to five, 3'x5' solar panels (about 600 watts to 1,000 watts) used for small lighting, a fan and a small refrigerator. No generator is involved but about five deep-cycle vehicle batteries provide the electric backup for night and overcast days.

The cost for the above limited EMP installation ranges from about $5,000 to $7,500, but becomes less in time as quantity production and installations increase into mid and late 2010 decade.

Note. It may be that many Tier 3. category inhabitants may opt to go the route of the community cottage-shed developments, that are EMP protected homes with solar rooftops built around a waterfront pond or lake. These are described in detail in Chapters 8-12.

Tier 4 - EMP Survivalists

This group differs from the above three tiers, in that the EMP survivalist are independently operating. Their motivation to spend time and their own money for EMP protection is in recognition of earlier-mentioned government apathy and the fear of the consequences (see Fig. 3.5). This has been exacerbated by the fact that the civil sector has done almost nothing and they perceive that there exists little evidence that the civil sector will be doing much anytime soon. However, their EMP survival preparation experience has developed a wealth of basic existence know-how.

Fig. 3.5 - Partial listing of items EMP survivalist will seek to acquire.

Water	Electric & Electronics
Bottled	Light appliances
Canned	Flashlights
Well, hand pump	Batteries
Charcoal & sand filtered	Battery charger
Soft drinks	Shortwave radio
Brook or creek	Police Scanners
Food	CB radio
Canned food	Cell phone
Freeze dried	Small Solar
Vegetable garden	Inverter
Cows and pigs	iPad and/or iPod
Deer and squirrel	Microwave oven
Medications	**Computer & Peripherals**
Prescription drugs	**Candles and housing**
Vitamins	**Cooking**
Ointments	Propane heater
Pain killers	Propane storage tank
First aid kit	Charcoal
Splints and bandages	Box oven
Oxygen or other	Tin Can & Dutch ovens
Weapons and Ammo	Eating flatware
Pistols & revolvers	Kitchen utensils
Hunting rifles, shotguns	
Ammunition	
Machete	**Security**
Carving knives	Trip alarms
Bow and arrows	Proximity alarms

A browse through the Internet under an "EMP Protection" keywords or related search provides over 100 advertisers and listings of items for sale including a few books. The table in Fig. 3.5 lists most of what may be found with such a search. One of the more comprehensive books the reader may want to buy under $10 is *EMP Survival* by Larry and Cheryl Poole. It may be found on Amazon Books.

Note. As already been mentioned for Tier-3 Groups, it may be that many Tier 4. category inhabitants may opt to go the route of the community cottage-shed developments, that are EMP protected homes with solar rooftops built around a waterfront pond or lake. These are described in detail in Chapters 8-12.

3.5- Evaluating Progress: Quick Overview

It is remembered that EMP protection is less expensive for new homes when incorporated, only achievable during new home construction. The data gained and lessons learned will be incorporated into Phase-2 developments. The options for small cottage-shed community developments are covered in Chapters 11 and 12.

Progress throughout the two years of Phase-1 will be known to each selected county on a periodic or continuous basis so that all will benefit from the good vs. not-so-good choices with supporting rational (via bottom-up management of Chapter 5). In a different vein, throughout the entire program a number of seminars and webinars will be run nationally and locally so that the non-technical readers as well as professionals will be informed nationwide. To add to the national interest and participation, there will be cash awards for submitted design and implementation improvements from the general public. After all, there is a wealth of creativity spread throughout the country, and the government must participate, promote, encourage and capitalize upon these resources.

3.6- A Peek at Phase 1 Costs, Jobs & Expectations

Discussed in depth in later chapters, this section gives the readers a peek at expectations regarding costs and jobs, first for Phase-1, EMP-Solar, Pilot Project (experiment or study) described in this chapter 1. Then, when carried through Phase 2 - the entire USA by 2025.

Fig. 3.6 – Summary of General EMP Protected, Tier Classification and Cost Estimates for Phase II

	A	B	C	X	D	E	F	G	H
Row #	Tier Class.	Population	Exist/New	Sq.Ft.	Homes#	Cost $	Homes$M	Commercl$M	Total $M
1	Tier 1	10,000	Existing	5,000	3,860	65,000	251	402	653
2	Tier 1	3,000	Existing	3,800	1,158	50,000	58	93	151
3	Tier 2	5,000	Existing	2,300	1,930	35,000	68	108	176
4	Tier 3	3,000	New CS	1,400	1,158	21,000	24	39	63
5	Tier 4	NA	New CS	NA	NA	Below	13	20.8	33.8
6	160 SF Cottage	NA	New Home	160	200	20,000	4	6.4	10.4
7	400 SFCottage	NA	New Home	400	200	45,000	9	14.4	23.4
8	2+2+2 +2	NA	NA	NA	9506	Total	414	662	1076
Row #	A	B	C	X	D	E	F	G	H

Notes: Estimated EMP Protection + solar cost is shown at Cell E (excludes basic house = $100/SF)
Average house + protection + solar per household for 160 sq. ft. = E6 + $100*X = $36,000
Average house + protection + solar per household for 400 sq. ft. = E7 + $100*X = $85.000

Figure 3.6, in a spreadsheet form, gives a glimpse of the various element data and their totals on the bottom line. Column B is the town or village population involved and Column C identifies if the home to be EMP protected is existing or a to-be-built small community cottage-shed home is selected. Column D is the approximate number of homes involved, based on an average household of 2.6 persons. Column E is the rough cost per average home for EMP protection including adding a solar rooftop. Column F is the total home cost in units of million dollars ($M) for the Tier shown in Column A.

The electric utility industry reports that 38% of their electricity load (users) are residential and 62% is a combination of commercial plus industrial. The latter is 62/38 = 1.6 times the residential load. So, as a first estimate, Column G is 1.6 times the amount of column F. Finally, Column H is a total of both Columns F and G. Remember, the numbers here are very rough since there are many expenses and variables involved and the lower cost of government participation and support has not yet been added.

Figure. 3.6 shows that the cost for housing and commercial installations for Phase-1 over the first two years is about $1.1 billion (total at bottom in cell H8). This is spread over eight counties with the first two, serving a town population of 10,000 and 3,000 (cells B1 and B2) which is the highest cost at about $806 million. The average population of all 3,141 US counties is (317 million USA/3,141 counties) = about 100,000 people/county. The (U.S. census) estimated net worth is about $55 trillion/3,141 counties = average of $17 billion/county. Highest income counties may approximate $40 billion and the lower income about $4B. For a high-income county of 100,000 population, $40B net worth corresponds to $400,000 per person. The Tier-3 counties have a average per person net worth of less than $40,000.

The $804 million of Column H1+H2, towns in Fig. 3.6 is spread over a 200,000 county population and amounts to about $4,000 per person. However, this is not relevant since, as mentioned earlier, the money comes from the issuance of county and corporate bonds from investors, retirement funds, and annuities. From the previous paragraph, $4,000 is about 1% of the county per capita wealth; so this is no financial challenge (in other words, it is readily affordable) via county bonds and some corporate bonds.

Regarding jobs, the $1.1 billion pilot, Phase-1 cost (bottom line, Fig. 3.6, Column H8) is the total direct cost exclusive of government participation. Forty per cent (40)% is arbitrarily added (CBO estimates not available) to account for government participation cost, some volunteer time contributed, publicity and education costs, plus items not identified in Fig.3.6. So the $1.1 billion becomes about $1.5 billion cost for Phase-1.

Since an estimated $225,000 of money spent back into an economy represents one job created with a $48,000 average annual salary), the number of jobs created from Phase I is above $1.5B/$2250k = 6,700 job-years (see Fig. 3.7). Because this is spread over two years, this represents 3,350 jobs lasting for two years.

For Phase II, over eight years, assume only 50% of the families have their homes, partial homes, or apartments EMP protected (some home or apartment roofs are not suitable for rooftops. This will approximate the above 6,700 job years for Phase I out of a total 122 million homesteads = 0.5x6,700/[Cell-D8/USA homesteads] = 0.5x6,700/(9,506/122M)] = 43 million job-years, or averaged over 8 years = 5.4 million U.S. Jobs. The above financial information is admittedly rough, but adequate to get a first order evaluation of the doability of Phase-1.

The above data are plotted in Fig. 3.7 graph. The horizontal axis is 12 years from 2015 to 2017 for Phase I and 2017 to 2025 for Phase II. The vertical axis is the number of jobs/year in millions. The

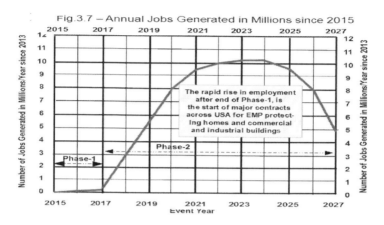

Fig.3.7 – Annual Jobs Generated in Millions since 2015

The rapid rise in employment after end of Phase-1, is the start of major contracts across USA for EMP protecting homes and commercial and industrial buildings

peak years are around 2023; thereafter the number of jobs falls off as fulfillment is achieved.

3.7- Phase I – Timeline, Two-year Planning Chart

For each of the counties involved, all states, and the fed, there exists a two-year planning chart, subject to weekly updating so that everyone is on the same page. Of course each of the three levels has its own timeline chart. The one below is shown for Phase I by quarters to get some idea what it will look like. The real one will be shown by months and contain many more entries.

Phase I Gantt Timeline General Planning Chart, Yrs. 2015-2016

Line			2015				2016			
#	Project ID	TBD	1Q15	2Q15	3Q15	4Q15	1Q16	2Q16	3Q16	4Q16
	Column Head	A	B	C	D	E	F	G	H	I
1	Awareness & Media									
2	What to Do?									
3	Minimum Preparations									
4	Replenishments									
5	Join Community Groups									
6	Seminars & Webinars									
7	Forum									
8	Radio and TV Talk Shows									
9	Blogs & Social Network									
10	Design, Build & Test									
11	Basic Building									
12	Cottage Shed									
13	Small Home									
14	2k SF Home									
15	3500 SF Home									
16	Solar Rooftop									
17	Public Lighting									
18	Financing									
19	Police & Sheriff									
20	Water Works									
21	Sewage Disposal									
22	Fire and EMS									
23	Clinic, Doctors/Dentists									
24	Underwriter/Berrial									
25	Motel/Hotel									
26	Meetimg Hall & Rooms									
27										
28										
29										
30										
Line			2015				2016			
#	Project ID	TBD	1Q15	2Q15	3Q15	4Q15	1Q16	2Q16	3Q16	4Q16

3.8- Phase II, EMP Protection Fulfillment

As previously remarked, Phase II's mission is for the vital EMP protection to become instituted nationwide over an eight-year period. The two years of Phase I preparation is then followed by a methodical, mass-production type approach, as awareness, product and service problems are mostly all thought out, and eight village and town installation prototypes and templates are history, along with lessons learned, both good and bad.

The above also includes the continual improvement in materials and production techniques over a period of time. More training and time reporting via trade journal articles, symposia and conferences, seminars and webinars will also assure the lowering of costs with volume productions.

Since eight years seems like a long time, a few percent of the entire production fulfillment costs are earmarked for continual creative new product and service updates and developments. These cover the gamut of a continual shift from first generation, silicone solar panels to second generation, lower cost, thin-film, Cd Te, panels (First Solar of Tempe AZ reports a production efficiency of 20% has been reached by cadmium telluride)).

In fact, third generation, BIPV (Building Integrated, Photovoltaics) will start to be implemented. This is a solar paint placed on the sides of buildings which contain no solar panels because of unfavorable angles between the sun and vertical building walls. However, since BIVP paint is so cheap, this will be used to extend the four-floor building limitation of solar rooftops due to only one solar roof feeding multiple floors with electricity. Thus, a major solar limitation imposed upon the solar viability of cities with tall buildings can be mitigated. The 10-floor building-height dream for solar electrical sources may be achieved. Maybe in time, even more. Perhaps, DHS in its new 2015 HR 3410 mission can add additional unsolicited proposal enhancements here.

In summary, remember the positive side of all this Phase I and Phase II efforts is the generation of:

• "Free" electricity both before and after an EMP event.

• An influx in property values and property taxes due to an influx of security minded individuals and companies.

• An enormous insurance against the catastrophic EMP event in that respectable percentages of lifestyle continues due to timely EMP preparation and implementation.

73

• A wake-up call to the over 500,000 existing USA solar rooftop owners and their contractors and to the Community Solar Gardens programs now under way to at least do the *screen cover roof under solar installations.* At a tiny additional cost, this permits EMP protection to be done later– otherwise EMP protection can not be be added to those installations except at a relatively high cost.

• Generation of many new businesses performing new products and services, not otherwise likely to happen.

• Creates millions of new jobs, increases the standard of living and creates hope. Good qualities, such as *Positive Accountability* and ideals taught by www.roycewhite.com who shows how to develop leadership, how to discover or enhance your passions, start a new business, and enhance capitalism while still providing the more meritorious selections of socialism.

• Provide a real opportunity to meaningfully pay down our National debt which has just crossed $18 trillion and is heading higher.

Do you really know how devastating and ugly the outcome of an EMP incident can be? You lose your job, income, digital wealth, social security check, sewer, water transportation & communication.

Chapter 4
The Players, Organizations, Product & Service Providers

Chapter Overview

In any large activity, especially involing a nation, far better and smoother operations are possible by knowing and understanding who the key players are. Thus, this chapter identifies the companies, agencies, organizations and suppliers of EMP related products and services.

This identification is done in two tiers: first a triangle identifying the three principals (1) the EMP community because this is the main subject, (2) The EMC community because these are the folks who provide the the products and know-how for EMP protection and (3) the solar rooftop manufacturers and suppliers since post-EMP lifestyle without electricity will be very hard, restrictive and tend to shorten one's life.

The second tier brings in additional structure including the federal, state and county role in EMP protection. Also participating is the real-estate community since escape cottage sheds locally and in the country will become very popular, because they will be EMP protected and have built-in solar electricity.

The last group is the EMP Survivalists and Preppers, totaling about 1% of the USA population. They hoard water, 25-year food, medication, bartering items and guns and ammo for survival with a somewhat dismal lifestyle, usually without electricity.

4.1- The EMP Community

The Electromagnetic Pulse Community, or simply, *the EMP Community*, consists of three major communities plus several smaller ones (Fig. 4.1). This is shown in the following triangle diagram. The major components are: (1) The EMP Community (Survivalists who are not "plugged in" with and don't enjoy the technical savvy and products that the EMC Community offers, nor do they have access to EMP protected solar energy generation), (2) The EMC Community and (3) the solar rooftop and solar farms community.

Fig. 4.1 – The broad EMP Community

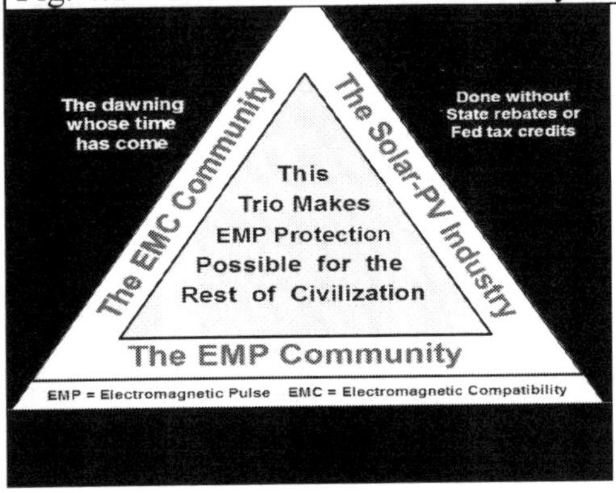

The dawning whose time has come

Done without State rebates or Fed tax credits

This Trio Makes EMP Protection Possible for the Rest of Civilization

The EMP Community

EMP = Electromagnetic Pulse   EMC = Electromagnetic Compatibility

4.1.1 EMPact America

EMPact America is a non-profit organization formed by Henry Schwartz, owner of a food distribution center, Steuben Foods, in upstate New York. He realized that after an EMP attack, no food would be distributed. He would have no food products coming into his facility, and nothing would work at his facility in a post-EMP situation anyway. Food distribution would simply grind to a halt.

One of the first significant activities of EMPact America was a major conference on EMP in Niagara Falls, New York in September, 2009. The conference was open to anyone, and most of the speakers were scientific and engineering professionals who were able to explain the EMP threat in a way that anyone could understand. Many speakers also discussed the threat of geomagnetic storms. Some other speakers discussed dangerous geopolitical developments and shared information that EMP weapons are being developed by countries that have threatened to destroy the United States.

The two-day conference was attended by about 700 people from around the world. The two day event, hosted by *EMPACT America*

Inc., explored the threat, the potential impact on America and options to protect our critical infrastructures and our homes. The conference concluded with a special interactive session to lay out an action plan.

This conference was intended as a watershed event, helping to build a national consensus on the urgency to end our unprecedented vulnerability to a weapon that may already be in the hands of rogue nations or terror groups dedicated to our destruction. As nuclear technology spreads over the 21st century, many additional nations may acquire nuclear EMP capability. Reports from the Congressional EMP Commission and the National Academy of Sciences characterize electromagnetic pulse as a potentially catastrophic threat.

EMPact America, in partnership with Breitbart News Network and the Center for Security Policy, hosted the "National Security Action Summit II" on Monday, September 29th, 2014. The program featured remarks from Dinesh D'Souza, Dr. Ben Carson, Allen West, Judge Jeanine Pirro, Andrew McCarthy, and many more. The event can be viewed in its entirety on www.HomelandThreats.com. There was a panel on the importance of grid security with former Director of Central Intelligence, James Woolsey, Judge Pirro and Rep. Trent Franks (R-AZ), who spoke via video. It can be found under "Summit Recordings, Session 6."

To Contact EMPactAmerica:
General Information: info@empactamerica.org
Phone: (716) 435-7873
Mail: EMPact America, PO Box 124, Elma, NY 14059

Other EMP Symposia

• Other symposia have been conducted in recent years by the US DoD Department of Defense, but are of a classified nature and will not be covered here.

• The Department of Defense (DoD) and the Department of Energy (DOE) announced that the 30th Hardened Electronics and

Radiation Technology (HEART) Conference was held in Monterey, CA, March 13 - 16, 2012. The HEART Conference provides a professional forum specifically for classified or sensitive research and development investigations. The HEART Conference and the HEART published proceedings provide a unique, classified and export controlled colloquium for authors who desire the professional recognition associated with fully scientifically-refereed publications. This type of publication is the choice for reporting superior, exclusive results.

Of particular interest are experimental or analytical observations that are new and significant to the design, testing, or economics of hardened systems. Two types of technical papers are invited for consideration in the conference program. The first is classified up to the level of Secret Restricted Data (no CNWDI); the second is unclassified but restricted by export control (ITAR). Papers of special interest, that are not classified or ITAR, will be considered on a case-by-case basis. Attendees must have security clearances certified by DoD and DOE officials to attend the classified sessions. ITAR attendees must be US citizens or U.S. resident aliens with a Permanent Resident Card (Green Card).

Based on the positive reception at previous conferences, demonstration space is provided for those who are developing desktop computer programs in all radiation environment effects, and all related topic areas. The HEART Conference will continue to provide a forum for research and development investigations in space radiation, nuclear, electromagnetic pulse phenomena, and EMP/HPM effects on systems and subsystems. The final program will have a balance of electromagnetic and solid-state physics phenomena. Papers on new and emerging technologies in related fields are also encouraged.

4.2- The EMP Preppers & Survivalist Communities

Preppers are individuals, a family or family group who prepare in varying degrees to survive a natural or man-made catastrophe, such as a hurricane, tornado, electromagnetic pulse, volcano, earthquake, tsunami, Nor'easter, floods, fires, and large mudslides. They spend their own time and money in varying degrees for preparing for survival over a few days to over a year. It is estimated that about 1% of the US population are Prepper members.

Trade Journals dedicated to the survival mission are

(1)- Survivalist, bimonthly journal, CDI Publications, Inc.

(2)- Disaster and Recovery,

(3)- The Prepper Journal,

Doomsday Preppers is an American reality television series (now in its fourth season as the year 2015 starts) that airs on cable and hulu and prior seasons are available on Netflix. The program profiles various survivalists, or "preppers", who the National Geographic Channel shows preparing to survive the various circumstances that may cause the end of civilization, including economic collapse, societal collapse, and electromagnetic pulse. The quality of their preparations is graded by the consulting company Practical Preppers, who provide analysis and recommendations for improvements. There are some myths and Hollywood poetic license added.

EMP Survivalists are a survival subset group of Preppers, sometimes not identified with the Preppers. Their mission is geared entirely or mostly to EMP protection. The book *EMP Survival* , by Larry & Cheryl Pool comprehensively addresses the EMP Survival mission. It may be purchased on Amazon.

The EMP Survivalist emphasizes storage of water and 25-year, freeze-dried food, medications, bartering items, ammo and guns. Their seventh item is to have a place in the county to retreat to when an EMP event happens. The problem here is that bare survival has almost no lifestyle. If a gasoline/diesel vehicle is used, they may not even get to the county. They have no plan for an EMP protected enclosure or solar rooftop to significantly improve their lifestyle. However, there is evidence that EMP preppers are starting to get the message

4.3- The EMC Community and IEEE/EMC Society

EMC Stands for Electromagnetic Compatibility. This means the control of electromagnetic interference of all types. Examples include transmitters inadvertently jamming each other or other receivers, electrical and electronic devices disturbing communications, and the crowded frequency spectrum spilling over into devices occupying the skirts or harmonics of other user devices or equipments.

To make EMC happen, their community of many manufacturing companies have developed an arsenal of components and technologies involving, structure shielding, bonding, grounding and cable shielding, surge suppression and filtering. Part of this community is the IEEE (Institute of Electrical and Electronic Engineers), EMC society of over 4,000 members and 37 chapters in the USA and about 30 other countries. The IEEE, EMC Society holds an annual symposium in different cities in and outside the USA and publishes a quarterly record called "Electromagnetic Compatibility Magazine". You may contact IEEE/EMC on their website, www.emcs.org.

They are the dominant source of technology and components for the EMP community in protecting all kinds of electronics and electrical devices and equipment from an EMP event. At the risk of repetition, it bares repeating that EMC probably makes and utilizes more than 80% of the products and services that will be used in EMP protection fulfillment.

4.4- The Solar-Electric Community

The Solar Photovoltaic Community is a world-wide gathering of people and organizations with a solar PV mission. Their end product is a solar installation in the form of solar rooftop or utility or privately owned solar farms. Its importance is envisioned as the big backup to the electric utility if and when it goes down. Actually it goes beyond the EMP threat in that nearly all installations provide "free" electricity where the electric grid does not reach.

To get some idea about the large size of the the solar industry, visit the website: www.enfsolar.com. Therein are listings of over 20,000 global organizations, divided into eight categories from about 70 countries:

- Equipment
- Sellers
- Components
- Installers
- Materials
- Applications
- Panels
- Services

For example, in USA there are listed 2,863 Installers, averaging 57 installers per state or nearly one per county. Exceptions acknowledged, each installer can provide to www.enfsolar.com the size of his company in number of employees, phone and fax numbers, web address, mail address and possibly more for website visitors. Among the principal suppliers of EMP protection products and services are those shown in Table 4.2 on the next page.

Fig. 4.2 – Some of the Principal EMC and Solar Players

Manufacturers of Source Materials and/or Serices which may be used for HEMP & Solar Hardening

#	Company Name	Tel. Number	Fax Number	E-mail	URL-Website	SR	SC	SW	SH	BD	GR	SS	FT	TL	CS	#
1	Chomerics	781-935-4850	781-933-4318	Chomailbox @												1
2	ETS-Lindgren, Illinois	630-307-7200	630-307-7571	info @ets-lindgren.com	www.ets-lindgren.com											2
3	ETS-Lindgren, Texas	512-531-6400	512-531-6500	info @ets-lindgren.com	www.ets-lindgren.com											3
4	Holland Shielding	31-78-613-1366	31-78-614-9585	info @hollandshielding.com	www.hollandshielding.com											4
5	Metatech Corporation	805-683-5681	806-683-3023	info @metatech.com	www.metatechcorp.com											5
6	PanaShield	203-866-5888	203-866-6162	help @panshield.com	www.panashield.com											6
7	Protection Technology Group	800-882-9110		sales@protectiongroup.com	www.protectiongroup.com											7
8	Renewable Energy Creations	941-743-7633	941-743-7633	drjw9@aol.com	www.emp-protection.org											8
9	Retif Testing Laboratories	703 533-1614	703 533-1612		www.Retif.com											9
10	RFI Corporation	631-231-6400	631-231-6435	rfisales@rficorp	www.rficorp.com											10
11	Schaffner	800-387-5566	732-225-4789	ken.bellero @schaffner.com	www.schaffnerusa.com											11
12	Schurter	707-636-3000	707-636-3033	info @shurter.com	www.schurerinc.com											12
13	Spectrum ASP	814-474-1571	814-474-3110	susan @altman-hall.com	www.spectrum.com											13
14	Tech-Etch	548-747-0300	548-746-9639	bmcallister @tech-etch.com	www.Tech-etch.com											14
15	Zippertubing	800-321-8178	310-767-1714	orders @zippertubing.com	www.zippertubing.com											15

#	Company Name	Tel. Number	Fax Number	E-mail	URL-Website	SR	SC	SW	SH	BD	GR	SS	FT	TL	CS	#

A Few Solar Panel & Inverter Manufacturers and Solar Magazines

#	Company Name	Tel. Number	Fax Number	E-mail	URL-Website	SR	SC	SW	SH	BD	GR	SS	FT	TL	CS	#
16	First Solar	877-850-3767	602-414-9400		www.firstsolar.com	Panels		Inverter	b Magaz.							16
17	Suntech Power	866-966-6655	415-882-9923		www.suntech-power.com											17
18	Sun Power Corp..	800-786-7893			www.us.sunpowercorp.com											18
19	Yingli, China/USA	888-686-8820	212-886-8806	info @yingliamerica	www.yinglisolar.com											19
20	Canadian Solar	925-866-2700	925-866-2704	inquire.us @canadian	www.Canadian-solar.com											20
21	Solectria Renewables	978-683-9700	978-683-9702	inverters @solren.com	www.solren.com											21
22	Delta Products Corp	877-460-5851		sales.usa @www.solar-inverter.com	www.solar-inverter.com/na											22
23	Global Solar Technology	239-245-9284	239-236-4682	arae@globalsolartechnology.com	Www.globalsolartechnology.com											23
24	Solar Industry	800-326-6745	203-262-4680	info @solarindustry.com	www.solarindustry.com											24
25	Solar Today	303-443-3130	303-443-3212	ases@ases.org	www.ases.org											25
26	Photon.Info	617-874-5500	617-262-4309	info @photolnfo.con	www.Photon.info.com	Panels		Inverter	b Magaz.							26

#	Company Name	Tel. Number	Fax Number	E-mail	URL-Website	SR	SC	SW	SH	BD	GR	SS	FT	TL	CS	#

Code: SR = shielded rooms, enclosures. SC = Shielded cables, connectors. SW = shielded windows, glass panels. SH = shielded materials, windows, building siding, other. BD = bonding. GR = grounding related products and subjects. SS = surge suppressors. TL = Testing Labs, CS = consulting

Note: we will be expanding this list in our next printing. If you wish to be listed, please provide your credentials

There are four magazines and trade journals serving the Solar-PV community (note: PV is added to mean photovoltaic from the sun - not from heating blankets and pipes for water and pools):

- PV Magazine: www.pv-magazine.com
- Solar Industry magazine: www.solarindustrymag.com, 100 Willenbrock Road, Oxford, CT 06478, Phone: 800-325-6745, Fax: 203-262-4680, e-mail: info@solarindustrymag,com
- Solar Power World: www.solarpowerworldonline.com
- Solar Today (American Solar Energy Society), 2525 Arapahoe Ave, Ste E4-253, Boulder, Colorado 80302, Phone: 303-443-3130, Fax: 303-443-3212, e-mail: info@ases.org
- Home Power Magazine: www.homepower.com, Phone 800-707-6585 or 541-512-0201
- Solar Pro Magazine: www.solarprofessional.com
- pv magazine: www.pv-magazine.com
- Solar Builder Magazine: www.solarbuildermag.com, Benjamin Media Inc. 10050 Brecksville Rd. Brecksville, OH 44141 USA, www.benjaminmedia.com

4.5- Small EMP Protected Homes & Builders Communities

Many of the EMP protected homes in the next few years will likely be small, second homes, like cottage sheds built in large groups on farms or by real-estate developers (Chapter

Small, Early EMP Protected Development of Cottage-Sheds for Sale or Rental
See other "Circle-the-wagons" development layouts

12). These are mostly factory-built homes ranging in size from 160 sq. ft. (8x20) to roughly 480 sq. ft. (16x30). The larger ones have provisions for EMP protected parking of a vehicle plus an electric golf cart and additional storage. Their main attractions are their relatively low price with "free" electricity, located on a pond or lake, providing pleasant weekend entertainment in the administration building, and additional security offered by a community size. Multiple financial options are available.

In addition to small factory-built homes, other home sources include Amish homes and shipping container homes (described in Chapters 9 and 12).

4.5.1- Community Solar Gardens

Today, there is a big movement in Community Solar Gardens (sometimes called Community Solar Projects). A CSP is a solar power installation that accepts capital from and provides output credit and tax benefits to individual and other investors. In some systems you buy individual solar panels which are installed after your purchase. In others you purchase kW capacity or kWh of production. The farm's power output is credited to investors in proportion to their investment, with adjustments to reflect ongoing changes in capacity, technology, costs and electricity rates. Companies, cooperatives, governments or non-profits operate the farms.

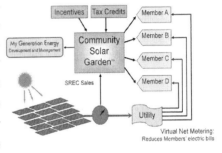

Community Solar Gardens are discussed further in Chapter 12.

Chapter 5
Bottom-up Management - County Planning & Operations

Chapter Overview

As mentioned earlier, the national perception is that the government has abdicated its fiduciary responsibility to provide EMP protection for the nation and its citizens. That's why roughly three million Americans have taken EMP survival into their own hands. Thus, unless America gets new credible leadership, more things can and will get done via bottom-up management. This means that nearly all the necessary EMP protection planning and actions will initiate from the county rather than the feds or the states. This includes issuing county bonds for financing rather than costly subsidizing actions which have often resulted in waste and fraud.

Bottom-up management means that EMP awareness, planning, teaching, and media outreach, construction, test certification and financing are orchestrated at the county level. This will economically streamline the production and implementation of new ideas and products while curtailing waste, abuse and fraud.

The county Economic Development Office, local Chambers of Commerce, local professionals and installers, bank financiers, and developers will form a County Group of Seven to orchestrate and expedite EMP planning. The state role will be to minimize duplication of efforts and manage systemic voids.

The federal role is building prototype and template villages to ensure that all paper designs and plans are physically realizable at competitive costs. There are many other roles described in Chapter 3.

5.1- Bottom-up Management

The traditional way of running an organization or project, government or industry, is from the top down. This is called *Top-down Management*. When the top managers display sound, innovative, flexible and empathetic leadership things generally get done in a timely, creative and purposeful manner.

Conversely, if the top managers lack leadership, the organization and its otherwise productive output, become subject to failure. When the organization is government it has the unfortunate image of a "bureaucracy", where things take a longer time to get done and often in a way that tends to result in waste, abuse and sometimes, fraud. Industry, far better in performance, also is subject to examples of the weakness of a bureaucracy, usually because of poor leadership.

Exceptions acknowledged, the main reason that government performance is perceived in a poor light, is because they are taught to spend money, not earn money. Contrast this with capitalistic industry, geared to create and develop a return on investment or ROI. It has been suggested that one requirement for serving in upper government management positions is to have had five years of prior industry experience.

The opposite of Top-Down Management is *Bottom-up Management*. In this approach, things usually get done faster, on time with little to no cost overrun. They are more creative because producers at the bottom are not encumbered with meetings, distracting sideisms, including media and marketing and waste. Thus, lower management and their workers tend to be more agile and their mission and goals are more readily achievable. (The reader, not interested in more discussion on bottom-up management may skip the next two pages),

Significant changes are taking place in management and especially project management today. Organizations, like the New York

Times, Tribune Co, Ernst & Young, switched from traditional top-down management style to bottom-up management.

Others, including some of the world's biggest corporations, such as Toyota and IBM, implemented *bottom-up management style elements in some of their departments.* The popularity of the bottom-up approach to management is growing. Why have organizations become so anxious about changing their management style? If we compare the two management approaches, the answer to this question will be clear.

Top-down	Bottom-up
Inflexibility	Flexibility
Bureaucracy	Agility
Overall control	Collaboration
Imposed processes	Team-driven processes
No moral motivation – people feel that their opinion does not matter	High motivation – team members contribute to the way the project is developed

Project Management 2.0

Control and collaboration

Clarity of project goals and visibility of internal organizational processes

Coordination and collective intelligence

If you have tried introducing the best bottom-up practices to your organization, you have probably found it difficult to do that while utilizing traditional tools for project management. Traditional project management software, like Microsoft Project, was mostly designed to fit the use of the top-down approach and is not meant for the bottom-up management style. This software is focused on the project manager and places him in the center of the project communications.

Team members very often have read-only access to the project plan and cannot make any contributions or changes. The employees send their updates to the project manager in disconnected files via e-mail. The project manager then has to collect all the data and put the information manually into the project plan. After that, he has to communicate the changes to the corporate executives. All these routine procedures lead to a situation where the project manager's talents and time often are buried by the routine work. The huge amount of mechanical control/ synchronization work often leaves little very time for leadership from the project manager.

The good news is the above situation is changing thanks to the transformations going on in how people share and receive information. More methods for the successful implementation of the bottom-up management best practices have emerged. These methods include Enterprise 2.0 technologies – wikis, blogs, social networks, collaboration tools, etc. They come into organizations and change the original way of executing projects. They turn traditional project management into Project Management 2.0 and bring new patterns of collaboration, which are based on collective intelligence.

Collective intelligence is a collection of valuable knowledge from different fields that each project team member is an expert in. This knowledge is now successfully collected and shared in a flexible, *collaborative environment* brought by second-generation project management software. The project manager is the one to conduct the work of his team and choose the right direction for the project development, based on the information received from the individual employees.

Thus, the role the project manager plays in the project changes. Project Management 2.0 software facilitates delegation. It means that people become less dependent on the manager as a to-do generator. The project manager turns from a taskmaster into a project leader. His role is to facilitate the team communications, provide a creative working environment and guide the team. He becomes a visionary able to leverage the team strengths and weaknesses and adjust the project development, based on various external changes. Individual team members still have the freedom and responsibility to find their way to the next milestone.

So that all readers are on the same page, remember that Bottom-up Management was first introduced in Chapter 3. A variation of that EMP protection organization chart for the US Government EMP is shown in Fig. 5.1. The bottom third of the chart applies to nearly all the 3,421 USA counties where Bottom-up Management resides.

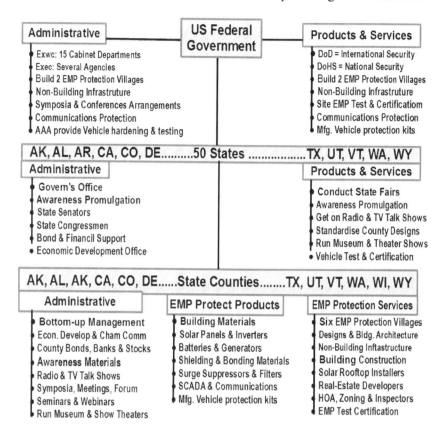

EMP protection can best be implemented by applying Bottom-up management, starting at the County Level for the following reasons:

● Homes, buildings, infrastructure and solar rooftop architects and engineers exist at the county level and activities are applied primarily within their own familiar locations.

● Similarly, construction foremen and workers, builders, and support personnel are mostly local and know the "ropes.".

● Counties have their own government tailored to the variables of their location, climate, mountainous or seashore, ethnicity, etc.

89

Thus, they are more pragmatic and effective at getting things done on a timely basis.

● Most of the financing is done with county bonds and some corporate bonds executed via local stock brokerages and banks. Of course, the states have their role in this process ensuring uniformity and oversight protection. This leads the reader to the next section.

5.2- County Configuration and Demographics

Each of the fifty USA states is subdivided into counties. There are 3,142 counties (a few are county equivalents) in the USA. The average number of counties per state is 63. The average county population is close to 100,000 inhabitants and the average county area size is about 1,100 sq. miles (2,800 sq. km).

There are 10 counties with over one million population and 14 under 1,000 population. The small ones can join a contiguous county to have at least 10,000 in population. Since the big and small counties constitute less than 1% of the USA county number, they will not be addressed now in favor of the leading 99%. Local state congressman and senators are county contacts to the state capitol. Each county has a direct dedicated contact at the state capital. The state will ensure timely dissemination of material to other counties and interested parties to avoid duplication of efforts. It will also see that all pertinent EMP issues are timely addressed, such as, the installation of 4,000 ft., mat-dirt replenishment runways as addressed in later chapters.

5.3- County EMP Planning Group

The county planning group has seven members and a full-time secretary. One of the seven is the group leader who works full time. The remaining six are part time working for

90

their normal companies. Included in the group of seven are:

5.3.1- County Economic Development Office

The chief county officer is usually named County Administrator. The group that makes rules and regulations for the county is the Board of Supervisors (sometimes called Board of Commissioners). Chief contact for the responsibility of present and future planning for county growth is the Economic Development Office. They focus on bringing into the county, manufacturing, tourism and retirees who will spend money in the county that they earned elsewhere

The Economic Development Office provides one person for the new EMP Protection task group. His new role will also be to interact with companies that want to take root and grow in an EMP concerned community as well as initiate EMP protection activities.

5.3.2- County Chamber of Commerce

Representing the business side of the county and the Economic Development Office is the *Chamber of Commerce*. Covering small and big businesses, the CoC includes real estate developers, builders, installers of solar rooftops and solar farms, private utilities, retailers, banks and stock brokers and many others. One representative from the CoC is assigned to the County EMP protection Group.

5.3.3- County EMP Planning and Fulfillment Group

The County EMP Group of Seven consists of one member from:

- Group Leader, full time & primary contact for outside the county
- Economic Development Office
- Chamber of Commerce
- Architect or Engineer and coauthor of publications
- Real Estate Developer
- Banker or Stock Market Specialist
- EMP Survivalist or Prepper
- Full time secretary – Good Girl Friday

The Group meets at least once a week. Each member has a specific mission and goals and a monthly updateable time line or Gantt Chart. They are responsible for developing in a timely manner the following:

- EMP awareness, planning, construction, test, & other documents
- Request for Quotations and bidding contracts for construction
- Designing EMP protect details, cottage sheds, homes, buildings
- Development of escape Cottage Shed and related communities
- Installers of solar rooftops, farms and their test certifications
- Frequent radio and TV talk shows and media contacts
- Training classes, seminars and webinars on how-to-do-it
- Issuing county and corporate financing bonds

The activities and performance of the county EMP planning group is discussed in later chapters

5.4 Roles of the Federal and State Governments

5.4.1 The Federal Government

Some have criticized the feds as having abdicated their fiduciary responsibility for protecting its citizens from rogue nations and terrorists initiating an EMP event over America. Chapter 2 addressed this matter in two parts: (1) active protection by anti-missile lasers and other means, and (2) defensive EMP protecting homes, building and other infrastructure. Number 2 is the big failure. But, ask ourselves: what should the Fed's role be and what are the specifics and timing?

One may generalize and say the Fed's defensive civil role is some-what similar in *concept, but to a lesser and more relevant degree,* to what it has done to protect the military weaponry such as:

- EMP harden Navy fighting ships so they still function after an EMP event.
- EMP protect all the supply functions so that ammo and functioning weaponry are available when needed
- Protect ammunition storage dumps
- Secure communications so there exists enough protection and

redundancy.

• Since a lot of military equipment depends upon microprocessors to continue functioning after an EMP event, an enormous shielding and surge suppression effort, was developed.

The military needs a functioning civil world after an EMP event in order for it to discharge its mission. Domestically, all military and government employees wear two hats: one at work and one civil hat for after working hours. They call home on their cell phones, stop to get gasoline and groceries before arriving home, eat dinner, play with the kids, then go to sleep, and arise for work again the next morning. The military is not fire-walled against a collapsed electric grid and a dysfunctional destroyed country. A functioning civilian sector supports a string military.

Here are the main civil actions the government must do for EMP protection of its citizens:

(1)- Communications, such as phone, cell, ipad, satellite, radio & TV talk shows, Internet (e-mail, webinars, forum, blogs), and some social networking are vital. Also, that information is available on EMP awareness; what does the citizen do; when and how? The government needs to ensure that vital communications can survive an EMP attack.

(2)- Information developed in Phase 1 of EMP preparedness, such as The *documents* produced by the county groups of seven, discussed in Chapter 5, can be printed and disseminated by the feds. Educating about EMP is vital to ensure the timely adoption of EMP protection and aftermath application techniques

(3)- *Long distance vitals supply and replenishments:* When the lowest likely EMP bomb is detonated at, say, 20 miles (32 km km) altitude, all non-EMP protected electronics, including electrical power becomes dysfunctional over a radius of about 490 miles (750,000 sq. mi. or 1.9 million sq. km.). Thus, most replenishment deliveries cannot be carried out in a timely manner, and citizens may starve, die of disease or malnutrition or other missing vitals.

A network up to 150 relatively inexpensive, 4,000 foot, metal-mat covered earth runways can be built around the country in needed locations not having airports. This will allow a a Globemaster III cargo plane (with a 70-ton payload) to resupply the damaged area from an undamaged base more than 500 miles away.

(4)- AAA and the vehicle susceptibility reduction

As reported in Chapter 1, The U.S. EMP Commission, EMP tested a number of cars and trucks at the Army's *White Sands Proving Grounds*. The results of the tests were inconclusive since they tested at lower EMP field strengths, not wanting to destroy the vehicles. Their vintage ranged from 1980 to 2002. In the past two decades the number of vulnerable micro-processors on vehicles has significantly increased, thereby exacerbating the susceptibility problem by unknown amounts.

As part of the solution to this problem is to require the auto manufacturers to perform simulated EMP tests on their autos and trucks to document their EMP susceptibility profile. They also need to develop a booklet for buyers on how to protect or mitigate against an EMP. However, in the shorter term the government needs to come to an agreement with the AAA (American Automobile Association) and or individual vehicle manufacturers to do two things: (1) perform an EMP susceptibility profile for some vehicles each year, and (2) offer an EMP susceptibility mitigation kit for sale to reduce vulnerability.

The U.S. EMP Commission also tested a number of 1986 to 2001 model trucks at the Army's White Sands Proving Ground.

(5)- EMP protected villages. In earlier chapters it was mentioned that two of the Phase I prototype/template, Cottage-Shed villages can be constructed in areas near two selected Army, Navy and Air Force field laboratories. This benefits for laboratory employees, if

an EMP event occurs when off hours and ensures the military is participating in the civil-side of the EMP-protection program.

Ed. Note: Since the Federal Government has provided for decades a 90% guarantee to the banks for all Small Business loans, a smaller percentage of this may be considered for county bonds to be used for EMP protection.

5.4.2- EMP Protection Support from States

As mentioned in Chapter 3, there exists an average of 63 counties per state – an enormous span of supervision in number, ethnicity, culture, wealth, climate, etc. To ensure that Bottom-up Management works, the state will be tasked to ensure timely EMP protection awareness and understanding, as well as eliminating gaps in preparedness and duplication of county efforts. State senators and congressmen will help in this process. But, timely awareness and communications will best be structured correctly from the start. Here are a few examples:

• New county developed awareness documents, discoveries, and new ways and means will be promptly submitted to the state for quick feedback.

• The state assists in getting out the word on EMP protection via local radio and TV Talk shows. The latter gets more difficult as the producers and advertisers make it harder for the less well-known participants to join the hosts.

• State fairs and participating symposia and conferences having a partial EMP mission will be monitored by the state. The mission is to ensure counties have an opportunity to participate as visitors, booth participants, and those presenting technical papers and sessions.

• The average state has three of the previously mentioned 4,000 ft mat-covered dirt runways for vitals, Globemaster III replenishment enhancements. This translates to one such runway for the least populated states to about 12 for the most populated.

- Provide backup support to the issuance of County bonds that finance most of the EMP protection. This is done by assisting the counties and stock brokerage houses with providing timely information in the correct format.

5.4.3- Potential Fed Role: EMP Protection Agency:.

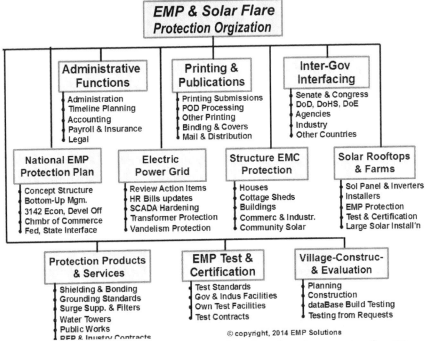

© copyright, 2014 EMP Solutions

One could develop an argument for the development of a New Federal Agency, called *EMP Protection Agency*. The primary benefit is that the country can focus thereon and Congress can appropriate funds. However, we remember what happened to the Environmental Protection Agency today vs 50 years ago. Perhaps we should try Bottom up Management and the Scrum effect first and see how that works.

(Note: Scrum is a way for teams to work together to develop a product. Product development, using Scrum, occurs in small pieces, with each piece building upon previously created pieces. Building products, one small piece at a time, encourages creativity and enables teams to respond to feedback and change, to build exactly and only what is needed.)

Chapter 6
National & Local EMP Educational Media

Chapter Overview

This chapter addresses EMP educational media available on the Internet and elsewhere. If one is new to EMP, one starting point is www.futurescience.emp; another is www.emp-safeguard.com.

Books are the more traditional starting place. There are eight published EMP protection and related books, including two novels, for sale on Amazon, the above websites and elsewhere.

There are a few animated and narration slide shows on EMP and EMP protection. These are especially good for awareness and education as they have both the printed and spoken word. Videos can't do this, for example, if the video is stopped to examine an image, voice is lost and written word may not exist.

There are many EMP-related videos on the Internet, but they are mostly demonstrating how bad an EMP event can be rather than educational on EMP prevention. National Geographic has a few which are useful, but once it goes Hollywood, myths are introduced and it becomes a novel.

Blogs and forums are available on the Internet. There are many hundreds of blogs, but they are more in response to a specific topic, leaving most subjects not addressed. Forums are fewer in number, but tend to be better as they convey more information.

From time-to-time, Fox Studios runs some TV talk shows with several experts testifying on EMP, solar flares, the Shield Act but rarely on EMP protection. EMPactAmerica (www.EMPactAmerica.com) has an archived talk show on EMP related matters.

6.1- The Internet

The Internet is replete with all kinds of information on EMP and Solar Flares. The later is less devastating because solar flares are less dysfunctional to electrical and electronic devices which have hard-wire line connections shorter than 500 feet (producing induced levels 50 dB down from an intercepting 100 mile [160 km] transmission lime). This is because Solar Flares produce very low frequencies requiring long lines to couple meaningful damaging induced currents.

There is also a lot of myths on the Internet about potential damages and potential fixes or mitigators of EMP protection. Some apposing articles negate these Myths with supporting rationale.

Unfortunately, most of the Internet information focuses on the damage that EMP can cause to infrastructure, housing and vehicles, because (1) yes, negativity sells, and (2) there is far more negativity on the Internet than what can be done to EMP protect victims. Most exceptions involve small items like cell phones, ipads, where aluminum foil- lined envelopes do the EMP shielding, or shoe boxes and trunks which also have foil-lining and protect portable radios and larger items. These shielded small items use what is called "Faraday cages" or "Faraday shields" named after the English Physicist, Michael Faraday.

The most popular Internet source for credible EMP information on the Internet is www.emp-futurescience.com. It is regularly updated and expanded and has been on the Internet for years.

The author's website, www.emp-safeguard.com, is far less expansive than the futurescience website. However, it contains perhaps the most information of any other website on how to perform EMP protection on cottage sheds, houses, buildings, infrastructures and solar rooftops.

The best detailed EMP protection product sites are the manufacturers in the EMC (Electromagnetic Compatibility) Community who make shielding, bonding, grounding, and cable surge suppressors and filters and testing. Most are shown in the table depicted in Chapter 4.

6.2- Books on EMP Protection

There are about ten books on EMP and/or EMP protection listed on the Internet. Most are sold on the Amazon site. In inverse chronological order, from Chapter 3, they are repeated here for convenience.

- *A National EMP Protection Plan,* by Don White, EMP Solutions, LLC, Jan. 2015
- *EMP Protecting Housing & Solar,* aka *EMP Protecting Cottage Sheds, Homes, Buildings and Infrastructure with Solar Rooftops,* by Don White, EMP Solutions, 2014
- *EMP – Protect Family, Homes and Community, 3rd Edition,* by Don White and Jerry Emanuelson, EMP Solutions & Renewable Energy Creations, 2013
- *A Nation Forsaken,* by F, Michael Maloof, 2013
- *Electric Armageddon: Civil-Military Preparedness for an Electromagnetic Pulse Catastrophe,* by Dr. Peter Vincent Pry, 2013
- *Contrasting EMP Survivals – A Tale of Two Towns,* a novel or sequel to *One Second After,* by Don White, EMP Solutions & Renewable Energy Creations, 2013
- *Disaster Preparedness for EMP Attacks and Solar Storms, by* Arthur T. Bradley, PhD., 2012
- *Nuclear EMP Threats – What Next?,* by Don White. Renewable Energy Creations, LLC, 2012
- *EMP Survival,* by Larry and Cheryl Poole, self published. 2011
- *Solar Flare Survival,* (Protect Yourself and Your Electronics with Faraday Cages) , by Marc Remillard, 2011
- *One Second After,* by William T. Forstchen, 2009

6.3- Slide Shows on EMP Protection

There appears to be few slide shows on the Internet for EMP protection. They are:

- EMP Protection Slide show – YouTube, 90 seconds
  www.youtube.com/watch?v=ODgE5m-yz-
  Jun 11, 2012 - Uploaded by Donald White

● A National EMP Protection Plan with Strategies, Ways & Means and Surprise Payoffs", www.emp-safeguard.com/slideshow.html

6.4- Videos on EMP Protection

The Internet has many Videos on EMP and a few on EMP protection. Here are some of the more informative ones:

6.4.1- EMP Threat

● EMP Bomb Threat Scenario – YouTube, Fox News
www.youtube.com/watch?v=vn6OVLK0MBI May 12, 2013 - Uploaded by TopGunMilitary

● Is U.S. Prepared for Electromagnetic Pulse Attack?
video.foxnews.com/.../is-us-prepare... Fox News Channel, Dec 13, 2011

6.5- Seminars and Webinars

There may be few people on earth who have taught more seminars than this author. For a period of 23 years, I have taught two to five-day seminars on EMC subjects (shielding, bonding, grounding, surge suppression and filtering). They have been taught in five continents to 14,000 engineers in 29 countries. The ability to teach, understand, calibrate other professionals, and give them creative solutions are my cherished challenge and legacy.

At seminars, I have the pleasure of seeing a student's countenance to help calibrate the degree of understanding at any moment of the teaching process. Questions were asked at any time - not once an hour or when the subject has changed to another. Instant questions short of letting the instructor finish his paragraph, was especially appreciated by the rest of the students. Allow as much as 20% of the course time for Q&A when doing seminars.

The best part was the last half day of the course, where a class was divided into groups of 3-4 students and given a problem to solve and a computer to numerically get the solution and options. Each group selected its own group leader, who usually operated the computer. Later he stood in front of the classroom and presented the group problem and solutions with transparencies or slides, as the class asked him questions. It was a great learning process.

Today it is a lot more impersonal as webinars on the Internet have taken over most of the teaching process. Since all sessions are recorded, along with live Questions and Answers, the best can be used for teaching teachers or for students to review in private for more in-depth understanding.

The best of the above can be redone in the sister EMP world to cover about ten related facets of EMP protection, somewhat remindful of the 19 chapters of this book. The EMP courses can occupy a range of 2 hours, 1/2 day, 1 day or two days, While there are very few classes offered on the Internet, and they are by special arrangement only, seminars and webinars are the best way to go for intensive learning.

All seminars can be tailored to the company or agency mission and goals. They are called dedicated (or customer site located) classes and those taught at specified times and dates are known as published courses.

6.6- Computer and CD Materials

Two computer software programs regarding EMP and EMI (electromagnetic interference) protection have been identified:

• #3500, *Shielding Effectiveness* (Electromagnetic Radiation Blockage): Program computes shielding effectiveness for 36 metals from 10 kHz to 10 GHz for metal thicknesses from thin foils to sheet metals to plates. Results are plotted for any distance between source and metal shield. Results are graphed for 0 to 150 dB shielding for E and H fields and plane waves.

• #3600, *Shielding Aperture Leakage Control.* Computes the shielding effectiveness of enclosure apertures, unprotected windows, vents, seams, covers and component holes between 10 kHz and 30 GHz. Shielding data are presented in graphical and tabular form or a selected frequency. Program permits running "what if?" comparisons.

Both computer software programs are available from *EMP Solutions and Renewable Energy Creations, LLC* at website: www.emp-safeguard.com

6.7- Blogs and Forums

6.7.1- EMP Related Blogs

A blog is a regularly updated website or web page, typically one run by an individual or small group, that is written in an informal or conversational style. The blog usually comments on an article or on remarks made by previous bloggers of the article subject.

The Internet has, perhaps, a hundred websites providing comments about an EMP topic or EMP prevention subject, too many to enumerate here. Usually it is a page promoting a product or service website or an observer or user of a product or service.

6.7.2- EMP Related Forums

A forum is defined as an assembly, meeting place, television program, Internet website, etc., for the discussion of questions of public interest. Also called on-line **forum**, Internet **forum**, Web **forum**, message board.

There are some forums on the Internet relative to EMP and Solar Flares. Here are a few:

- **Electromagnetic Pulse (EMP) | Doomsday Prepper Forums** www.doomsdayprepperforums.com › ... › Types of Disasters Doomsday Prepper **Forums**- for serious Doomsday Preppers and for those who .... China's military is developing **electromagnetic pulse** weapons that Beijing..

  - EMP (electromagnetic pulse) - EMPact America - Prepare Hub www.preparehub.org/forums/Topics.aspx?forum=*132321*. Shortly after I read "Lights Out", it is also an **EMP** story line and scary as hell!Hey guys, this reminds me that I was going to add a **forum** to this web site for people.

• Electromagnetic Pulse - EVE Online Forums
https://**forums**.*eveonline.com/default.aspx?g=posts&t=326078*
Mar 1, 2014 - 5 posts - 4 authors. While both work well according to the situation I am proposing a third option – an **electromagnetic pulse**. This could be a smart bomb.

• Directory: Electromagnetic Pulse (EMP) - PESWiki
peswiki.com/index.php/Directory:**Electromagnetic_Pulse_(EMP)**
Directory of technologies and resources pertaining to **electromagnetic pulse**, ...**Forum** responses: Most panels have bypass diodes fitted to the discrete series ...

• Solar Flare Forum - Topix
www.topix.com/**forum**/news/**solar-flare**
Forum and message boards for **Solar Flare**. ... Second **solar storm** hits Earth, auroras expected... Sep., 2014, Kid_Tomorrow · 1 · **solar flares.**

• Flare Sci-Fi Forums flare.solareclipse.net/
Forum, Posts, Last Post, Moderators. Administration ... **Flare** Sci-Fi **Forums** Recent Visitors: 85. guest(s) ... 1999-2008 **Solareclipse** Network.

6.8- National Radio & TV Talk Shows

• TV Fox News of 1211 Avenues of the Americas, NYC has from time-to-time, guest speakers on EMP topics:
  • Megyn Kelly, weeknights, 9 P.M. EST
  • Bill O'Reilly, weeknights, 8 P.M., EST, The O'Reilly Factor
  • Mike Huckabee, (was on weeknights). Now, off-the-air
  • Jon Hannity, weeknights, 10 P.M., EST
  • Judge Jeanine Pirro, Sat. night, 9 P.M., EST

BTW, rare exceptions acknowledged, the reader will notice that almost all EMP talk shows, including the host and guests, discuss how the EMP threat, its impact and how disastrous it is, with only a very small time discussing remedies. **Note:** to the producers. Yes, negativity sells, but think of the audience response when you talk about solutions. Now, you have a positive approach (no spin) that produces listener response, interest, intrigue and the ability to do something about the EMP threat other than the little, post-EMP no lifestyle of Preppers and EMP survivalists! Don't continue to miss these opportunities. Optimize your approach.

- EMP Threat - Shows - CoShows Jan 3, 2013 -Former policy analyst for the Dept. of Defense, and currently WND's Washington senior reporter, Michael Maloof, discussed how everything...Coast to Coast AM

  www.coasttocoastam.com ›

- 'End is near': Radio star issues dire warning – WorldNetDail
  www.wnd.com/.../end-is-near-radio-star-launches-emp-w...
  Aug 4, 2014 – The threat of an electromagnetic pulse event or attack on the United...of "Coast to Coast AM," the most-listened-to overnight radio program.

- Expert: Iran ships a dry run for later nuclear/EMP attack ...
  www.washingtonexaminer.com/expert-iran...nuclearemp.../2544041
  Feb 14, 2014 - Iran's surprising decision to move warships off the Atlantic **coast** poses a potential catastrophic **threat** to America from a potential nuclear source .

Chapter 7
EMP Protection Materials

Chapter Overview

This chapter discusses the basic materials used to perform EMP protection via item or structure shielding, bonding, grounding, and cable surge suppression and filtering. The first two involve EMP radiation protection and the last two involve wire or cable conducted EMP protection. Grounding is common to both as a means to divert EMP source current flow away from the structure and force it to earth ground where it will dissipate without damage.

Generalizing, perhaps 90% of the EMP protection materials and techniques, cost and effort, goes into shielding the overall housing whether it be a protected shoebox or industrial park building. Regrettably there is a lot of misunderstanding and myths about shielding which this chapter will address. There is even a CD program attached to this book which helps the designer select any of the 20 materials of any thickness or screen-type for shielding. The CD also has another software program on aperture (holes; slots, tears) leakage control, which produces the compromise in shielding when apertures exist. Finally, for intended apertures, like air vents, a special program is given to prevent shielding compromise.

For cable entries to a house, building or other infrastructure, such as power lines, telephone, Internet access control or signal leads, EMP radiation may appear thereon via many different conductors leading to or from the shielded structure. Here, surge suppressors and filters are used to keep the EMP levels below conducted susceptibility limits.

In both radiated and conducted EMP penetration, grounding and grounding materials and techniques generally make a substantial difference in overall protection achievement. Sometimes this ages in time or even weather such as a rainy season or drought. The contiguous grounding soil type ranging from fertile to sandy soil has a substantial impact on the degree of protection.

7.1- Shielding and Bonding Materials & Techniques

Shielding is the process of completely surrounding an object (cell phone, envelope, shoe box, a large box, filing cabinet, pantry, big room, house, building, sprawling industrial complex building) with a metal or more than one metal type. Where shielded metal parts meet or come together, they must be bonded to ensure the integrity of the entire shield.

Before discussing shielding and bonding materials and techniques, here is an overview of how shielding works.

7.1.1- How Shielding Works

For the benefit of the non-technical reader, here is a relatively simple explanation of how shielding works, in two parts: (1) Every on-coming radio frequency or microwave radiation, even a high-powered EMP radiation, has a wave impedance. A metal blocking barrier, on the other hand, has a low impedance (because metal is a good conductor) and acts like nearly a short-circuit to the radiated oncoming wave; (2) a thicker metal shield than a thin shield absorbs more of the remaining radiation not reflected by the metal barrier of part (1). Combine the two together to get the total shielding effectiveness.

It is important to remember that the old term *radioflash* is very descriptive of what an EMP actually is. EMP can be thought of as being a blinding momentary flash of radio waves suddenly occurring over a wide range of frequencies, all at once.

The technical explanation of how shielding works is quantitative rather than qualitative. Figure 7.1 is a diagram explaining how shielding works. Basically, an EMP wave source (most = 377 ohms/square) at the upper left (marked E and H field) strikes a shielding barrier (usually metal having a tiny ohms/square) and it reflects back to the left at the same opposite angle. The ratio of the incident electric or magnetic field to the corre-

Fig. 7.1 – Shielding effectiveness of metal barrier

E

Metal Barrier

Inside of Enclosure

Incident Wave

Transmitted Wave (absorption loss, AL)

H

RL

E

Reflected Wave

H

E

Attenuated Incident Wave

H

E

H

E

H

Outside World

W

Internal Reflecting Wave

sponding reflected field is defined as the reflection loss (RL_{dB}) measured in decibels. (A decibel or dB is simply a ratio, defined as $dB = 20*log_{10}(E_{before}/E_{after})$.

A second loss, due to absorption (AL_{dB}) of the wave traveling through the metal barrier, is shown inside the metal. Shielding Effectiveness, SE_{dB}, is defined in Eq. (7.1) as a combination of both losses:

$$SE_{dB} = RL_{dB} + AL_{dB} \qquad (7.2)$$

7.1.2- Shielding Materials

Several options exist to shield different housing applications and sizes, ranging from a cell phone or iPad envelope, to a shoe box, cabinet, pantry, shed, house, commercial building an industrial structure, electric traffic lights, an automobile, aircraft, subway, boat, etc.

Conductive paints (such as those with aluminum or copper particles) have limited use because (1) of the several coats required to achieve the required 80 dB (default) shielding effectiveness listed in Table 2.2, (2) life expectancy is more limited, and (3) paints are also more susceptible to developing climate and exposure damage, and weathering than solid metals and screens.

Figure 7.2 tabulates the shielding effectiveness of different metal shields vs. frequency from 100 kHz to 1 GHz. The second column lists the required shielding in dB to protect electronic equipment as listed in earlier Table 2.1, repeated here for convenience, where it goes from 80 dB below 2.2 MHz defined in Chapter 2 against an upper atmospheric nuclear burst down to 0 dB at and above 1 GHz for the typical referenced EMP waveshape.

Fig. 7.2 – Shielding Needed for EMP Protection

Frequency	SE Needed
≤100 kHz	80 dB
1 MHz	80 dB
3 MHz	77 dB
10 MHz	65 dB
30 MHz	52 dB
100 MHz	30 dB
300 MHz	10 dB
≥ 1 GHz	0 dB

Fig. 7.2 - Shielding Effectiveness of different Shielding Materials

Shielding Material / RadFreq	100 kHz	1 MHz	3 MHz	10 MHz	30 MHz	100 MHz	300 MHz	1 GHz	$//SF	Notes
Shielding Effectiveness Reqm	80	80	76	65	52	30	10	0	NA	A
10 OPI screen shld	86	*75	*66	*55	*46	35	26	15		B
20 OPI screeen shield	92	81	*72	*61	52	41	32	21		C
30 OPI Screen shield	96	85	76	65	56	45	36	25		D
0.64 mil = Reynolds Wrap	88	89	89	90	90	94	97	107	0.04	E
0.93 mil HD Reynolds Wrap	91	93	93	95	97	103	112	146	0.07	F
1.4 mil XHD Reynolds Wrap	94	96	98	101	104	112	127	165	0.11	G
1/64" = 15.6 mil sheet Al	>165	>165	>165	>165	>165	>165	>165	>165	1.52	H

Notes: A- Required Shielding from Fig. 5.x based on Nuclear Burst producing 50 kV/m, and

Victim electronic device passing MIL-STD-462, RS-105 at 10 V/m. or EN 61000-4-3.

EMP pulse shape has rise time of 5 nsec and 50% height duration of 150 nsec.

B-D OPI = Openings per Inch rating of welded-screen schields

B-D Obtained from EMP-Solutions, Shielding Effectiveness Software Program #3600

The 3rd to 5th rows of Fig. 7.2 list welded metal screens (usually: aluminum. copper or stainless steel). Their screening density is defined in terms of their wire crossover distance or OPI = openings per inch. Except for 10 OPI and 20 OPI (see asterisk, in the cells of Fig. 7.2 for welded metal screens over a portion of their frequency range) all screens meet their shielding effectiveness needs. 20 OPI is selected as a default value since it is usually more rugged (larger wire diameter) than the larger number OPI.

The last four rows in Fig. 7.2 speak to three popular thin aluminum foils (0.64 mil, 0.93 mil and 1.4 mils thick. 1 mil = 0.001 inch = 0.0254 mm) and one sheet of thin aluminum stock (1/64"). There, it is seen that each provides more shielding effectiveness than required. Aluminum foil rolls of 12", 18" and 24" width (31 cm, 46 cm and 61 cm) of all three thickness come in lengths of 50 ft. to 250 ft (15 m to 76 m. (Their cost is very low, roughly $0.04 per square foot ($0.43/sq.m.). Note for large areas to be shielded, more expensive 20 OPI welded screen may be preferred since it is somewhat easier to work with, less prone to tear or puncture and easier to nail.

The next three chapters describe the different appl
shield type for a building foundation, siding and ro
without solar rooftops.

If the facade of the existing building permits the c
an aluminum foil, then the household, 1 mil (= 0.001 inches =
0.0254 mm) or a more rugged version (for example, 3 mils)
provides all the shielding
needed. For example, our
shielding effectiveness
computer program #3600
provides the following
shielding performance for
1 mil aluminum foil. One
One mil provides 97 dB
of shielding as shown in
Fig. 7.3 As discussed in
Chapter 2, 80 dB was
determined to be the

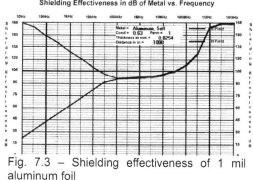

Shielding Effectiveness in dB of Metal vs. Frequency

Fig. 7.3 – Shielding effectiveness of 1 mil
aluminum foil

required amount of building skin shielding to protect against an
EMP incident for most applications. So there **is** sufficient
shielding. But how are sheets of foil to be bonded to their
mounting material and how are they mated together at their edges?

Basically, an adhesive spray is made on the mounting material
back and the foil is placed thereon. A squeegee may be used to
smooth the mounting. However, the foil overlap should in Fig. 7.4
approximate one inch (2.5 cm), and masking tape used to secure
the overlap junction. Do not
spray the foil adhesive in the
2.5 cm region as *metal must
be bonded to metal* without
any other material in be-
tween to ensure a high
conductivity.

METAL FOIL SHIELDS

Fig. 7.4 – Two layers of foil overlap to
The foil must end at each ensure against handling and aging effects
window sill or outside door
sill or frame as the window/door will receive its own shielding. An
electrical bonding agent or gasket (described below) is used to
electrically connect the shielded building facade with each window

.nd door periphery.

Suppose, then the mating metal parts are for an outside door, that is frequently opened and closed, what then? The gasket must be of a type permitting compression to fill the gap between the

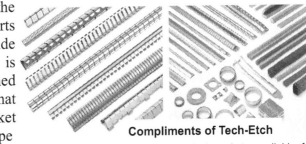

Compliments of Tech-Etch

Fig. 7.4A – Many different electrical gaskets available for selection of the correct type for any particular application. Right central wire mesh type for window sills.

door frame and the door. Fig. 7.4A shows options available from Tech-Etch for achieving this objective. The figure also shows other electrical gaskets useful in bonding other types of mating electrical parts.

To demonstrate the need for meticulous workmanship, suppose that a hole in the shield foil as small as 0.1 inch (2.54 mm) resulted. What is the new shielding performance of the foil with the hole? Fig 7.6 shows the resulting shielding performance of 58 dB at 64 MHz – the frequency of the second node in the EMP time-domain pulse discussed earlier is somewhat defic-

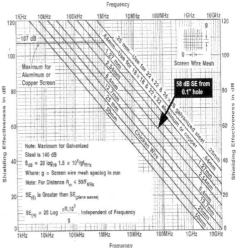

Fig. 7.5 – Shielding leakage with holes

ient). This hole can happen in many ways. One way: suppose a workman secured the foil with a screw into a plywood siding (accidentally or intentionally); then he removed the screw for whatever reason! This explains why two layers of foil were used earlier and two layers of wire mesh screen are frequently used on windows and solar panels.

One alternative to the above foil is to use copper or aluminum paint, applied by brush, roller or spray. One source (*LessEMF.com*, reveals a copper latex paint reported to produce less than 0.1 ohm/square (resistance across any square section)(shielding effectiveness of >72 dB below 1 GHz) for 2 mil deposit. Five mil in two coats will produce the required 80 dB at a paint cost of roughly $2 per square foot. ($21/sq.meter). Exclusive of windows, doors and other building skin discontinuities, a 20,000 sq. ft. building will cost $80k in conductive paint. (This is possibly reduced to ≈ $25k for quantity purchases of over 200 gallons.)

A finishing non-conductive protection coat of latex paint is applied. One major benefit of the paint approach is the relatively easy application by spraying and the avoidance of foil overlaps, and electrical gaskets except at windows, doors, etc.

Duralux Aluminum Marine Boat Paint Green, or equivalent may be a viable protection at a significantly lower cost per gallon ($85). In all cases the surfaces must be clean free of dust, dirt, oxides, etc. Sand blasting may be a necessary first step.

7.1.3- Compromises in Shielding Integrity & Solution Options

As illustrated in the next few shielding application chapters, building shields must be broken or penetrated for several reasons to effect their gainful use. This includes water mains entries and sewage pipes, ventilation pipes on roofs, attic fan and soffit ventilation, and cable and wire entry leads for AC power, telephone, Internet and control and signal leads (SCADA), as applicable. Thus, additional shielding measures are needed for wires and openings Note: the treatment for wires/cables is different since the cross section becomes a coax structure and must be converted to a capacitive filter

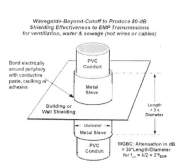

Fig. 7.6 – Application of WGBC.

For water and sewage lines coming into a house via the foundation or lower outside siding shield, any PVC, ceramic or other non-pe must be converted to a metal pipe (copper or aluminum) rt of entry over a distance of three times the pipe diameter ....,n in Fig. 7.6. This acts as a waveguide-beyond-cutoff (WGBC) to any EMP radiation leakage entry and provides 80 dB EMP attenuation as shown in the illustration. The periphery of the metal pipe at entry point is bonded to the aluminum sheet flooring hole via either wire-mesh shields or conductive paste, caulking or adhesive, as shown in the illustration.

Sold as a pack (12/pk), 3M Thermally Conductive Epoxy Adhesive TC-2707 is an aluminum metal filled, two-part, thermally conductive epoxy adhesive. 37 ml Duo-Pak Cartridge.

Another technique to the above WGBC blockage of a leaky shield entity, is to wrap two layers of 3-mil aluminum foil (such as heavy-duty Reynolds wrap) around the PVC periphery point of entry and bond with the wire mesh or conductive paste or caulking. Be sure to weather seal protect the aluminum foil.

When the entering pipe or tube shown above is not a simple circle or square, its depth can be shortened by breaking up the large aperture into a number of smaller ones as shown in Fig. 7.7. in the honeycomb air vents made by several manufacturers listed in the appendix.

Honeycomb Air Vent showing Hexagonal Cells and Mesh Electrical Gasket

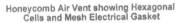
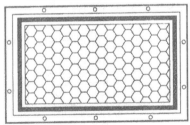

Fig. 7.7 – Honeycomb air vent shield

Other large shield penetrations, like windows, doors, vestibules and solar rooftops are discussed in building applications in later chapters.

7.1.4- Do You Just Want to EMP Protect Small Items?

Do you want to EMP protect one or more small (less than a few cubic feet) electronic devices with little effort that practically cost

nothing? Let's say you have a ham or short-wave ra(
want to use to get live emergency status info in the
EMP attack. Then, go to Walmart or wherever and bu, _ _   _
of Reynolds wrap (aluminum foil) for less than $4.00. Get the
bigger 18" wide variety if any dimension of your radio is over 12".

Take your power cord and fold it back and forth (8" to 12") in a
serpentine fashion and secure it with rubber bands or tape at both
ends and place flat on the radio surface. Do not coil the cord for
minimum pickup. If you have a telescoping antenna disconnect it
or compress it and fold it flat on the surface of the radio.

Make one 360° wrap with duct tape to hold the radio, power cord
and antenna around the middle of the face. Wrap the radio around
the four sides with the aluminum foil and secure the 360° periphery
wrap with about one or two inches of the foil overlap. Secure the
overlap with a few inches of the duct tape. Then turn the radio 90°
and repeat the aluminum foil top-side-bottom-side, overlap 1-2"
and secure with duct tape. Examine to see if all the radio is
completely wrapped with no uncovered areas exposed. If
something is showing, repeat in the exposed area with a taped
aluminum foil patch.

If there may be any areas that were sharp that could puncture the
foil cover with Scott paper towel and tape in place, You don't need
any more foil as you have provided over 90 dB shielding. But, if
you persist, you can make a repeat of the above with a second
wrapping. Do not use any insulation between the layers (a myth) as
you already have an overkill.

Look what you did and what you have now. A completely EMP
protected radio (or other device) for less than $2 worth of
aluminum foil and duct tape! Of course you can also repeat the
above procedure for other items to be EMP protected.

7.2- Grounding Techniques

Fig. 7.8 shows a shielded building including building skin, shielded windows, shielded HVAC (heating, ventilation air con-auditioning and elevator shacks and other external elements. The shielded building could float in space (like an airplane) without grounding and the shield works fine. No grounding is required.

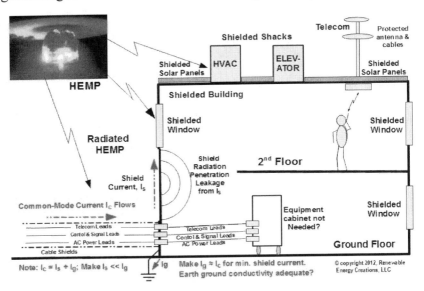

Fig. 7.8 – A Shielded building with compromising cable entries

However, there are other concerns such as if the shield becomes charged up to any voltage above ground due to whatever stray radiations (or accidental connection of a hot AC lead to building skin), it constitutes a shock hazard to entering and exiting people. Also, for lightning control. That's why the building skin must be grounded (low-impedance connection to earth).

Also, as shown at the lower left of Fig. 7.8 telecom leads, control and signal leads, and AC power leads must enter the building. These cables must also be shielded. Since the cable shield and the building shield may be at a different voltage, the entering cable shield must be bonded to the building shield (at usually a metal

114

plate). The object is to divert the EMP cable shield currents away from the building shield by grounding them to earth, where they are harmlessly dissipated. But, the devil is in the details!

The sketch of Fig. 7.8 illustrates the situation repeated thousands of times throughout a state or a country of a developed nation. Radiated EMI (electromagnetic interference or EMP) is coupled to a cable shield where EMI surface, common-mode currents, I_c, are grounded at the shielded building entrance (assuming a best case in which the building is shielded). It is typically assumed that the EMI currents will flow down the ground rod(s) (see I_g) and dissipate harmlessly into the absorbing earth. But, some EMI cable currents (I_s) still flow onto the building shield (that skin current is capacitive coupled back to ground to close the loop). Those currents residual cable currents may then penetrate into the building skin where they can upset or burnout internal electronic victims. So how effective (e.g., how low?) is the low-impedance grounding or earth system, and how successful is the building shield? It all gets down to the quality of each and attention to pertinent details.

Remember, the only shield current that should flow is from the terminated, direct radiated EMI onto the building shield, per se. It should not contain additional currents that come from any cable entry ground which can exceed the terminated EMI surface current on the building by large amounts. The degree to which it is exceeded is a direct measure of the reduction loss in building shielding effectiveness.

If the building were built on sand or some non-moisture holding soil, or a drought existed in the area, then the grounding system will not work as well. Or, if the ground Fargo clamps (Fig. 7.9) eroded out or became disconnected, then what? (Note Fig. 1.1, *Measurement of Soil Resistivity*, in MIL-HDBK-419 speaks in detail

Fig. 7.9 – Grounding wire, rod and pipe clamps

Fargo Clamp

Compliments of ElecDirect

115

to the number of ground rods, ground wells and earth electrode subsystem to achieve the grounding objectives).

The author of this book, has sadly witnessed over the years a plethora of meaningless grounded installations on multi-million dollar infrastructures and equipment. How often is a grounding system inspected and/or tested for numerical compliance? Probably not at all once it is installed for the first time. So then are all the thousands of cell-phone towers, TV, radio, telecommunication and other towers protected? Certainly, many or most are compromised. Does the insurance carrier ever inspect? Never or rarely, unless there is a fire or intrusion damage. So, unbeknown to many, an electrical or electronic system installation grounding system for shock safety and lightning control, may, in reality, be an injury or a death trap waiting to happen.

Can you testify if your own facilities or other installations are properly grounded? What criteria or standard do you use? Who signed off on the inspection? Still "grounded" five years later?

(Note from Don White): Here is a short illustration. While my visiting UK friends were at Jefferson's home, Monte-cello, in Charlottesville, Virginia, I departed from the line of waiting patrons, to examine the lightning protection system of the large majestic old oak trees. The lightning rods stood above the old magnificent oak trees and the #6 AWG down conductor was in place. But, the grounding Fargo clamp no longer was connected to the line – perhaps separated by a lawn mower hit. The oxidation of the two suggested that this may have happened years ago. What does this tell you?)

As it stands the entire discussion is academic from an EMP point-of-view since few non-government buildings are EMP protected. For those situations, all the interior electronics are fried in an EMP event – grounded or not.

EMP, lightning and EMI won't go away. Grounding is an important part of the protection system, but shielding and filtering are oi equal concern. Many of the details of shielding and filtering are too technical for this book. The hard-bound books, Vol. 2, *Grounding and Bonding,* and Vol.3, *Electromagnetic Shielding,* published by Donald R.J. White, *EMC Technology* in 1980 may still exist in thousands of global technical libraries and covers these technical details. Some newer books are also found on the Internet.

7.3- Cable Surge Suppressors & Filtering Techniques

Earlier, Fig. (7.8) showed that a second major EMP access route (radiation coupling) into a hut, home or building is via the entering or exiting building cables containing AC power mains, telephone and Internet access, control and signal leads (SCADA), and antenna lead-in cables, as applicable. All of these four types of cables act as a big antenna pick-up system to the radiating outside EMP pulse and bring induced currents into the building to burnout all electronics control, even when the structure is otherwise adequately shielded, as suggested in Fig. (7.8).

EMP protection for the AC power line entering the building in the lower left of Fig. (7.8) is provided by surge suppressors on the cable or its connector at the point of entry. Basically, the surge suppressors may be a high voltage clamping diode with an inductor or a capacitor, short circuiting the high-frequency components of the EMP burst while passing, without loss, the 60 Hz power-line current. The TV or communication line entry at the upper right of Fig. 7.8 uses a bandpass filter rated to withstand an EMP, high-voltage burst.

Surge suppressors are used on wiring and cables entering and exiting all structures. This includes power lines, telephone, control and signal leads. Cables act as "radiation pick-up antennas" with EMP voltage spikes up to 50,000 volts. As such, the spikes exceed wire insulation – arcing over, shorting and destroying devices connected thereto unless EMP protected.

ercial electronic surge ssors used for lightrikes do not clamp fast enough (clamp >100 nsec for lightning; need to clamp less than 5 nanoseconds for EMP, per Fig. 2.2 to protect against the near instantaneous effects of an EMP. Some also may not have great enough current carrying capacity. So it is important that EMP surge suppressors be used for any exterior wire/cable entrance from the outside world to the inside of the EMP-shielded building.

Fig. 7.10 – Two different types of many hardened surge suppressors

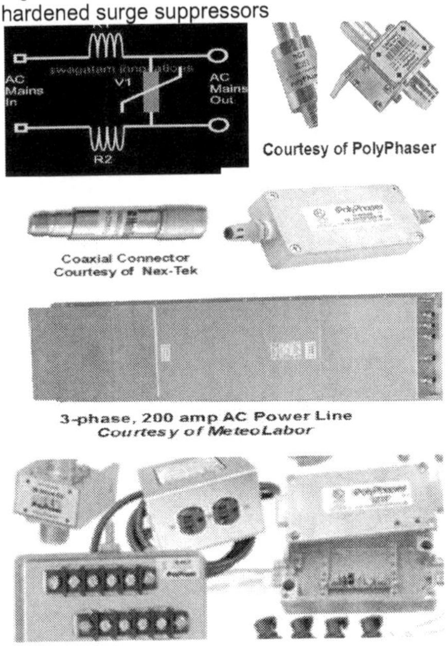

Courtesy of PolyPhaser

Coaxial Connector
Courtesy of Nex-Tek

3-phase, 200 amp AC Power Line
Courtesy of MeteoLabor

Fig. 7.10 shows a few of several EMP surge suppressors available for addressing the wide variety of needs and applications. (The surge suppressors used for high voltage transformers in substations to address surges from geomagnetic storms are different and are not shown here)

7.4- Sources and References

Measurement of Soil Resistivity, in MIL-HDBK-419
MIL-STD-188-125

Shielding and Bonding Materials

● ETS–Lindgren, Tel: 512-531-6400, www.ets-lindgren.com,1301 Arrow Point Drive, Cedar Park, TX 78613 (shielded windows and buildings; 4 ft x 50 ft rolls of screen wire)

● Chomerics, Tel: 1-781-935-4850, 77 Dragon Court, Woburn, MA, wflanders@parker.com

● Panashield, Tel: 1-203-866-5888, 185R West Norwalk Road, Norwalk, CT 06850,

• TWP Inc., Tel: 510-548-4434 or 800-227-1570, 2831 Tenth Street, Berkeley, CA 94710 USA, sales@twpinc.com

• Hebei General Metal Netting Co. Ltd. Of China, Tel: +86-318-855-7784, Fax: +86-318-775-7320, http://www.generalmesh.com, http://www.industrialwirecloth.com

Surge Suppressors and Filters:

PolyPhaser, Tel: 800-882-9110 , 10701 North Airport Road, Hayden, ID   83835

Transorb, Tel: 800-882-9110 , 10701 North Airport Road, Hayden, ID 83835

Protection Technology Group, 800-882-9110 or 208-772-8515, 10701 North Airport Road, Hayden, ID 83835

EMC/EMP Test & Certification

• Dayton T. Brown, Tel: 1-800-232-6300, Fax: 631-589-3648, Email: info@dtb.com, Email: test@dtbtest.com, 1175 Church Street, Bohemia, New York 11716, USA

• ETS–Lindgren, Tel: 512-531-6400, www.ets-lindgren.com,1301 Arrow Point Drive, Cedar Park, TX   78613

• Elite Engineering Inc. , Tel: 1-800-354-8311, 1516 Centre Circle,| Downers Grove, IL 60515-1082

• Most of the EMI test houses that perform MIL-STD-461E or later testing, also perform RS105 and CS-115 testing. Some of the labs have large chambers to be able to test vehicles for the Army

Government EMP Test Facilities

• White Sands Missile Test Range, New Mexico. In addition to military testing, EMP test simulation facility is rented to automotive manufacturers.
• Naval Air System Command has an EMP test simulation facility in Pax River, Maryland.
• Oak Ridge National Laboratory, Tennessee

- Naval Weapons Center China Lake, Ridgecrest, CA
- Sandia Labs, Albuquerque, NM has a bounded wave simulator (4x11x5 m).
- Air Force Weapons Lab at Albuquerque, NM has an HPD and a VPD. The largest open-air, EMP simulator in the world.
- Edwards AFB, CA (Also a site at Palmdale HPD for unique aircraft EMP testing.)
- Army at Ft. Monmouth, NJ. (May have moved its EMP facility to Aberdeen Proving Ground, Aberdeen, MD.

Chapter 8
How to EMP Protect Homes & Small Buildings

Chapter Overview

Previous chapters have provided most of the necessary information to make an EMP protected structure, capable of producing solar electricity, since the assumption is that the electric grid is down and electrcity is not available.

First consider a shed, home or building to be a simple six-sided (parallel-epiped) structure – a foundation, a roof, and four sides. The first section addresses the structure's foundation part and how to shield it, especially when there are penetrations, such as water and sewer-septic line entries, and wire and cable entries.

Homes with basements are more difficult to shield as the shield material is underground on the outer basement walls and more difficult to access. Above all, a new building under construction has very roughly 60% of the EMP protection cost vs. that of protecting an existing structure.

The second shielding area involves the four (or more) sides of a shed, home or building. As in the roof or bottom, EMP protection modes includes blocking by shielding Special optically transparent shielding is needed for windows, Shielded doors are treated differently with specialty bonding to the frame.

All wire cables entering the structure must be shielded and surge suppressed. Shielding includes proper bonding of mating shields (cable and building side shields) and grounding the cables at entry in order to keep the radiated pickup current from the cables off the housing shield and onto the earthing grounding cable.

Shielding the roof runs into obstructions and location access problems such as bathroom ventilation pipes, attic ventilation, and soffits. The first requires the use of metal-pipe insertions if PVC pipes are used. The others can use metal mesh screens to cover attic ventilation fan openings and soffit ventilation.

8.1- Shielding Materials

Some shielding materials have already been discussed in previous chapters. Conductive paints have limited use because (1) of the several coats required to achieve the required 80 dB (default) shielding effectiveness in Chapter 2, (2) life expectancy is limited, especially in warmer southern latitudes of the U.S., and (3) paints are also more susceptible to developing climate and exposure damage, than solid metals and screens.

Table 8.1 tabulates the shielding effectiveness of different metal shields vs. frequency from 100 khz to 1 GHz. The second row lists the required shielding in dB to protect electronic equipment against an upper atmospheric nuclear EMP burst. Note the required shielding goes to zero dB at and above 1 GHz for the EMP wave shape listed in the bottom of the table.

Table 8.1 - Shielding Requirements and Shielding Effectiveness of Shielding Materials

Shielding Material / RadFreq	100 kHz	1 MHz	3 MHz	10 MHz	30 MHz	100 MHz	300 MHz	1 GHz	$/SF	Notes
Shielding Effectiveness Reqm	80	80	76	65	52	30	10	0	NA	A
10 OPI screen shld	86	*75	*66	*55	*46	35	26	15		B
20 OPI screeen shield	92	81	*72	*61	52	41	32	21		C
30 OPI Screen shield	96	85	76	65	56	45	36	25		D
0.64 mil = Reynolds Wrap	88	89	89	90	90	94	97	107	0.04	E
0.93 mil HD Reynolds Wrap	91	93	93	95	97	103	112	146	0.07	F
1.4 mil XHD Reynolds Wrap	94	96	98	101	104	112	127	165	0.11	G
1/64" = 15.6 mil sheet Al	>165	>165	>165	>165	>165	>165	>165	>165	1.52	H

Notes: A- Required Shielding from Fig. 5.x based on Nuclear Burst producing 50 kV/m, and
Victim electronic device passing MIL-STD-462, RS-105 at 10 V/m. or EN 61000-4-3.
EMP pulse shape has rise time of 5 nsec and 50% height duration of 150 nsec.
B-D OPI = Openings per Inch rating of welded-screen schields

The next three rows list welded metal screens (usually: aluminum. copper or stainless steel). Their screening density is defined in terms of their wire crossover distance or OPI = openings per inch. Except for 10 OPI and 20 OPI (see asterisk, in the cells for welded metal screens over a portion of their frequency range) all screens meet their shielding effectiveness needs.

The last four rows in the table speak to three popular thin aluminum foils (0.64 mil, 0.93 and 1.4 mils thick (1 mil = 0.001 inch = 0.0254 mm) and one sheet of thin aluminum stock (1/64"). There, one can

see that each provides more than the shielding required. Aluminum foil rolls of 12", 18" and 24" width (31 cm, 46 cm and 61 cm) of all three thickness come in lengths of 50 ft. to 250 ft (15 m to 76 m). (Their cost is roughly $0.04 per square foot ($0.43/sq. meter).

Another foil material, but not shown in the table, is aluminum foil and aluminum laminate of standard 5.9 mil (and other thicknesses) and a bonded laminate of plastic aluminum or other material for strength and puncture mitigation such as made by ALCOA, as shown in Fig. 8.2. At less than $0.15/sq.ft. ($1.50/sq.m.) this can

become a base cover to lengthen the life of roof asphalt shingles. However, its main purpose is to provide the needed rooftop material cover for an unprotected EMP solar rooftop installed now, so that it can be EMP protected in the the future. Thus, for this low "insurance" price, the entire roof of an average 2,300 sq. ft (222 sq. m.) U.S. home can be covered for about $200 - $300 with aluminum laminated material for new, non-EMP protected solar rooftops.

8.2- Shielding of Building Structure Foundation

A building foundation is the mass of material that ties the building structure to an uncertain earth which may range from sand with/without watery content to rocky or unseasonably hard. The second shielding area mass is the four (or more) sides of a cottage shed, home or building. As in the roof or bottom, EMP protection modes include blocking by shielding the roof, sides and floor bottom or basement if applicable. Special transparent shielding is needed for windows, and the solar panel rooftop. Shielded doors are treated differently.

All wire cables entering the structure must be shielded and surge suppressed. Shielding includes proper bonding of mating shields (cable and building side shields) and grounding the cables at entry in order to keep the radiated pickup current from the cables off the housing shield and onto the earthing cable. The taller the building and weight, the bigger the challenge and more complex is the foundation. Since every building structure must have all six sides (or other number), consisting of four vertical sides, top (roof) and bottom (foundation) shielded, foundations may pose the greatest challenge.

For sheds. homes and small buildings, there are three types of foundations: (1) insulated slab foundations, (2) pier foundations and (3) crawl-space foundations.

If the owner intends to use an FHA loan to buy his manufactured home and land, he will need to have an insulated slab foundation installed prior to the home's delivery. This type of foundation is more costly than one consisting of just piers and tie-downs, but it will meet FHA's requirements, and will fulfill the criteria for having the county tax office tax his new property as real estate (another FHA requirement).

8.2.1- Insulated Slab Foundations

The slab foundation consists of a concrete pad, which has drain tiles or a customized way to keep the ground dry underneath the pad. Water draining under the pad can cause the pad to move (or "float"). This movement would cause the pad not to meet FHA's requirements. Insulating the pad from water drainage ensures its stability. With no water drainage issues, the ground underneath the slab

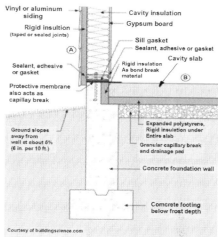

Fig. 8.3 Insulated Slab Foundation

stays dry and warmer than surrounding areas in the cold months of the year.

The home is set up on the concrete slab ("B" in Fig. 8.3), and is supported by concrete block piers. Anchors are embedded in the concrete, and steel tie-down straps are wrapped around the home's support beams, then attached to the anchors.

Fig. 8.3 is an overkill for simple sheds described in earlier chapters, especially those in the southern USA climates where single story, shallow roofs and no frost depth may exist. The foundation wall then may shrink to near zero height. The flooring and its EMP shielding are discussed in the next section.

8.2.2- Pier Foundations

If the owner is purchasing a mobile home with any loan except FHA (or for cash), a pier and ground anchor foundation may be used. This method of foundation is less expensive and time-consuming than the slab foundation and

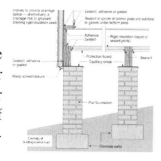

Fig. 8.4 Pier-type Foundation

125

is widely used all over the United States. Areas with soft ground soils, storms and high winds, and heavy snow may require more anchors and tie-down straps to secure the home to the ground as shown in Fig. 8.4.

This method uses steel jack stands or open cell concrete blocks stacked up to the required height of the home's support beams underneath the home. These stacks of blocks sit on a concrete pad. Screw-in ground anchors are used to secure the home against the uplift of winds from storms. Steel straps wrapped around the home's support beams are attached to the ground anchors, which are screwed into concrete (at a depth below the area's "frost line") to add security. The number of straps and ground anchors will vary in different regions of the U.S. and capacity of ground soils to securely hold the anchors. Areas of high storm activity and winds (such as Florida) require more steel straps and anchors to secure the home safely to the ground.

8.2.3 Crawl-Space Foundation

The most secure foundation, and the best for FHA lending and "real property" conversion, is the crawl space foundation, shown in Figs. 8.5 and 8.6. This method combines concrete block under-pinning around the perimeter of the home with internal, indepen-dent support points underneath. The home is tied down to ground anchors by steel straps attached to the perimeter support beams of the home. This method gives more resistance to the uplift of winds in storm areas. The underpinning

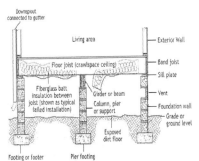

Fig. 8.5 Pier-type Foundation

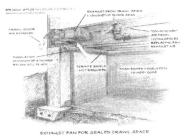

Fig. 8.6 – Some crawl space ceiling Integrity penetrations

gives a more "site built" appearance to the outside of the home. Block piers are used underneath the home for support. This type foundation is more expensive to construct than the slab or pier foundation method. There are no issues with drainage problems underneath the home since there is no concrete slab.

8.2.4- EMP Shielding the Foundation

The illustration on the right, Fig. 8.7, shows the concrete foundation floor slab area as a cut-away view of preceding Fig. 8.4 The heavy black line (thickness exaggerated for emphasis) at the left is the shielding material, identified as "A". This shield is under the siding (discussed in next chapter) and proceeds down to point "B", around to points "C" and terminates at "D".

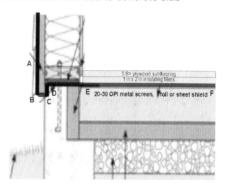

Fig. 8.7 Slab foundation showing metal shield bonded to concrete slab

The shield belonging to the the foundation begins at point "D" and proceeds to "E" and "F". At point area "D" the siding shield and foundation shield meet with at least a 2" (5 cm) overlap. The bonding of the two overlapped shields, discussed in Chap. 3. is via duct tape or other secure means. The entire interface area is weather coated and secured for long-term climate control.

Options for choosing the shielding material for the foundation are also discussed in the preceding chapter. A heavy duty screen, 20-30 OPI, may be preferred over aluminum foil as it is less likely to tear in handling it in the more difficult Point "B, C and D" areas.

8.2.5- EMP Shield Protection of Cables, Water and Sewage-line entries.

As mentioned in the previous chapter any wires, cables (for example: AC power mains, telephone lines, TV cables entry or supervisory control and data acquisition), water and sewage pipes, can destroy the shielding effectiveness of a housing or building shield. Radiated EMP pickup leaks in unless electrically sealed.

Wire and cables must be surge suppressed or capacitively by-passed to their shield (a shield is generated near the port of wire/cable entry), which in turn is bonded to the outer foundation shield. This, in turn is electrically grounded to earth as explained in the previous chapter.

For water and sewage lines coming into the house via the foundation or lower outside siding shield, any PVC, ceramic or other non-metal pipe must be transitionally converted to a metal pipe (copper, aluminum or iron) at the port of entry over a distance of three times the pipe diameter, Fig.8.8. This acts as a waveguide-beyond-cutoff (WGBC) to any EMP radiation leakage entry (provides 80 dB EMP attenuation

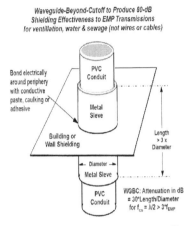

Fig. 8.8 WGBC acting as a "shield".

as shown in the illustration on the right). The periphery of the metal pipe at entry point is bonded to the aluminum sheet flooring hole via either wire-mesh shields or conductive paste, caulking or adhesive, as stated in the illustration and discussed further in the next chapter on siding.

Another technique to block the EMP leakage to the above WGBC blockage of a leaky shield entry, is to wrap two layers of 1.6-mil aluminum foil (such as heavy-duty Reynolds Wrap) around the PVC periphery point of entry and bond with the wire mesh or conductive paste or caulking. Be sure to weather seal protect the aluminum foil.

8.2.6- EMP Protection of Well & Septic Systems (if applicable)

Instead of a county public works, water and sewage service, the building owners may be on their own private well and/or septic system. For this condition, the previous diagram will apply for septic.

However, for a water well, there are basically, two types: (1) a shallow well and (2) a deep well. Figure 8.9 shows two varieties of a shallow well, and on the next page, a deep water well.

While submersible pumps (deep well) are more efficient than jet pumps in delivering more water for the same size motor, pump or motor problems will necessitate pulling the unit from the well casing (a job that's best left to a pro). However, submersibles are known for their reliability and often perform their role 20 to 25 years without servicing.

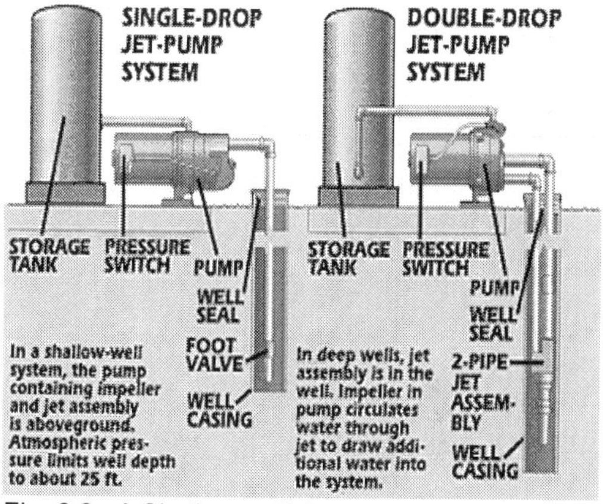

Submersible pumps may also be used in shallow wells. Silt, sand, algae and other contaminants, however, can shorten the pump's life.

Fig. 8.9 - A Shallow well, jet-pump system

Shallow well: The first question is where are the jet-pump, storage tank and well to be located? Typically, the first two are inside or near a garage; the well may be located some distance away. The only thing electrical or electronic is the jet pump. If the house and garage are EMP shielded, the wiring and pump needs no further protection.

If they are located outside a cottage shed, then the pump must be shielded and the AC power leads protected by a HV surge suppressor or filter capacitor. The need for a high voltage suppressor can be avoided by placing the interconnecting wires inside a conduit, secure at both ends to their respective shields. The source power leads between the inside of the shed protected power and the jet pump motor should be a shielded, twisted trio (hot, neutral and safety). Do not externally earth the pump as the green safety wire is connected to its shielded frame.

Deep Well: Fig. 8.10 shows the pump motor located near the bottom of the well, must be EMP protected by shielding its housing and cable leads. At the top of the well, the cable connector must have either a surge suppressor or filter (capacitor) rated to handle at least 1 kV. The other end of the cable providing the well pump motor, must also be surge suppressed at the point of entry into the cottage shed or home. The corresponding

Fig. 8.10 A deep well, submersible pump system.

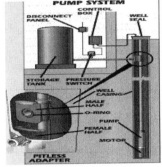

voltage ratings of the surge suppressors or filters can be greatly reduced if the intersecting cable is a sufficiently shielded, twisted pair or twisted pair inside a metal conduit as explained in the previous chapter.

8.3.- Shielding the sides of the Shed, Home or Building

Emphasis now shifts from EMP shielding the structure foundation to its sides.

8.3.1- Shielded Building Rooms and Cabinets (other than the first paragraph, the non-technical reader can skip this section)

Figure 8.11 illustrates that there exists three possible levels of shielding. The benefit of shielding the entire building to 80 dB means that nothing else inside needs to be shielded. Existing climate con-

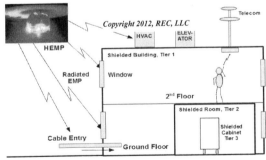

Fig. 8.11 – Three tiers of shielding: shielded building, shielded room and shielded cabinet or box.

130

trols, cell phones, iPhones, iPads, laptop computers, peripherals, and all the rest of electrical and electronic devices in chapter 3 can continue to be used.

However, shielding a building to 80 dB in some cases may become expensive (perhaps, for example, more than 10% of the entire building cost in 2014; and a lower percentage later). Consequently, one or more internal shielded rooms could be added where the more sensitive items would be located, and the entire building shielding can be correspondingly reduced. For example, suppose a 1 mil aluminum foil or sprayed copper paint on the walls, ceiling and floor (bonded and secured) is used for the inside building conductive skin to reduce its requirements to, say, 40 dB. This may appear to drop the price of the building shielding. Be aware, however, that the electrical wiring in the outside walls are still not protected; *therefore, this will not work.*

However, if the items in the proposed internal shielded enclosure have a radiated susceptibility below 10 V/m (the assumed conditions in chapter 3), the additional shielding can be achieved in an internal screen room or cabinet or box size, as applicable. Shielded enclosures of the quality offered by the EMC manufacturers are shielded to about 120 dB and represent a huge overkill and, therefore, would not be used here. (they also shield up to 10 GHz, and EMP needs no shielding above 1 GHz.)

The shielded building skin is best placed on the outside with sheet metal building walls bonded where joined and each of the four or more sides of the building is bonded along its entire length. Do not try to shield the wall board on the inside as this will not work as stated above because all the wiring trapped between the inside and outside skin will act as a gigantic pick antenna and destroy the shielded building performance.

The amount of shielding needed was computed in Chapter 2 from the ratio of expected EMP radiation level (50 kV/m per MIL-STD-188) to the susceptibility level of the victim devices (EU and other compliance levels are typically required to meet 10 V/m as the standard level. So 50 kilovolts per meter/10 volts per meter =

,000 ratio = 20*log(5,000) = 74 dB + 6 dB for safety margin = 80 dB. But, see earlier Table 2.1 for the shielding needed at any frequency.

Eq.(8.1), gives the simple additive formula in dB for the three levels of shielding shown in Fig. 8.11: (1) outside building skin, (2) inside shielded room, and (3) shielded cabinet, rack or console. Note: 80 dB is the total amount required for HEMP protection. But the illustration indicates that there are three levels of protection possible:

Total Shielding, $S_{dB} = Build_{dB} + Room_{dB} + Cabinet_{dB}$ (8.1)

for building skin, only, $S_{dB} = 80$ dB $+ 0$ dB $+ 0$ dB $= 80$ dB

where: $Build_{dB}$ = building outer skin shielding in dB

$Room_{dB}$ = shielded room (enclosure) in dB

$Cabinet_{dB}$ = shielded cabinet in dB

Fig. (8.11) shows that the windows, rooftop elevator shack, A/C heat exchanger, and all cable shields penetrating the building must not have SE less than 80dB (below 2.2 MHz) from earlier discussion in Chapter 2.

8.3.2- Shielding of the Building Facade

How do we shield the building facade (outer skin)? What constitutes the basic material under the building skin or envelope, such as with vinyl siding? In the U.S., it is typically a plywood lath sheathing in the North and concrete blocks, stuccoed over, for residential in the South. For commercial it may be aluminum composite panels, copper or stainless steel sheets, weather-board, etc. These and other materials are dependent on whether or not the building already exists or has not yet been designed or built. Most specifics of this discussion are beyond the scope of this handbook and involve important architectural matters.

There also exists BI-PV (third generation materials = Building Integrated, Photo Voltaics) in the form of paint, inks or dyes applied to the building facade. This is best applied to a new building. However, BI-PV cover would have to be first shielded. This forthcoming issue is not discussed in this book.

For further discussion on building facade metal siding, the reader is referred back to Chapter 7.

An alternative to the above foil is to use copper or aluminum paint, applied by brush, roller or spray. One source (*LessEMF.com*) reveals a copper latex paint reported to produce less than 0.1 ohm/square (shielding effectiveness of >72 dB below 1 GHz) for 2 mil deposit. Five mil in two coats will produce the required 80 dB at a paint cost of roughly $2 per square foot. ($21/sq.meter). Exclusive of windows, doors and other building skin discontinuities, a 20,000 sq. ft. building will cost $80k in conductive paint (possibly reduced to ≈ $25k for quantity of over 200 gallons).

A finishing non-conductive protection coat of latex paint is applied. One major benefit of the paint approach is the relatively easy application by spraying and the avoidance of foil overlaps, and electrical gaskets except at windows, doors, etc. as described below.

Duralux Aluminum Marine Boat Paint Green, or equivalent may be a viable protection at a significantly lower cost per gallon ($85). In all cases the surfaces must be clean free of dust, dirt, oxides, etc. Sand blasting may be a necessary first step. Application to new buildings is less expensive than retrofits to existing buildings.

8.3.3- Bonding of Adjoining sides of Building Shields

Remember, the building has six sides: the four vertical sides, usually 90° apart, the horizontal top and bottom. More complex facades (for example, dormers and gutters) have more faces; the same physics and engineering requirements still apply, but achievement becomes somewhat more complex. In any event, the remaining shielding involves bonding the adjoining meeting sides with the proper material.

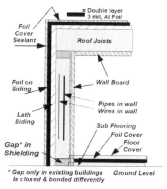

Fig. 8.12 – Detail showing shielding gap before closing in existing retrofit

Of the six sides, the only bonding access

133

problem is in *retrofitting* (not new construction) the bottom of the lowest floor of existing buildings. As shown in Fig. 8.12, there exists a gap between a foil or other conductive flooring on the inside bottom and the four vertical sides of the remaining shield faces on the outside.

How to close this gap? There are different methods, but they go beyond the level of this book. Of course, to a new building just being planned or being built, this is not an issue as the bottom floor shield is extended beyond the outer frame to be bonded to side shielding (Fig 8.12)

Regarding electrical gaskets used to seal the adjoining metal sides, Fig. 8.13 shows options available from Tech-Etch for the engineering community.

Fig. 8.13 – Tech Etch - Many different electrical gaskets available for selection of the correct type for any particular application. Right central wire mesh type for window sills.

The figure also shows other electrical gaskets useful in bonding other types of mating electrical parts, discussed elsewhere in this handbook.

8.3.4- Grounding of Shielded Building (tech readers)

Good Electromagnetic Grounds

Because RF (radio frequency) current flows on the outside conductor surface only at MHz and GHz frequencies, circular conductors are the poorest configurations (their cross sectional periphery-to-area ratio is the lowest). As shown in Fig. 8.14, a strap, cross section or better yet, a thin foil conveys the EMI from

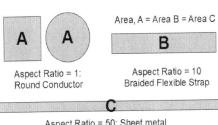

Area, A = Area B = Area C

Aspect Ratio = 1:
Round Conductor

Aspect Ratio = 10
Braided Flexible Strap

Aspect Ratio = 50: Sheet metal

Aspect ratio = width/thickness
A: For aspect ratio = 1, relative RF conductivity = 1 = fair
B: For aspect ratio = 10, relative RF conductivity = 5 = better
C: For aspect ratio = 50, relative RF conductivity = 25 = best

Fig. 8.14 – Performance of Grounding Conductors

the shield bond down to the earthing conductor rods more effectively.

If the soil has poor conductivity (sand, drought), it can be increased in the region by adding bauxite, bentonite or a proprietary grounding material. The answer is to make the I_g/I_s current ratio in Fig. 8.11 as high as possible or meet a specified numerical objective for a specified installation.

Numbers are not used here as they will bore most non-technical readers and have little meaning. However, those so inclined, may get a copy of MIL-HDBK-419A on the Internet and download for free. It is titled, Military Handbook, Grounding, Bonding and Shielding for Electronic Equipment and Facilities, Vol 1 and 2.

8.3.5- Shielding Windows, Doors & Other Skin Leakage

Windows cannot employ electro-chrom glass as this blocks light with little shielding, nor can one have a few microns (very thin film) of vapor-deposited metal on the window as a shield since one could not then see through the window. Although a one micron (very thin film) of silver deposited on glass offers an RF shielding effectiveness of 80 dB, it also blocks the optical transmission.

Fig. 8.15 – Wire mesh, shielded windows

Therefore, a metal screen mesh (Fig. 8.15) is considered for covering the windows which passes almost all the light (optically) but blocks the HEMP radiated transmissions by 80 dB below 12 MHz (depends on the mesh screen spacings). The required screen mesh separation distance, d, to achieve this shielding, is calculated by:

$$SE_{dB} = 20Log_{10}(150/(d*f_{MHz}) = 80\ dB \qquad (8.3)$$

where: f_{MHz} = 12 MHz from the geometric mean of the first and second corner frequencies in earlier Fig 2.2..

Solving Eq. (8.3) for mesh separation, d, produces a distance of d = 1.29 mm. This corresponds to 25.4/1.29 or 20 wire mesh openings per inch (OPI). This OPI is mentioned since mesh shielding is usually reported in OPI by manufacturers, and is available up to 100 OPI.

Do not use higher OPI on solar panels as the light transmissivity begins to suffer and this will adversely affect the solar panel efficiency of converting sunlight into electricity.

Fig. 8.16 – Shielded screen room with more than 85-dB shielding below 1 GHz

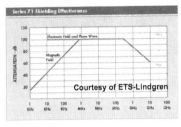

When using Eq. (8.3), graphed earlier, one word of caution: be careful. The manufacturers seem to show a shielding limit of about 60 dB. This is partly because of the use of wire mesh and because the perimeter of the shield is not bonded with a low enough conductive gasket. This is demonstrated by a copper screen shielded room which shows a lower limit more nearly 85 dB. While this topic is beyond the intentional technical limits of this handbook, Fig. 8.16 shows proof of this remark.

Shielded External Doors

One or more doors permit entry into and exit from the shielded building. For each such door, a vestibule must be generated such that a set of two doors is used with interlocks so that not more than one door can be opened at any time. This will avoid an unfortunate situation in which both doors are temporarily open at the moment an EMP incident occurs, which would otherwise compromise the entire integrity of the building shielding effectiveness.

The vestibule can be added either external or internal to the existing outer door, whichever is the more practical, considering available room, cost, etc. Whether external or internal, the vestibule must also be shielded on all six sides to preserve the building's shielding integrity

The doors may be shielded in any of several ways as already discussed for the building shielding. Bonded aluminum (or other metal) foil on either or both door faces covering all door five or six sides. Around the periphery of the door is bonded shielded finger stock, wire mesh or other

Fig. 8.17: EMP shielded building entrance/exit options.

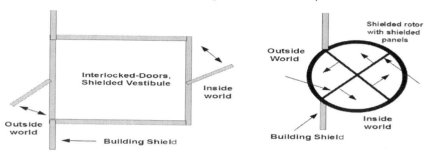

suitable bond (see Fig. 8.17). Finger stock is often used on door seams because its life expectancy goes into the thousands of times of openings and closures. The stock is mated with a bladed seam so that no contact can accidentally be made with the clothing of people entering/exiting.

The finger stock or mesh will have to be periodically replaced if the doors are opened hundreds of times per day. Therefore, a maintenance cycle must be established.

Fig. 8.17 also shows that another option to construct a rotating shielded entrance frequently seen on commercial office buildings. Here, of course, the entire assembly is shielded including the four rotor partitions.

8.3.6- Shielded Wires and Cable Entries

As shown in earlier discussions, three cable and wire classes enter nearly every building: (1) telecom (telephone, Ethernet, and other hard-wire communications) leads, (2) control and signal leads for controlling certain activities and reporting back elsewhere with status data, and (3) AC power mains to supply 120 VAC, 240VAC or other voltage to run the building's many operational loads. Unless the cables are already placed in conduit, buried and/or shielded, their shields must provide the required 80 dB below 64 MHz isolation to the entering leads.

The interconnecting wiring between and among all solar panels, the inverter (if micro-inverters are not used) and the down conductors to the service entrance panels must also be shielded to 80 dB. A solid thin wall copper tubing can also be used as the shield. However, to ensure the benefits of flexibility, if desired use knitted-wire mesh shielding on all cabling instead. Fig. 8.18 shows a compliant shield for interconnect wiring. All shielding must have an overcoat of weather sealant or outer jacket if not placed inside a conduit.

Courtesy of Tech-Etch

Fig. 8.18– Wire mesh, cable shields

As explained above, the cable shields are bonded to the building shield usually at a metal grounding plate welded to the building shield at cable entrance (see above discussion on building grounding).

8.3.7- Surge Suppressors & Cable Filter Connectors

Surge suppressor and filter details are also discussed in the last chapter.

Do not suppose that each of the three building cable types contain EMI (electromagnetic interference) or some residual EMP protection. This, of course, depends on several variables such as cable type, buried above or below ground, inside a metal conduit, length of cable before building entrance, etc.

The telecom cables require a surge suppressor rated to clip all surge voltages above some minimum, such as 100 volts (well above the intentional levels), that may result from a residual EMP. The control and signal leads are confronted with a similar situations. Filters are not used as they may not cut off at high enough frequency unless all future data rates are known well in advance.

AC power mains is another matter since it is supposed to contain only 120 VAC, 240 VAC or other service voltage values. The cutoff frequency should not be just above 60 Hz (or other power line frequency) since the inductors and capacitors become big, bulky, weighty and expensive. Therefore, most have a low-pass cutoff frequency at about 1-10 kHz.

To protect against insulation burnout of the filters with a EMP incident, they are preceded by a surge suppressor rated at one of the above voltages. The capacity of the surge protector depends on whether the AC service is furnished underground or above ground, enclosed in its own cable shield, length of cable runs, if the feeding distribution transformer is protected, etc. The next chapter gives a few examples.

8.4- EMP Protecting Roofs

8.4.1- Applying Roof Shielding over Plywood/OSB Decking

How and where the roof shield material is applied over the top of the shed or home structure depends upon the structure, per SE. One of many roof types is shown in the Fig. 8.19 below.

Typically, plywood or OSD (oriented strand board) decking is used to cover roof rafters. For 18" rafter spacing, 1/2" decking thickness is used while 5/8" is selected for 24" spacing. Other decking materials include fiberboard, bamboo, and rubber board. Fiberboard is stronger, heaver, but does not hold screws as well.

Fig. 8.19 plywood or OSD decking for shield attachment

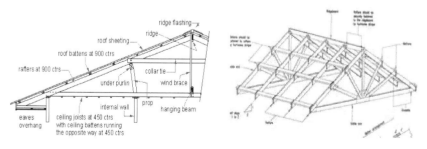

The aluminum shield may be bonded to the decking with spray or brush applied adhesive and, for foils, pressure rolled to ensure good bond. Nails, staples and use of applicable guns are not desired for foil covers as they might tear the thin aluminum or metal screen unless aluminum laminates are used. Where sections

139

of aluminum foil meet, one of two practices may be used: (cover the meeting gaps with 2" adhesive-back aluminum tape, or (2) allow the aluminum foil to overlap about one inch and cover the exposed ends with the same aluminum tape. The second method is preferred since the overlap is a direct metal-on-metal connection, while in the first method, the adhesive material on the tape directly touches the metals. Thus, it acts like a high capacitance bridge (low-impedance bond) connection. The metal overlaps are shown in the accompanying figure.

Usually asbestos shingles will be nailed over the top of the aluminum foil or sheet with nails piercing the shields. This is OK, since the shield will not be torn and the metal nails or staples fill the piercing holes to preserve the shielding integrity.

Extend the metal foil roof around the decking cover edge and under the soffit and end with a turn to the top of the siding where subsequent mating shields can be engaged. As discussed later, the house metal sidings will be bonded to this metal roof cover extension to make a continuous and sound electrical shield with no seam or other leakages to compromise shielding effectiveness.

8.4.2- Bonding Roof Ventilation Pipes to Shielding

Bathroom ventilation pipes exit the roof. The roof shielding is either an aluminum foil or 20-30 OPI screen as previously described. In either case, around the periphery of where metal pipes penetrate the foil or metal screen, a conductive paste or caulking, such as Parker Chomerics CHO-Bond 4660, or equivalent is used. If the exiting ventilation pipes are non conducting, such as PVC, then a WGBC approach is used, as described in Fig. 8.8.

8.4.3- Shielding & Screening Soffits & Fan Louvers

Where a house has an attic, the soffits and ventilating openings are covered with a 20-30 OPI screen shielding in regions where the roof shielding joins the house side shielding as described in the previous chapter.

8.4.4- Shielding the Chimney

Chimneys are obsolescent in new houses being built in USA today although they may still be designed and installed in some homes, especially in the North and more remote locations in rural regions where the house is heated by wood fuel.

Shielding options include selecting 20 OPI stainless steel, heavy duty screen, discussed earlier, for going over the chimney top and down the sides. Where screen meets screen down the sides at the four corners, overlap the screen by at least 1 inch (2.5 cm). Bond the overlap with an epoxy adhesive. Bond the screen to the chimney brick (or other chimney material) with the same bonding epoxy. Ensure that there are no holes or gaps in the chimney installation at the top and along its downward length.

The metal shield continues from the top of the chimney to the bottom of the chimney where is then bonded to the outside metal siding with the same epoxy adhesive.

8.5- Sources and References

Shielding and Bonding Materials

• ALCOA, Aluminum Company of America (Reynolds Wrap). Alcoa Corporate Center, 201 Isabella Street, Pittsburgh, PA, 15212-5858, USA, Phone: 412-553-4545. Fax: 412-553-4498

• ETS–Lindgren, Tel: 512-531-6400, www.ets-lindgren.com,1301 Arrow Point Drive, Cedar Park, TX 78613 (shielded windows and buildings; 4 ft x 50 ft rolls of screen wire.

• Tech Etch, Tech-Etch, Inc.45 Aldrin Road Plymouth, MA 02360,

Tel: 508-747-0300, Fax: 508-746-9639

• Chomerics, Tel: 1-781-935-4850, 77 Dragon Court, Woburn, MA, wflanders@parker.com

• Panashield, Tel: 1-203-866-5888, 185R West Norwalk Road, Norwalk, CT 06850,

• TWP Inc., Tel: 510-548-4434 or 800-227-1570, 2831 Tenth Street, Berkeley, CA 94710 USA, sales@twpinc.com

• Hebei General Metal Netting Co. Ltd. Of China, Tel: +86-318-855-7784, Fax: +86-318-775-7320, http://www.generalmesh.com, http://www.industrialwirecloth.com

Surge Suppressors and Filters:

• PolyPhaser, Tel: 800-882-9110 , 10701 North Airport Road, Hayden, ID   83835

• Transorb, Tel: 800-882-9110 , 10701 North Airport Road, Hayden, ID 83835

• Protection Technology Group, 800-882-9110 or 208-772-8515, 10701 North Airport Road, Hayden, ID 83835

EMP-protecting a building is "old hat" to those with clearance who have done this for decades at classified government sites. Since the authors have no current security clearance, and nothing appears on the Internet, we re-engineer expectations so the rest of the civil community can benefit.

Chapter 9
Adding a Structure Solar Rooftop

Chapter 9 Overview

This is the first chapter that solar-PV (PV is photovoltaic to distinguish it from solar thermal for heating water and a pool) is discussed in detail. Solar is "green" (no carbon pollutions) energy and in 2014 in some locations provides electricity at a price less than that provided by the electric utilities. Generally, solar electricity is expected to be on par with fossil fuel electricity costs by 2017-2018). Solar (or another renewable energy) provides some electricity after an EMP incident when the electric utility has become dysfunctional and can no longer produce electricity for perhaps a year or more. The next chapter addresses the EMP protection required for solar and how it is accomplished.

This chapter provides an overview of typical solar rooftop installations *before* solar EMP protection. This chapter also discusses the three generations of solar (crystalline silicon; thin films; and solar paints, inks and dyes). "How solar works" is also reviewed.

The rest of the chapter introduces the exposed solar component victims not addressed in earlier chapters, since they will also have to be EMP protected. They include solar panels (and solar panel mounting racks), inverters or micro-inverters, new wiring,. a controller (for battery charge regulation) and possibly, a smart meter (makes the installation more EMP susceptible). Generators are not used in an EMP protected system since they require fuel.

The chapter closes with a section on solar cost expectations, break even and ROI from 2014 up until 2020.

9.1- Prologue: About Solar-PV Rooftops

There are three reasons for adding solar-PV rooftops to cottage sheds, homes and commercial buildings that may apply in the mind of the beholder:

(1) Reduce or eliminate the electric utility and the monthly billings. The economics of this depends on the hourly utility rate of the location state, site and mountings, and the degree to which sufficient solar panels are installed. However, unless other power backup (like batteries and/or generators) exists, the occupants need the utility power at night and for overcast days for a normal lifestyle.

(2) Solar electric power (or possibly another renewable energy source) is also needed in the event of an EMP incident as there is then no surviving electric utility power for the cottage shed, home, or building. If both the building and its new solar installation follow the 80-dB shielding guidelines of Table 2.1, then the installation becomes nearly self sufficient, provided additional supporting battery backup is added. This statement excludes the need for replenishments and vehicle protection for an EMP event

In the case of a disaster, such as tornado, hurricane, earthquake, volcano, tsunami, and assuming the building was not directly hit, the power outage in the area can typically vary from a few hours to two weeks in USA (like the 13 days of author's home in Hurricane Charley in SW Florida in 2005). After that period, lifestyle usually returns to normalcy. Contrast this to an EMP disaster in which lifestyle may be lost or severely compromised for many months or years, with loss of life running up to 90% in the first year from starvation and disease as some forecasters have projected. Of course the solar-PV backup would be of no consequence if not also EMP protected as discussed in the next chapter.

(3) Solar is "green" - a reason that appeals to many people.

Regarding the economics of solar rooftop power, *Solatel* scores for

145

each of the the 50 USA states become compelling since this determines a major measure of expected degree of performance and beneficial yields. (Other impacts not included are local weather, rooftop orientation to the sun, shadows from trees or buildings.) Solatel scores are defined:

$$\textbf{Solatel} = \textbf{Sol} \times \textbf{el} \times \cos(\textbf{lat}) \times \textbf{N} \qquad (9.1)$$

where, **Sol** = % bright days in a state in terms of 365 days/year
el = electric utility charge in cents/kWh (kilowatt-hour)
lat = median state latitude in degrees
cos(**lat**) is used as solar brightness is proportional to
the cosine of the angle of the site's latitude
N is a normalizing/scaling factor

When Eq.(9.1) is computed for the 50 USA states, Table 9.1 results, and is organized in descending Solatel state ranking.

Table 9.1 – Solatel State Location Scores for Solar Rooftop Viability

US State	State Rank	Solatel Score	Cos() Latit	Bright Day%	cents /kWh	US State	State Rank	Solatel Score	Cos() Latit	Bright Day%	cents /kWh
HI	1	100.0	0.93	75	23.2	IL	26	50.5	0.77	61	11.4
CA	2	93.7	0.83	79	15.1	WI	27	50.4	0.72	61	12.1
CT	3	90.2	0.74	63	20.4	KS	28	47.9	0.78	67	9.7
FL	4	83.4	0.9	79	12.4	MI	29	47.1	0.73	60	11.3
NY	5	83.1	0.74	64	18.3	IA	30	46.9	0.74	65	10.2
NV	6	83.0	0.79	87	12.7	MS	31	46.9	0.84	67	8.8
MA	7	79.0	0.74	64	17.4	OK	32	44.7	0.81	68	8.6
NJ	8	77.8	0.79	63	16.6	UT	33	44.5	0.77	71	8.6
AZ	9	74.2	0.83	87	10.8	OH	34	44.1	0.77	57	10.7
TX	10	72.2	0.87	69	12.8	LA	35	43.9	0.86	63	8.5
MD	11	72.2	0.78	64	15.2	TN	36	43.1	0.81	65	8.6
RI	12	70.4	0.74	64	15.5	MN	37	42.9	0.69	64	10.1
NH	13	69.8	0.73	61	16.5	IN	38	42.2	0.77	62	9.4
DE	14	65.6	0.78	63	14	WY	39	42.0	0.73	71	8.5
NM	15	63.2	0.82	80	10.2	MO	40	40.8	0.79	63	8.6
WA	16	59.5	0.68	52	17.8	NE	41	40.7	0.75	67	8.5
VT	17	58.1	0.72	57	15	AK	42	39.5	0.48	50	17.2
SC	18	56.3	0.83	69	10.3	KY	43	39.4	0.79	63	8.4
VA	19	54.9	0.79	69	10.7	SD	44	39.3	0.72	69	8.4
GA	20	54.2	0.84	66	10.3	MT	45	37.1	0.68	65	8.8
AL	21	53.6	0.84	63	10.6	ID	46	36.0	0.72	69	7.6
CO	22	53.3	0.78	74	9.8	OR	47	32.6	0.71	56	8.7
NC	23	52.6	0.81	68	10.1	ME	48	31.1	0.71	63	7.3
PA	24	52.5	0.75	63	11.7	ND	49	29.4	0.67	63	7.3
AR	25	50.6	0.82	68	9.6	WV	50	28.6	0.79	49	7.8

So the higher the Solatel score, the more likely the solar rooftop is to pay for itself and generate extra savings.

In examining Solatel Scores in Table 9.1, the most promising states are in the upper decile (10 percentile), to wit, (Solatel score from 100 down to 85) Hawaii (best), California, Connecticut, Florida and New York. CT may appear as the odd state here because it has a higher latitude than the other four. However, its electric utility rate is high, making it a more successful candidate for competitive home solar rooftop installations.

Conversely, from Table 9.1, the lower decile in Solatel scoring (score 29 to 36) results for the states of West Virginia (lowest), North Dakota, Maine, Oregon and Idaho. All are higher (northern) latitude states except, WV, which ranks lowest This is because WV has relatively low electric utility rates ($0.07/kWh) and has the lowest amount of bright days (49%) of any state making solar rooftop installations less competitive there.

The above discussion invites the question of what are the six median scoring Solatel group states? What do they have in common? Answer: North Carolina, Pennsylvania, Arkansas, Illinois, Wisconsin and Kansas. They all seem to be middle latitude states (excepting WI) with middle electric utility rates as seen in Table 9.1.

In summary, Solatel score rankings from HI (#1) to WV (#50) corresponds to a yield/cost ratio performance range of 100/28.6 = 3.5:1. Solar rooftop installations are more generally marketable in the higher Solatel scoring states. Remember, all this is without regard to the EMP protection discussed in the next chapter.

9.2- Solar-PV Generations and Performance

There are currently three generations of solar-PV technology:

1st Generation, Crystalline Silicon solar represents the most popular solar-PV with about 82% of the solar installations as of 2014. It is the most expensive and is about 20% efficient in

147

converting sunlight into electricity. It is the oldest of the solar technologies and has a 25 year guarantee and a 40+ year life expectancy for most locations.

Table 9.2 – Solar rooftop technology and median installed price

Solar Rooftop Technology and Median Installed Price

Solar Generation & Technology		2014 Efficiency*	2014 Price $/Watt	2016 Efficiency*	2016 Price $/Watt
	1st Generation				
1st Generation	Crystalline Silicon	20	$3.00	22	$1.50
2nd Generation	*2nd Generation*				
Thin Film	Amorphous Silicon				
	Cadmium Telluride	14	$2.00	17	$1.00
	CIGS	12		8	
3rd Generation	*3rd Generation*				
Inks and Dyes	Solar Paints	Rooftop		5	$0.30
		Siding		2	

2nd Generation, Thin-Film solar is made from amorphous silicon (the least favorable of the 2nd generation), or from popular cadmium telluride (CdTe) or copper, indium, gallium, selenide (CIGS) cells. In thickness it is less than a human hair in diameter, but mostly formed into rigid, glass-covered panels. Efficiencies are reported at about 14%, but First Solar, Inc. reported that they can manufacture new ones with a 20% efficiency in early 2014. Note: 2nd generation efficiency values are contentious, as they are based on a different measure of efficiency than first generation. This is discussed below.

3rd Generation, Paints, Inks and Dyes, still, mostly in experimental stages and in a few years expected to become practical, competitive, and provide inexpensive installations. It also generates more visual aesthetics to incorporate into building surfaces.

While applied vertically along the outer skin of a building, their solar conversion efficiency is low (equivalent efficiency about 5% at best) but their cost is very low. So the resulting yield/cost ratio is becoming favorable. Because the 3rd generation solar is still in its early stages, it is not discussed further in this book.

More on Solar Cell Generations and Efficiency

Many, if not most who are knowledgeable about solar cell technology, say that first generation silicon solar is more efficient, reliable, and has a longer life expectancy than second generation, thin-film, solar technology. They further argue that silicon solar technology has been around for more than 50 years, used by NASA in space, and has a large reliable data base, while thin-film has only been out for about 17 years. The confusion or problem here is that the *measurement criteria* and other metrics of performance *are different* for the two solar generations. And, there is always the "turf politics" problem of NIH (not invented here). CdTe solar cells are predicted to grow the fastest in the next several years for reasons discussed later.

Thin-film solar companies are often weary of being asked about their conversion efficiency, which is basically defined for the first generation as the amount of sunlight a solar panel can convert into *peak* power when pointing directly at the sun. Part of the problem is because the thin-film manufacturers say the efficiency standard is flawed. Therefore, some thin-film companies are pushing for a new and more meaningful or relevant standard.

The measurement criteria for first generation solar is based on questionable assumptions. For example, peak power output (not average or under conditions representative of a real-world installation) is used for silicon. Proponents of second generation solar (for example, CdTe and CIGS) argue that the total kWh energy output per kW of power installation over a unit of time is the real-world use and test. Most first generation advocates say "no" (because this will make their product appear less favorable and even more expensive).

Another reason for discord is that thin-film solar can make electricity in diffuse light (for example, overcast skies), while regular silicon-based panels need more direct light. Thin-film advocates say this means thin films can produce more electricity throughout the day if graded by not using the silicon standard of measurement.

The discussions here are not based on a contentious efficiency term based on peak power output, but rather the kWh/kW/day approach. (kWh/kW/day = kilowatt-hours of energy per kilowatts of installed power per 24-hour day). When this is used, thin film becomes more "comparable" to silicon daylight conversion, even though its silicon definition places it at roughly 70% "efficient" relative to silicon (e.g: best: 24% vs. 17%).

In summary, it is absolutely essential that the matter of silicon peak power efficiency vs. thin-film kWh/kW/day be resolved ASAP. Otherwise one is dealing with apples and oranges, and saying that they are both fruit resolves nothing, but only exacerbates and prolongs the problem and communication misunderstandings. Thus, when requesting bid quotations from installers be sure to ask if they can quote proposal prices for both generations and their corresponding kWh/year outputs.

9.3- *How Solar Rooftop Installations Work*

The accompanying illustration shows the six principal parts of a solar rooftop installation for a residential application.

Courtesy of **Solar Direct**

Fig. 9.3 – Solar rooftop system installation showing six major parts

(1)- Solar-PV (photovoltaic) modules convert sunlight (or diffused solar) into electricity by the photo-electric effect. The PV modules, generally organized into solar panels, generate low voltage DC (direct current) electricity. Their DC output is connected to an inverter to convert to AC (alternating current) voltage for consumer appliances and other loads.

As explained in a later section, a PV cell is most often made of a thin wafer of silicon modified with small amounts of other materials that give the silicon wafer special electrical properties. When sunlight hits a PV cell, it produces an electric current. PV cells are connected together in a solar module, which has a non-reflective glass front, a protective insulating back sheet, and aluminum frame for strength and mounting.

(2)- The inverter transforms the 12-48 volt solar DC power output into 120-240 VAC (alternating current) electricity for household consumption. The inverter may also provide safety functions such as automatic shutdown of the solar electric system in the event of a grid-connected power failure.

(3)- Existing electrical panel, containing circuit breakers for each circuit between 10 and 50 amps. The panel gets its input from either the power company (electric grid) or the AC output from the solar inverter, depending on which is connected.

(4)- Electrical loads, consisting mostly of appliances (air conditioning, water heater, clothes dryer, oven, stove-top burners), electric hand tools, and electric lighting.

For systems with a battery backup (optional, but usually located in off-the-grid areas where the electric grid does not exist), the inverter often regulates the charging of batteries or an added controller does this as shown below in Fig. 9.6. The electricity stored in the batteries can be used at night, or during overcast days or electric blackouts. The battery output is connected to an inverter, similar to the solar cell output.

(5) A valuable feature of photo-voltaic systems is the ability to connect with the existing utility electric power grid which allows solar owners to sell unused electricity back to the utility with a plan known as "Net Metering."

(6) At times when the electricity produced is not being used, the meter will run backwards - selling the electricity back to the utility power grid at retail rates, usually that which they charge the consumer (sometimes lower).

For smart metering installations, the entire system is linked to a Performance-Monitoring Reporting System (PMRS). The PMRS measures and monitors all electricity generated by the system, performs system diagnostics and sends alerts regarding system or equipment issues. The PMRS also tracks weather and generates reports that link weather conditions to kilowatt-hour output.

An application of the above for an 8 ft. x 16 ft. (2.44m x 4.66m) backyard cottage shed, as discussed Chapter 11, is shown in Fig. 9.4. This is a 24/7 installation of a 1.2 kW service, using a solar rooftop and battery system. There are many different versions depending upon the site Solatel score and other variables. For example, the number of 12-volt batteries needed to support a single 200-watt panel may vary from one for SW USA to three in lower bright-day Solatel States in Table 9.1.

Fig. 9.4 – Battery back-up installation for a solar rooftop system.

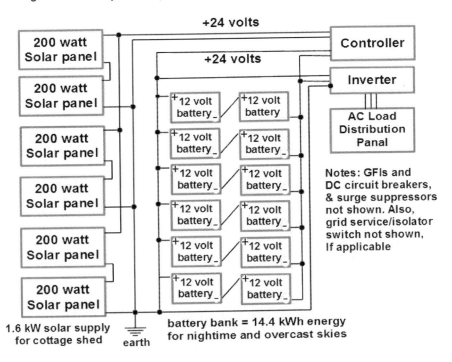

9.4- A few Examples of Solar Rooftop Installations

A few examples of solar rooftop installations are shown in the eleven photos below in Fig 9.5:

Fig. 9.5 – Eleven solar rooftops of residential, commercial & industrial installations

In contrast to residential, 62.5% of the electricity developed in the U.S. goes for commercial and industrial use. Fig. 9.6 illustrates many of the uses and users of electricity in America. Commercial use shows the wide span of building types and uses.

So, it is concluded that commercial applications will be the dominant driver of the feasibility and the financial viability of EMP protection as well as solar rooftop power – at least in the formative years.

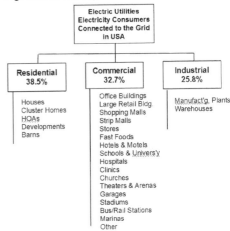

Fig. 9.6: Electricity consumers identification

9.5- Solar Site Location, Seasons, Daytime & Other Variables

This first step in a potential solar rooftop installation, is usually carried out before a proposal is submitted to a solar prospect customer. It is important, that there is no site blockage, Fig 9.7, of the rotating sun by trees or buildings from 20° above the horizon up to the zenith (90° straight up) and back down to 20° before sunset. solar energy production suffers when part or all of the panels are in the shade.

Be sure that the sector between the two paths from summer solstice (21 June) when the sun rises highest in the Northern

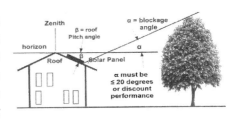

Fig. 9.7 - Solar Obstacle Restrictions

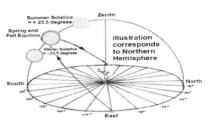

Fig. 9.8– Solar-Earth Seasons

hemisphere to the winter solstice (21 Dec) when the sun rises 47°
lower (Fig. 9.8) has been included in site obstruction checks.

Impact of Other Solar Variables on Solar Rooftop Performance

By combining the variables, latitude, southern-facing roof slope
angle, season and time of day, Table 9.3 is derived to compute the
loss of solar generated electricity for potential solar sites in
different seasons and times of day.

Table 9.3 – Solar Brightness Corrections for Variables

Site Latitude - Roof Slope in degrees	Spring & Fall Equinoxes			Winter Solstice Noon	Summer Solstice Noon
	Noon 12 p.m.	10 a.m. & 2 p.m.	8 a.m. & 4 p.m.		
A	B	C	D	E	F
0	100%	87%	50%	92%	92%
10	98%	85%	49%	90%	93%
20	94%	81%	45%	86%	98%
30	87%	74%	39%	79%	95%
40	77%	64%	31%	69%	84%
50	64%	53%	21%	57%	72%
60	50%	39%	9%	43%	57%

Note: Based on the cosine of resulting solar angle

For this example, a cottage shed to be installed in Newark, NJ, has a latitude of 40°, a shallow roof slope of 10°. Column A latitude of 40° - roof slope of 10° produces the column entry angle of 30°. For equinox conditions at high noon, the most effective luminance is 87%.

At 8 a.m. and 4:00 p.m., the equivalent efficiency has dropped to
39% = a huge loss. 85% of the daily solar energy for equinox
conditions at Newark, occurs during the six hours of 9 a.m. and 3
p.m. Thus, to estimate the daily number of kWh (kW hours)
producible, multiply the power available at noon x the efficiency x
six hours. For the 1.2 kW solar panels on the 8 ft x 16 ft cottage
shed, the daily available energy is 1.2 kW x 6 hours x 80%
efficiency = 5.8 kW hours.

To improve the efficiency of the Newark example, the latitude –
roof slope angle should be less than 15° in Column A for a 90+%
performance in Column B. This can be done by either having a
steeper slope roof, say between 25° and 55°. Perhaps an A-frame
roof with solar panels tilted at an additional angle of 15° so that the
existing roof at 10° brings to an effective slope of 25° for the
Newark example. These two options would increase the previous
example of 5.8 kWh to 6.4 to 7.1 kWh = a daily energy efficiency
improvement of 10% to 29%.

The above illustrates the importance of knowledgeable design for
optimal performance.

9.6- Solar-PV Panel Racking

At construction time, solar panel *racks* are among the first things to erect in place since they secure the solar panels The mounting integrity is especially important here because the installation, if later EMP protected, must be shielded by 80 dB (Table 3.1) for an EMP incident protection. No small task! This situation is discussed in the next chapter on solar panel EMP protection.

Fig. 9.9– Examples of Panel Mounting Racks

9.7- Solar-PV Panels

Solar panels represent roughly half of the solar installation cost. This percentage has reduced significantly since 2012-2013 as panel prices have come down because of the oversupply glut from subsidy withdrawals. Solar panels are sealed, low-reflecting glass housings containing a number of interconnected silicon (or thin film) solar modules that typically produce an output of about 200 watts ± 20%. The corresponding size is roughly 3 feet x 5 feet (91 cm x 157 cm). Other sizes are available. The frame and backing are made of aluminum Fig. (9.10) and are usually mounted onto the solar racks illustrated above in Fig.9.9.

For second generation, thin-film silicon, CdTe or GiGS modules, solar panels are flexible and sealed

Fig. 9.10 – Solar panels

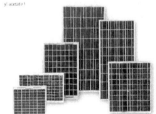

Courtesy, 123rf.com

in their own non-rigid

156

housings. Average efficiencies of CdTe runs about 14% in contrast to roughly 20% for silicon. But, their weight is considerably less than silicon and the price per watt is lower.

Table. 9.11– Examples of 2014 Source Solar Panels

Solar Panel Brand & Model Number	Power Watts, DC	Minimum Quantity	Price $/Panel	Efficiency Rating	Country Origin	$ per Watt
Eoplly EP125m-72-185	185	10	$165	14.49%	China	$0.89
Ritek PM230	230	24	$259	14.05%	Taiwan	$1.12
Trina TSM240PA05 Black	240	20	$240	14.71%	China	$1.00
Conergy PM-240P	240	25	$230	14.40%	China	$0.96
ecoSolargy ECO240S156P-60	240	30	$209	14.00%	China	$0.87
SolarWorld SW-240 Poly	240	10	$255	14.30%	USA	$1.06
Sharp ND-240QCJ	240	10	$279	14.70%	USA	$1.16
Canadian CS6P-245M	245	10	$250	15.23%	China	$1.02
Conergy PH-250P	250	25	$245	15.20%	China	$0.98
Yingli YL250P-29b Poly	250	10	$250	15.30%	China	$1.00
Eoplly EP156MB-60-250 Mono-Black	250	10	$229	15.30%	China	$0.91
Samsung PV-MBA1BG250-Silver	250	20	$294	15.33%	Korea	$1.17
SolarWorld SW-250 Mono	250	10	$269	14.90%	USA	$1.07
Helios 6T-250	250	20	$339	14.50%	USA	$1.35
CEEG CSUN260M Mono	260	10	$270	16.02%	China	$1.04
BenQ PM250P00-260	260	20	$290	15.90%	Taiwan	$1.15
Eoplly EP156P-72-280	280	24	$245	14.38%	China	$0.87
Ritek MM300T	300	24	$329	15.39%	Taiwan	$1.10

Source:

Although Table 9.11 is not especially detailed, it does contain information useful for applications elsewhere on this book. For example, if an average 2,300 sq. ft. home requires 8 kW of power, the above table suggests that 8kW/200W/panel = 40 panels are required. At $200/panel, 40 panels cost $8,000. If solar panels are roughly 50% of the installation cost, the contract price may approximate $16,000 before application of Federal tax credits to expire in 2016.

9.8- Solar Inverters and Micro-inverters

The micro-inverter is a small DC-AC inverter that accepts a typical 12 VDC output from a solar panel and converts it to 120 VAC or other voltage. As appropriate, they are connected in series and/or parallel to produce the desired load voltage as previously illustrated in Fig.(9.4). A small micro-inverter may be built into the solar panel near its output connector (this is done at the time of solar panel assembly back at factory) or more often mounted adjacent to the panel (Fig. 9.12).

Micro-inverters have several advantages over conventional larger central inverters. Even small amounts of shading, debris or snow lines in any one solar panel, or a panel failure, does not disproportionately reduce the output of an entire array. Each micro-inverter obtains optimum power by performing maximum power point tracking for its connected panel.

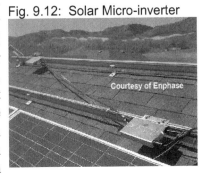
Fig. 9.12: Solar Micro-inverter

Courtesy of Enphase

Their primary disadvantages are that they have an initial higher equipment cost per peak watt than the equivalent power capability in a central inverter, and are normally located near the solar panel, where they may be harder to maintain. These issues are, however, surpassed by the greater durability and simpler installation of micro-inverters.

Fig. 9.13 – Solar Inverters

225, 500 kW

10, 13, 15 kW   60, 82, 95 kW   Courtesy of Solectria Renewables

When the total rooftop solar load exceeds roughly 10 kW, micro-inverters are usually not used and the inverter takes over. Fig. 9.13 shows three inverter sizes ranging from 10 kW to 500 kW.

9.9- Electric Meters and Smart Meters

Figure 9.14 shows two typical, well-known electric meters. Unless or until they are replaced later by smart meters, nothing needs to be done here. However, the next chapter addresses how to

Fig. 9.14 – Typical Utility Electric Meters

158

protect an unshielded smart meter (and its electronic circuits) or meter, per se, to 80 dB and their input leads surge suppressed.

9.10- Interconnecting Wiring

Nearly all the AC wiring from the electric utility transformer serving the customer load, is unshielded. Unless it is coming from an exposed utility pole transformer, as shown in Fig. 9.15, the electric wiring is routed down the pole to the ground transformer sitting on a concrete pad. The wiring to the customer is buried directly in a trench or

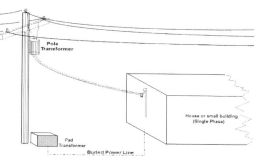

Fig. 9.15 - Small Customer Service Entrance

placed inside a plastic pipe in the trench. Then, it continues to the service entrance all of which has no shielding in a civil world. Remember, all this will be treated in the next chapter on EMP protection.

The customer premises are also served by cable TV, telephone, Internet access (VOIP) or one or more of its derivatives. For the commercial and industrial world, add control and signal leads (SCADA) derived from other sources. Remember, all the wiring and cables act like a huge radiation pickup antenna system and will become especially vulnerable in an EMP incident unless measures are taken for their protection as explained in the next Chapter.

9.11- Cost Considerations, Break Even and ROI

The objective here is to take a rather complicated math compu-
tation of the economics of a solar rooftop installation and to
convert it to a few relatively simple steps that the reader can
readily do for himself in a few minutes after learning the
procedure.

Fig. 9.16 Years for solar installation to break even vs. several variables.

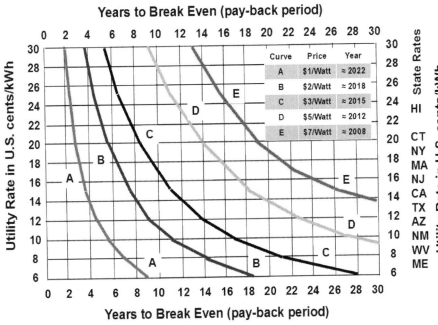

The graph, Fig. 9.16, above depicts the years to break even (X-axis
= recover your Investment) vs. electric utility electricity rates (Y-
Axis) for solar rooftop installations, costing $1/Watt, $2/Watt,
$3/Watt, $5/Watt and $7/Watt with no rebates or tax credits (which
can also be factored in).

Assumptions include average five hours of sunlight/day. This is
averaged over the seasons, in which there is a 47° change in the
elevation of the sun from summer solstice (June 21 in the northern
hemisphere) to – winter solstice (Dec. 21) as previously shown in
Table 9.3. Note, nothing is said about, the installation site latitude,

160

the compass orientation of the roof, the roof slope angle as well as the photovoltaic performance in different latitude and climate locations. These impact how close/far the solar panels are pointing

Fig. 9.17 – City Solar-PV Cumulative Intensity and City Latitudes.

City and State	Intensity kWh/m²/Yr	Multi- Plier	Latit. degr	City and State	Intensity kWh/m²/Yr	Mult- plier	Latit. degr
Atlanta, GA	1800	1.00	33	Mojave Dsrt, CA	2500	0.72	35
Austin, TX	1900	0.95	30	Los Angeles, CA	2100	0.86	34
Baltimore, MD	1600	1.13	39	Newark, NJ	1600	1.13	40
Boston, MA	1500	1.20	42	New York,NY	1600	1.13	40
Chicago, IL	1600	1.13	41	Philadelphia, PA	1750	1.03	39
Cleveland , OH	1600	1.13	41	Phoenix, AZ	2400	0.75	33
Dallas, TX	2000	0.90	32	Pittsburg, PA	1550	1.16	40
Denver, CO	2200	0.82	39	San Francisco, CA	2050	0.88	37
Detroit, MI	1700	1.06	42	Seattle, WA	1300	1.39	48
Fairbanks, AK	1300	1.39	64	St. Louis, MO	1700	1.06	38
Hartford, CT	1600	1.13	41	Sacramento, CA	2100	0.86	38
Honolulu, HI	2100	0.86	21	San Antonio, TX	1700	1.06	29
Houston, TX	1600	1.13	29	San Bernardino, CA	2100	0.86	34
Indianapolis, IN	1650	1.09	39	San Diego, CA	2100	0.86	32
Jacksonville, FL	1850	0.97	30	San Jose, CA	2100	0.86	37
Miami, FL	1850	0.97	25	Tampa, FL	1850	0.97	27

at the sun in the declination axis (North-South direction).To correct for (site latitude - roof slope) angle, first use the table in Fig. 9.17 above, to get the latitude of your solar installation site infrom NREL solar-PV map of the U.S. (Fig. 9.18), use the correction factor obtained from Fig. 7.19. These corrections result in:from NREL solar-PV map of the U.S. (Fig. 9.18), use the correction factor obtained from Fig. 7.19. These corrections result in:

Fig. 9.18 – NREL Solar-PV Map

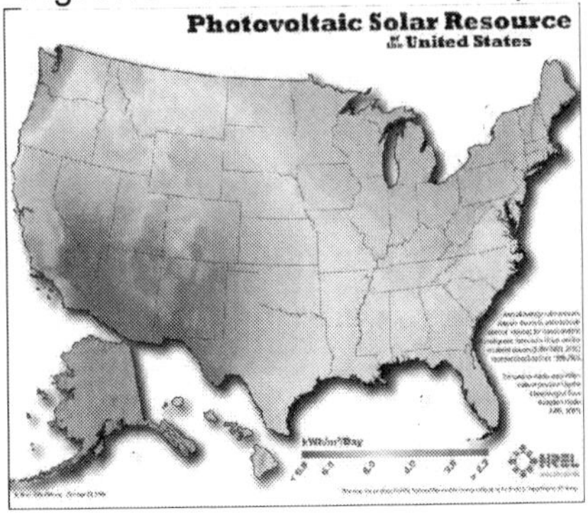

Photovoltaic Solar Resource
of United States

Fig. 9.19 – Correction of: Latitude – Roof Slope

Latit-Slope	Cos(L-S)	Error	Brk Even x
0°	1.00	0%	1
10°	0.98	2%	1.02
20°	0.94	6%	1.06
30°	0.87	13%	1.15
35°	0.82	18%	1.22
40°	0.77	23%	1.30
45°	0.71	29%	1.41
50°	0.65	35%	1.54
55°	0.57	43%	1.75
60°	0.50	50%	2.00

BE=Graph x Corr1 x Corr2 (9.2)

where: BE = break even in years
Graph = value from the Fig. 9.16.
Corr1 = Correction from Fig. 9.17
Corr2 = Correction from Fig. 9.19.

Illustrative example: Consider a thin-film, CdTe, solar panel installation costing $3.00 per watt near Newark, NJ. Assume a flat roof (slope = 0 degrees) on a commercial office building. The latitude for Newark is $40°$. Latitude – roof slope is $40°-0° = 40°$. Fig. 9.19 indicates the multiplier correction, Corr1, is 1.30.

From the graph, Fig. 9.16, $0.16 electricity cost Y-axis (NJ) intercepts the Curve C ($3/Watt) at about 10.5 years.

The second correction, Corr2, is from Fig. 9.17 for the solar climate of the location. For Newark this is 1.13.

So, calculate the corrected value for break even, BE, from the above equation. Since the flat roof has a slope of $0°$, the (latitude – roof slope) is:

BE = 10.5 years x 1.30 x 1.13 = 15 years.

This is not adjusted for any state subsidy or federal tax credit, if available. However, if subsidy is available, BE is reduced in USA by about 30% for a 30% state rebate and/or 30% (more) if a federal tax credit applies. For example, if both apply here, the corrected

162

break even is:

BE = 15.4 years x (1-0.3) x (1-0.3) = 7.5 years. This could have been combined into the original table, but the trend is to discontinue subsidies as the manufacturing and installation prices come down.

Some general trends are observable from the above. For example, it is clearly seen that:

• Electric utility rates below roughly $0.10/kWh "never" permit break even for solar rooftop costs above $3/watt. Roof life expectancy may also be exceeded.

• For states where rates are above ≈ $0.18/kWh, break even is less than 16 years for 2010 costs approximating $5/Watt.

• When solar rates approximate $1/Watt to $2/Watt (≈ 2015), break even is roughly four years for utility rates above ≈ $0.16/kWh.

• One strategy is to estimate the result using half the electric consumption now at, say, $4-$5/watt, on the southern slope, and the other half in a few years at $2/watt on the eastern and/or western slope. Thin-film, CdTe can be used on the northern slope at a later date.

The trade-off considerations here involve a straddle between deferring a few years more to install solar rooftop in recognition that the price comes down by Moore's Law vs. not having the beneficial use of solar.

• With respect to ROI, it is negative until break even, and it begins to payoff thereafter. Exceptions acknowledged, until solar installations reach $1/watt and only for higher utility rates as shown in the upper left region of Curve A of the graph, would an investor likely go for solar. However, the argument is quite different for non-grid connected installations as the motivation and judgment criteria are then very different. Also, because of their MWatt production, solar farms will enjoy shorter break evens and larger ROIs.

163

9.12- About the Solar Rooftop Market

The following is excerpted from Fortune Magazine, May 6, 2013, by Brian Dumaine, senior editor-at-large from an interview with Jim Hughes, CEO of First Solar of Tempe Arizona. Why is Hughes optimistic about First Solar's prospects now? For one thing, prices have finally stabilized. In the first quarter of 2013, prices of PV panels stopped dropping for the first time in five years and even rose slightly. A major reason is that the huge surplus in manufacturing capacity is starting to abate. According to the research firm Greentech Media, in 2008 there were more than 200 PV-funded solar startups in the U.S. Over the past few years more than one-third of them have been acquired, closed, or gone bankrupt.

Meanwhile, demand is soaring -- for a variety of reasons. China plans to install an ambitious 10 gigawatts of solar capacity this year. In the U.S. the solar industry grew 76% in 2012 as PV manufacturers installed a total of 3.3 gigawatts of power, or the equivalent of a new nuclear power plant. Generous state subsidies in California and elsewhere have driven sales, as well as the fact that 29 states now have requirements that a certain percentage of power come from renewables. And new solar financing models -- in which installers such as Solar City (backed by Google (GOOG, Fortune 500), among others) and SunRun lease solar systems to customers for little or no money down -- have taken off and now account for a fast-growing share of all new solar installations.

Hughes says his company is ready to ride this wave. First Solar's competitive advantage is a next-generation technology called thin-film solar. Most PV panels today are made with silicon. But First Solar uses cadmium telluride, which it spreads over very thin sheets. This less expensive manufacturing process allows First Solar to make its panels for a near-industry best of 64¢ a watt.

The challenge with thin-film solar panels, however, is that they are not as efficient as silicon panels, as measured by the amount of sun converted into electricity. Silicon panels average around 16% efficiency while First Solar achieves 13%. That means you'd need to install more First Solar panels to generate the same amount of electricity as silicon. (For this reason, First Solar has concentrated mostly on big utility-scale projects.)

Hughes argues that First Solar makes up the difference through lean manufacturing, low cost of capital, and less expensive installation. By 2016, he says, his solar farms should produce electricity for as little as 7¢ or 8¢ per kilowatt-hour, competitive in many instances with fossil fuels. And the efficiency gap may soon close. This spring First Solar's lab hit a new record for thin-film efficiency: 16%. That would make it competitive with silicon.

9.13- Sources and References

Largest Solar Panel Manufacturers

- First Solar, USA (thin film, CdTe), Tel:
- Suntech, China
- Sharp, Japan
- Q-Cells, Germany
- SolarWorld, Germany
- Yingli, China
-

Adding EMP protection of solar-PV rooftops to an EMP protected home increases manyfold the family lifestyle over those called survivors & Preppers.

1. 520.0 MW,JA Solar
2. 400.0 MW Kyocera
3. 399.0 MW Trina Solar
4. 397.0 MW SunPower USA
5. 368.0 MW Gintech

Solar Inverter Manufacturers

Use the website ENF solar directory, www.enfsolar.com or many manufacturers and suppliers

Chapter 10
EMP Protecting the Solar Rooftop

Chapter 10 Overview

This chapter explains how to EMP protect a solar rooftop on an EMP protected building. Of course, this is only an EMP protected building such as described in Chapters 7-8. For new constructions, both building and their rooftops are EMP protected at the same time which provides a cost reduction and expected better performance than if it is done separately.

Based on an EMP threat, all solar rooftop components must be EMP-protected, as addressed in previous chapters. This includes adding shielded solar panels and inverter or micro-inverters, shielding all rooftop and related wiring, and the new smart meter to replace the older electrical meter, if applicable. (A smart meter containing electronic circuits is more EMP susceptible and needs additional shielding unless inside the shielded building).

Since internally-shielded solar panels are a few years from off-the-shelf availability, one interim solar rooftop protection option is a reel-type, roll-on screening over the entire solar-rooftop area for ease of . maintenance and upkeep.

On-site, performance testing of the combined installation for EMP protection compliance is discussed in the next chapter. Because everything ages and because of adverse climate and weather effects, maintenance is addressed here in Chapter 10.

10.0- A Moment for Reflection

The following will provide an overview of where we have recently been and where we are headed. Then, we resume with some details of shielding and EMP protecting the solar-PV rooftop.

The diagram below starts with the question about whether the subject structure already exists or is about to be built? The reason for this is that a new structure offers solar rooftop and EMP protection options, that are not available to existing structures. Much of this is due to access limitations of existing structures, especially for bonding of different shields.

Follow the structure flow in the diagram below. The second question from the left asks about adding the solar-PV rooftop now. Assuming the answer is "yes", then some consideration needs to be made re the owner possibly wanting the solar rooftop panels (and building) to be EMP protected either now or at a later date (third question). Since this involves both costs and implementability, the "no" branch suggests that a low-cost aluminum foil laminate (for later solar shielding) should be added first before the solar panel racking is installed. Otherwise, later solar shielding update becomes nearly impossible.

Fig.10.1- Flow diagram when and how to EMP protect solar rooftop

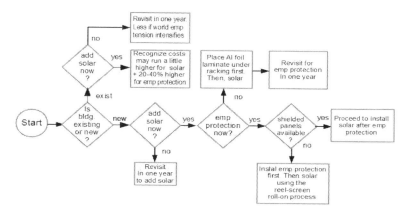

A second major question (fourth in the diagram) involves how to shield the solar rooftop in general and the solar panels in particular.

It has already been stated that internally shielded solar panels are not-yet commercially available till, perhaps, 2016. So the "yes" is not yet available. The "no" decision speaks to a method that to our knowledge has not yet been done for civil applications. It involves a concept somewhat similar to a swimming pool cover, reel-in approach. The system provides tightness for the wire mesh cover over the solar panels. It is not intended that the cover be reeled in and out except for infrequent maintenance, such as once a year. Some details are discussed herein on how this works and how the above screen is peripheral bonded to the screen below racking. While this system is an option for the present, the other option of using an available manufacturer-supplied, internal solar panel screening after 2016 is certainly preferable and likely to be less expensive.

10.1- Preliminary Solar Rooftop Considerations

The first question for solar rooftop installation is "what is to be optimized" and how to achieve the mounting of the solar panels to the roof? Some of these variables were addressed in the previous chapter. For a simple cottage shed, having less than about ten 3 ft x 5 ft (0.9m x 1.5m) solar panels (providing 1.2 kW of power), the number of variables is fewer and direction is quite simple; this is discussed later on. Otherwise, most of the principal variables are:

- Remaining life expectancy of roof and expected life of solar panels
- Electrical kW power objective for solar rooftop
- Southern roof exposure angle = degrees off South axis. (hopefully, under 30°= for 95% efficiency) for Northern hemisphere installations.
- NREL location brightness Index (see Table 3.1)
- Electric Utility price per kWh = Varies from 7.9¢ to 33¢/kWh
- Useful area of southern roof in sq. ft. or sq. m. Silicon panels produce about 13 watts/sq. ft and thin film about 10 watts/sq. ft.
- Solar roof site location latitude
- Roof elevation angle (slope). Efficiency = k*cos(latitude-slope)
- Roof elevation angle to be adjusted for seasons? (see Table 7.3)
- Trackers to be used for "daily rotating sun"? Solar Farms only? (can buy up to extra 25% efficiency over fixed, solar panels
- Roof type: asbestos, tile, or metal (impacts method of securing)

- Hardware for direct solar panel mounting
- Rack mounting for indirect solar panel mounting

In summary, lessons learned:

(1)- Southern solar roof pointing direction: keep angle from South under 30° off axis. For cottage shed, consider elevated racks for Northern latitudes. For Northern latitude homes, consider A-frame roofs or slope-enhanced racking which also permits greater kW power output and better snow-load run off.

(2)- Keep site (location latitude - roof slope) under 20°. Otherwise consider solar panel racks mounted at angle (for a fully adjustable tilt racking system, contact Lock Solar company).

It is important to ensure that the remaining life of the roof exceeds the life expectancy of the solar panels being installed. The default life period for most solar rooftop installations is 20 years. Most asphalt shingles in northern U.S. states have a life expectancy of about 30 years, while in southern states life may be shortened to 15 years because of greater solar heating.

Life expectancy of silicon solar panels may be 30 years or more while second generation thin film, CdTe, may have a 20-year expectancy. Thus, never allow the remaining roof life to be less than that for the solar panels to be used. This is an especially important consideration in areas where significant hail is common.

Since unprotected solar cells inside a solar-PV panel are susceptible to instant burnout or destruction from an upper atmospheric EMP event, solar panels must also be shielded. Unlike EMP screen shields used to cover windows (Chapter 7), *solar-panel* screen specifications are considerably more demanding. The object is to block the EMP originated, radio-frequency radiations below 1 GHz, but be as transparent as possible optically to the higher frequencies of sunlight. (the solar panel wire screen acts as a one-stage, high-pass filter, cutting off at about 22 GHz (Fig.2.2) to produce 80 dB rejection at 2.2 MHz for 20 OPI screen).

In Chapters 3 and 10 "Chapter Overview", it was mentioned that screen shields, built into normal solar panels are not yet off-the-shelf, commercially available for civil applications (classified applications in the 1980 versions notwithstanding, as the technology is well understood). It is estimated that solar panels, with internal screen shields will make their first civil market appearance about 2016, but it may take a year or two more to settle quality control and price reductions. Therefore, the *"reel-in screen"* shielding concept can be used for solar rooftops in the interim. As discussed later, this screen may be susceptible to storm. snow, sleet and hail damage

10.2- Solar Panel Mounting and Racking

Fig. 10.1 Several Roof Racking Configuration Options

While Solar panels can be directly mounted on asbestos roofing, they rarely are because the rafter cover, decking thickness may typically be only 5/8 inch (16 mm) – not deep enough to hold lag screws in heavy wind or sleet storms over years. Stud finders are used to locate the rafters, where racking is secured to the roof. Also, for tile roofing, racking is needed between the solar panels. Fig. (8.1) shows a number of rack configurations for solar rooftops and the tile roof to access the rafters for anchoring lag screws.

As previously remarked, the solar panel installation efficiency is proportional to the cosine of the (rooftop site latitude - roof slope) angle. So, for example, if you lived in metro Washington DC (latitude 38°) and have a flat roof, cos(38°-0°) = 79% efficiency.

170

To increase your solar efficiency by 27% to get 100% (ignoring for the moment daily and seasonal and other considerations), solar panel racking installation angle can be set to 38° as shown in the right images of Fig. 10.1. Be mindful of the increased wind and snow-load susceptibility of high-angle, solar racking. Maybe an A-frame roof is better.

10.3- Solar Rooftop Screening Options

Remembering that the solar panels must be completely covered with a bottom shield and an upper solar see-through screen for system shielding, a plan view is shown in Fig. 10.2. Around this installation the entire

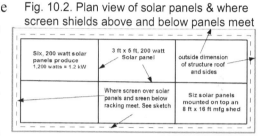

Fig. 10.2. Plan view of solar panels & where screen shields above and below panels meet

Six, 200 watt solar panels produce 1,200 watts = 1.2 kW

3 ft x 5 ft, 200 watt Solar panel

outside dimension of structure roof and sides

Where screen over solar panels and sreen below racking meet. See sketch

Siz solar panels mounted on top an 8 ft x 16 ft mfg shed

periphery of the solar panel screen is bonded 360 degrees to the lower screen rooftop cover as shown in Fig. 10.2 for a flat roof installation.

After mounting the roof cover bottom, the solar panel racking and the solar panels in place, two approaches may be used to top cover the solar panels with the high-transparency screen:

(1)- Reel, roll-over screen sheet rolls may be used to cover the entire solar panel area, including associated interconnecting wiring and micro-inverters, if used. Depending on the material source company, the widest available screen will vary from 36 inches (91 cm) to 6 ft (1.83 m).

171

Fig. 10.3. Hand mechanical & electrical methods of covering solar panel screen taken from pool cover approaches

The reel concept is a take off from the solar thermal blanket cover for swimming pools. Of course, significant changes or adjustments are needed at the beginning and end of the screen.

Since the screen top and lower rooftop shields meet around the periphery, one bond config- uration can be an arrange- ment such as shown in Fig. 10.4. The clamps are replaced with lag screws for maintenance cycles of greater than about every two years. For best electrical bonding performance, each screen should be folded

Fig. 10.4. Twist-clamp lock to bond screens

back about 1/2 inch in meeting its mate or use spring fingers stock illustrated in Fig. 7.4A in Chapter 7. Readers wishing to discuss more detail may contact "Electrical Interconnect Solutions, Inc.", via: Vern.Shrader@ gmail.com.

The DIY reader is reminded that the more northern states exhibiting sleet storms and large snowfalls may find the reel, roll-over screen cover approach to be too susceptible to bad weather damage. In the interim, contact a local architect or local solar rooftop installers for their securing opinions or considerations.

(2)- A more economical and easier approach securing top and bottom screens is suggested in Fig. 10.5 for the interim years before built in solar panels become available off the shelf.

As before, the wire mesh screen or aluminum foil composite over the asphalt shingles is shown at the bottom. The top screen is shown stretched over the solar panels. To connect the top screen cover with the bottom shield at the periphery, an S-shaped sheet metal bracket is used. Where the brackets meet, edge-to-edge, an aluminum adhesive foil cover is used. To ensure good electrical bond, spring finger stock (See Fig, 7.4A Chap.7) is sandwiched in between the bracket and mating screens. When infrequent maintenance is needed the lag screws are readily removed with an electric power drill.

Fig. 10.5. Mechanical method of connecting upper and lower solar panel screen shields/

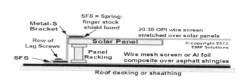

10.4- Selection of Solar Roof Screen Cover

In addition to screen OPI (openings per inch) being about 20 or 30 as described earlier, solar panel applications suggests that the screen wires of this shield application be thin, yet rugged enough to handle rain, snow, sleet, hail, and dust storms. Thus, for EMP protected rooftops for interim years, the earlier approach of reel-in screening is used for solar panel cover.

In Chapter 2 it was demonstrated that a 20 or 30 OPI (openings per inch) screen mesh cover would provide adequate default shielding effectiveness. There are a few suppliers (see Sect. 8.9 list at end of this chapter) who make this. One is shown in Table 10.1.

Column A is the OPI in inches. Col. C is the wire diameter in mils (1 mil = 0.001 inch). Col. F is the important solar light blocking area in

Table 10.1. – Specification List of Ultra-thin Stainless Steel Wire Mesh (extracted from data from Habei General Metal Netting of China)

A	B	C	D	E	F	G
Mesh per Inch	Wire diameter d in mm	d in mils	Mesh Opening w in mm	Opening Area In %	light blobk In %	Weight (kg/sq m)
16	0.04	1.6	1.55	95	5	0.01
25	0.06	2.4	0.96	88	12	0.05
32	0.05	2.0	0.74	88	12	0.04
36	0.05	2.0	0.66	86	14	0.05
42	0.04	1.6	0.57	87	13	0.03

per cent. For example, a 16 OPI wire mesh produces light blocking of only 5%, so that a low 5% of converted sunlight in watts will be

173

lost from the wire shadow for a 90 degree overhead sunlight. Since the screen wire shadow increases before and after noon, the conversion to electricity will also decrease (the blocking per cent increases).

More overhead sunlight is lost since we don't live on the equator during the spring and fall equinoxes, corresponding to 90° perpendicular solar panel, solar illuminated situations. The wire shadow also changes during the time of day with noon casting the least shadow. Table 10.2 shows the additional shadow loss for site latitude and roof slope of solar mounting, season and time of day.

Table 10.2 – Solar Brightness Corrections for Variables

Site Latitude - Roof Slope in degrees	Spring & Fall Equinoxes			Winter Solstice Noon	Summer Solstice Noon
	Noon 12 p.m.	10 a.m. & 2 p.m.	8 a.m. & 4 p.m.		
0	100%	87%	50%	92%	92%
10	98%	85%	49%	90%	93%
20	94%	81%	45%	86%	98%
30	87%	74%	39%	79%	95%
40	77%	64%	31%	69%	84%
50	64%	53%	21%	57%	72%
60	50%	39%	9%	43%	57%

10.5- Some additional remarks for screen-over solar panels & for future shielded solar panel manufacturers
(This section by Jerry Emanuelson)

Covering the front surface of the solar panel with wire mesh is best done at the factory. Unfortunately, at the time of this writing, such shielded solar panels are not yet available. It is emphasize that we have not yet tried this method although it is based upon, not only known shielding methods, but also upon techniques used by some of the more professional do-it-yourself makers of solar panels.

It is cautioned that how well the retrofitting technique described below works can vary greatly among different types of solar panels and different kinds of solar panel frames.

(1) A wire mesh of any kind that is not flat against the front surface of the solar panel will likely be damaged by any one of a wide variety of hazards. That damage may not happen for several years, but it will occur in any outdoor environment facing the sky.

174

(2) An uncovered wire mesh on the front of the solar panel will accumulate dust and snow that will be difficult to remove until it can be safely hosed down with water. This contrasts with a smooth glass-faced solar panel where, unless icing conditions are occurring, snow normally slides off, or can be easily brushed off, of the front surface glass of a solar panel.

(3) The wire mesh on the front of the solar panel must be sufficiently durable that a second layer of shielding is not needed. A second layer of wire mesh will begin to diminish transparency; and, however it is done, will only add to the problems stated above in (2).

(4) The problems of adding wire mesh to the front surface are sufficiently complex that the front surface shielding should be considered as an entirely separate matter from shielding the remainder of the solar panel and solar power system.

(5) A wire mesh lying flat on the front of the solar panel has the advantage of being a small heat sink, conducting heat away from the center cells to the frame. Heat is the main enemy of solar panel efficiency on all types of solar panels. All of the extra electromagnetic shielding on both sides of the solar panel has the advantage of also serving as additional heat sinking.

Keep in mind that only a high-transparency wire mesh can be used on the front surface of the solar panel. Although ordinary aluminum window screen appears fairly transparent to the unaided eye, this is a trick of automatic adjustments made by the human brain. So be sure to use only wire mesh with an actual open space area of 88 percent or higher.

The bottom of the solar panel must also be shielded, but this is a much simpler process since neither transparency nor flatness of the wire mesh is an issue on the back side of the panel.

10.6- Adding Shielded Micro-inverter or Inverter (shield only)

The micro-inverter is a small DC-AC converter which takes a typical 12 VDC output from a solar panel and converts it to 120 VAC or other user load value. As appropriate they are connected in series and/or parallel to produce the desired load voltage. A small micro-inverter can be built into the shielded solar panel

Fig. 10.7 – Shielded Micro-inverter

Courtesy of Enphase

near its output connector (this is to be done at the time of solar panel assembly back at the factory) or mounted separately next to the panel as shown in Fig. 10.7 at the right. Unless the entire solar rooftop assembly is to be shielded separately, as discussed elsewhere, the shielded unit in Fig. 10.7 would require a surge suppressor at both input and output cable connectors.

Micro-inverters have several advantages over conventional central inverters. Even small amounts of shading debris or snow lines on any one solar panel, or a panel failure, does not disproportionately reduce the output of an entire array. Each micro-inverter obtains optimum power by performing maximum power point tracking for its connected panel.

Their primary disadvantages are that they have a higher initial cost per watt than the equivalent power in a central inverter, and are normally located near the solar panel, where they may be harder to maintain. These disadvantages are usually surpassed by micro-inverters having higher durability & simplicity of installation.

When the total rooftop solar load exceeds about 10 kW, micro-inverters are usually not used and the inverter takes over. The photo at the right shows three inverter sizes ranging from 10 kW to 500 kW. If they were located outside the EMP shielded

Fig. 10.8 – Shielded Inverter Cabinets

225, 500 kW

10, 13, 15 kW   60, 82, 95 kW   Courtesy of Solectria Renewables

building they would have to have cabinet shielding of 80 dB plus cable surge suppressors and shielded cabling. To avoid this, if possible, they should be placed inside the 80-dB shielded building so existing models can be used with no further shielding retrofit required.

10.7- Adding EMP Surge Suppressors and Filters

Surge suppressors are used on wiring and cables such as power lines, telephone, control and signal leads entering and exiting all structures. Cables act as "radiation pick-up antennas" inducing EMP voltage spikes up to 50,000 volts. As such, the spikes exceed wire insulation – arcing over, shorting and destroying connected devices connected thereto unless EMP protected.

Commercial electronic surge suppressors used for lightning strikes do not clamp fast enough (clamp >100 nsec for lightning; need to clamp less than 5 nanoseconds for EMP, per Fig. 2.2) to protect against the near instantaneous effects of an EMP. Some also may not have great enough current carrying capacity. So it is important that EMP rated surge suppressors be used for any exterior wire/cable entrance from the outside world to the inside of the EMP-shielded building.

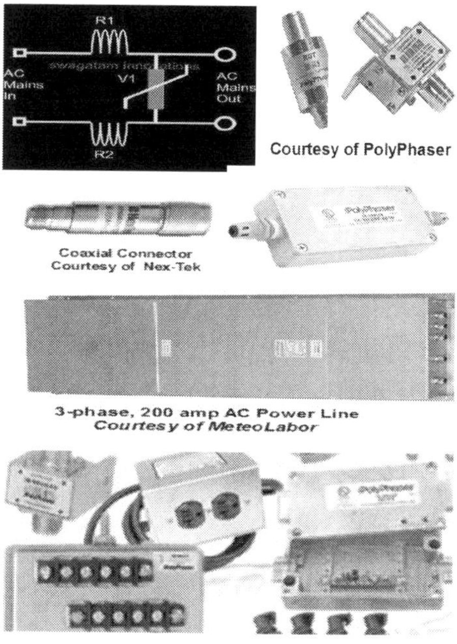

Fig. 10.9 shows a few of several EMP surge suppressors available for addressing the wide variety of needs and applications. (The surge suppressors used for high voltage transformers in substations to address the geomagnetic storm needs are different and are not shown here).

Fig. 10.9 – Two different types of Many hardened surge suppressors

Courtesy of PolyPhaser

Coaxial Connector
Courtesy of Nex-Tek

3-phase, 200 amp AC Power Line
Courtesy of MeteoLabor

10.8- Adding the Shielded Smart Meter

A smart meter (Fig. 10.1) is usually an electrical meter that records consumption of electric energy in intervals of an hour or less and communicates that information at least daily back to the utility for monitoring and billing purposes. Smart meters enable two-way communications between the meter and the central system. Unlike home

Fig. 10.1: Wire mesh, screen shielded meters

energy monitors, smart meters can gather data for remote reporting. Such an advanced metering infrastructure (AMI) differs from traditional automatic meter reading (AMR) in that it enables two-way communications with the meter.

Since the smart meter is mounted on the outside of a building, it will have to be shielded to 80 dB to match the EMP time-domain threat. This can be accomplished by using the same 20 OPI wire mesh engulfing the *entire* meter on the front and back discussed earlier.

The addition of smart meters will make EMP susceptibility of the electric grid at the consumer end more severe. The reason is that more microprocessors and communication networks are involved. Thus, this matter needs to be addressed in protecting installations with or without solar rooftop added

10.9- Sources and References

Shielding and Bonding Materials

- ETS–Lindgren, Tel: 512-531-6400, www.ets-lindgren.com, 1301 Arrow Point Drive, Cedar Park, TX 78613 (shielded windows and buildings; 4 ft x 50 ft rolls of screen wire)

- Chomerics, Tel: 1-781-935-4850, 77 Dragon Court, Woburn, MA, wflanders@parker.com

- Zippertubing, Tel: 800-321-8178 or 480 285-3910. Fax 480-

285-3997, 7150 W. Erie St. Chandler, AZ 85226

• Panashield, Tel: 1-203-866-5888, 185R West Norwalk Road, Norwalk, CT 06850,

• Holland Shielding, Tel: 31-78- 613-1366. Fax: 31-78-614-9585. www.hollandshielding.com,

• TWP Inc., Tel: 510-548-4434 or 800-227-1570, 2831 Tenth Street, Berkeley, CA 94710 USA, sales@twpinc.com

• Hebei General Metal Netting Co. Ltd. Of China, Tel: +86-318-855-7784, Fax: +86-318-775-7320, http://www.generalmesh.com, http://www.industrialwirecloth.com

Surge Suppressors and Filters

• PolyPhaser, Tel: 800-882-9110 , 10701 North Airport Road, Hayden, ID 83835

• Transtector, Tel: 800-882-9110 , 10701 North Airport Road, Hayden, ID 83835

• Protection Technology Group, 800-882-9110 or 208-772-8515, 10701 North Airport Road, Hayden, ID 83835

Chapter 11
Special Small EMP Protected Homes

Chapter 11 Overview

This chapter is about factory-built, manufactured and modular homes and shipping container homes. Advantages and limitations of one type home over the other are identified. The most affordable option is a small EMP protected, livable shed, called a cottage shed with its solar rooftop.

Increased quality, appearance and other considerations have improved the reputation of manufactured homes today, nearly removing all the earlier negative remarks of yesteryear. Many manufactured homes and shipping container-built homes are of such quality that it is nearly impossible to discern the differences. The internet is replete with sources.

To meet the modest needs of many EMP survivalists, who want to improve their post-EMP lifestyle, cottage shed sizes begin at the 8-ft x 16-ft (11.9 sq.m.). This can be equipped with eight EMP protected solar panels providing enough electricity (1.6 kW) for two or three fans, several electrical lights, a short-wave radio, computer and a small fridge.

Because it's inexpensive when made in quantities, for community developments discussed in the next chapter, a modified double cottage shed measuring 16 ft. x 20 ft, (29.7 sq.m.) will likely become the most popular as it also contains provisions for a vehicle shelter, an electric golf cart, more storage and a construction work area. Its protected solar rooftops provide up to 4 kW of power.

11.1- Factory-built, Manufactured Homes

As mentioned in later chapters, the cost of EMP protecting a new home structure being built may range from roughly 55% to 75% of the cost to retrofit an existing home. This savings increases further with a new factory-built, manufactured or shipping container home as further cost reductions become possible.

Other factory-built home benefits are;

• Costs of the building materials are less due to bulk purchases in factory-built homes.

• No site-stolen building material loss and lower insurance rates.

• Lower labor costs since there is no down time waiting for a delinquent electrician or plumber to arrive at the site or bad weather delays.

• Higher quality control, since the same people are building the same or similar units, year after year in factory-built homes.

• Somewhat similar arguments exist for installing an EMP protected solar rooftop in regards to quality control.

• Some of the savings can be put back into a more expensive tile roof so that the life expectancy is over 50 years vs. 15 years for asphalt roofs in southern states. This is important in considering the longer life expectancy of solar panels in certain climate conditions and location latitudes.

• Site EMP protection test and certification costs are reduced, especially when one or more fix-and-retest cycles must be done on site, since in time all factory-built homes will have the simulated EMC/EMP test equipment right in their factory.

11.1.1- Background Summary of Factory-Built Manufactured Homes

This section is a composite of different Internet articles along with our own additions and deletions for consistency and balance. It sets the stage for the next few sections in this chapter.

What Is a Manufactured Home and a Modular Home?

A manufactured home is built entirely in a factory, transported to a site, and installed there. It is distinguished from "modular", "panelized", and "pre-cut" homes, which are also factory built but are assembled at the site including the roof. Manufactured homes are limited to one floor whereas, modular homes can be two floors or more.

Note, manufactured homes already have their roofs intact when they leave the factory, in contrast to modular homes. So EMP shielding for manufactured homes is conceptually better controlled back at the factory than at a site including solar rooftops

Manufactured houses are frequently built without knowing where they will be sited, and are subject to a Federal building code administered by HUD. Modular type of factory-built housing are not assembled until the site is identified, and they must comply with the local, state or regional building codes that apply to that site. They are financed in the same way as houses constructed entirely on-site.

Manufactured housing may not be eligible for mainstream financing. Many, if not most, purchasers of manufactured housing, are shut out of the main-stream mortgage market. They must find loans in a parallel market, which is much like the unsecured personal loan market. Lenders in this parallel market assume that loss rates on manufactured house loans will be high, as they are on personal loans, and they price them accordingly. They view manufactured houses as poor collateral that provides them with little protection.

One reason for this view is that manufactured houses can be moved. Before the HUD building code went into effect in 1976, manufactured houses were called "mobile homes", and this term is still widely used. Even though few ever leave their first site, they remain somewhat tarnished by the image of mobility.

Distinction Between a Manufactured Home and a Modular Home

While both are factory built, the manufactured home is assembled in the factory and towed as a trailer to the final site. Thus, considering its wheels and trailer frame, it is already roughly two feet (52 cm) off the ground. This is apparent in the first photo. Thus, a manufactured home requires about four steps up to its entrance. The modular home shown below is anchored to a concrete slab on the ground or in some cases a basement in place.

The above manufactured home is about eight feet high above its bed + another foot for the shallow slope roof to total nine feet (2.5 meters). Add an extra two feet for the wheels and the highest point is about 11 feet (3 meters) above the ground or road when being towed to the final site. Thus, the driver must plan his course very carefully to ensure he will be below the lowest overpass or bridge along the journey to the site.

The modular home appears the same as a site-built home as shown in the photo to the right. It is frequently two stories high and has a roof slope considerably steeper than the manufactured home. Thus, it is seen why the roof has to be delivered separately not attached to the modules and assembled at the site. The solar rooftop, is added at the home site and does not enjoy the quality control possible of a solar roof added to the manufactured home back at the factory.

11.1.2 Some tips on purchasing a manufactured house

(1)- Do not buy a home from a dealer in a package that includes installation, site, and financing. Tempting as it may be, one-stop shopping in this market is a sure way for overpaying and not getting what you want. Take it one step at a time. It is easiest to compare the houses offered by different dealers if the price applies only to the house. Bundling muddies the waters.

(2)- Find the site first. Decide where you want your house to be located, and whether on rented or owned land. If your credit is good and you have enough cash to buy your own plot, you will be eligible for mainstream mortgage financing. The savings in financing costs and in rent, if converted into a "present value", will probably be well in excess of the cost of the land.

If you rent because you can't find a plot or don't have the cash to buy one, but your credit is good, you may still be eligible for mainstream financing. This requires that you obtain a proper lease, which is one that has a term of at least 5 years, and provides the other legal protections required by lenders.

Freddie Mac will buy mortgages on manufactured houses secured by leaseholds in some but not all states. Freddie's requirements are complicated and you may need a lawyer to determine whether any particular lease is in compliance.

If you can't purchase a plot or obtain an eligible lease, you will be obliged to settle for personal loan-type financing, paying 2-3% more. Even so, you will want to pay careful attention to the lease terms, which can vary widely. If you accept a monthly term, or the landlord's right to approve a purchaser, you will be at the landlord's mercy. Before you sign, talk to the residents of the park about their experiences.

Get a warranty on installation: Installation of manufactured houses remains trouble-prone. The dealer may want to include installation in the price. That is a type of bundling that makes sense, provided the dealer assumes responsibility with a strong warranty. If the dealer will bundle installation, but won't provide an adequate warranty, either ask for a price without installation, or walk.

If you buy the house without installation, you have to hire an installer yourself. This is no small matter, which is why so few buyers do it. The MHIA requires states to develop installation programs that include installation standards, training and licensing of installers, and inspections, but compliance has been spotty. Check your own state from *Implementation of MHI Act of 2000.* In addition, ask local owners for recommendations, ask installers for references, and make sure they are insured.

11.2- The Manufactured Home Cottage Shed

For EMP Survivalists, Preppers, (roughly 5,000,000 USA citizens), and others with more restricted budgets, or simply those wanting to take EMP protection in two steps, the EMP protected shed may be ideal. Although available in other sizes, the 8 ft x 16 ft manufactured shed is likely to become a popular choice.

This 128 sq. ft. (10.7 sq m) shed is constructed in a similar manner to previously discussed manufactured homes. The floor-plan of the shed to be EMP protected is shown at the right. It has two

Fig. 11.3 – Combined EMP Shielded vehicle enclosure and backyard Cottage Shed.

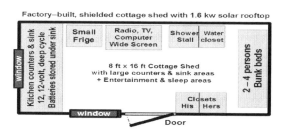

windows and one outside door. A stacked 2-4 person bunk is at one end and the kitchen counter, sink and cabinets at the other end. A clothes closet is at the lower right and the water closet (toilet) and shower are at the upper right. Entertainment center and work area are located at top center.

The shed may be annexed to the normal living home, e.g: the back yard, or hidden in the mountains or elsewhere, or placed on a farmer's property within the watchful eyes of an affiliate farmer in the country. The sketch shown above is one of scores of possible layouts, which when combined with different house sizes, offer an enormous range of designs with the flexibility to meet a wide-range of needs.

Now, considering the addition of an EMP-protected, backyard vehicle enclosure, deed restrictions of a development or other local constraints may not permit the addition of any other structures except a small shed. So, then what are other options for EMP protecting a vehicle? One would seem to be to use the garage of your house to both (1) serve to replace the backyard cottage shed and (2) protect a vehicle from the EMP threat.

The above assumes the owner does not want to incur the cost and displacement to convert the entire house. In this case assume the garage approximates 20 ft x 20 ft (6.1 m x 6.1 m). However, you may want the garage to be partitioned between 40% for living pace and 60% vehicle parking and workshop and garden tool storage. Figure 11.4 suggests one floor plan of many.

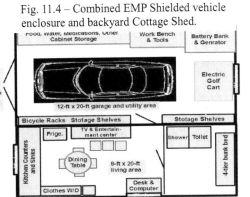

Fig. 11.4 – Combined EMP Shielded vehicle enclosure and backyard Cottage Shed.

In contrast to a detached structure discussed in earlier chapters, the concept of shielding an **existing** attached garage, built as part of the existing home structure, poses problems. For example, does one shield the outside or inside of the garage walls and roof? One immediate reply might be shield the outside since shielding the inside leaves all the exposed outside wall wiring to act as an enormous octopus-like, EMP radiation pick-up antenna system as discussed back in earlier chapters. But the inside, if not EMP protected, is already contaminated as the electrical entrance and breaker panel are located on the garage inside wall that conducts the EMP pickup from the rest of the house wiring. There may appear to exist three solution to this dilemma:

(1)- Shield the inside garage walls, ceiling and the breaker panel, fluorescent ceiling lights and duplex outlets. Each of the last three items has a shield zippertubing (or equivalent) around three of four sides to permit maintenance access. The shielded solar rooftop output cable has an an independent entrance into the shielded garage as discussed earlier. **This system will fail** as the unprotected garage fluorescent lights and power service panel will burn out in an EMP event.

(2)- Shield the outside garage walls and ceiling and use surge suppressors at the panel service entrance, and shield the common wall (garage and home) duplex outlets. This is complicated and requires a detailed electrical wiring construction beyond the scope of this book. Problem: many expensive surge suppressors are needed.

(3)- Since shielding a garage only admits the burnout of all the rest of the house electrical and electronics, drop the idea of shielding the garage or any other single room. EMP protect all or none of the house as explained in Chapters 7 and 8. Instead, consider adding an "attached" garage which shares a common attached wall, assuming the building codes property line distance and deed restrictions are in compliance. Then, complete the EMP protection by following the details of earlier chapters.

The reader is reminded that the questions of EMP protecting an existing structure vs. a new one favor the latter in cost by roughly 30% ± 10%. Thus, Solution #3 above may be regarded as a default decision for the most economical home approach ending with the essence of an "attached backyard cottage shed and vehicle garage".

Options #1 and 2 are doable, but at a significant relative cost.

Shown below are twelve types of cottage sheds illustrating various styles and models available. They range in size from 8 ft x 12 ft to 16 ft x 30 ft. The price listed by several sources listed in Section 2.7 range from $2,500 to $14,500 with an average price of about $26/square foot. Seems low? Yes, they are, but understand the land is not included and the insides are frequently austere without counter tops and many accommodations provided by most homes selling for around $100/sq ft.

The above prices do not include transportation, insurance and taxes. The solar rooftops and EMP protection add to the final cost.

The shed is to be EMP protected as described in later chapters. After EMP protection testing and certification checkout at the factory site, it is trucked to the installation site in a low-belly trailer, which will lower by nearly two feet, the height of the shed en-route to the installation site. This allows more route choices or allows a roof of greater slope. As discussed later, the optimum roof slope for a shed is equal to the latitude of the location site. This suggests sheds (and homes) have a shallow roof slope in the southern U.S., roughly 25°, but need a steeper slope in the northern U.S., up to 40°, for maximum solar-PV conversion efficiency (Alaska needs more and Hawaii needs less).

11.3- About Shipping Container Homes

Container homes are houses built using shipping containers as structural shells. The several sizes and shapes of such containers ares suited for architectural uses and there are a number of innovative ways to use shipping containers in home design. Companies specializing in conversion of shipping containers for residential uses can provide prefab homes shipped on demand and can design a custom home for a specific site.

Shipping containers are built to take considerable abuse while weathering a broad variety of conditions. When used as a structural shell, they can be laid end to end or side by side, stacked, and upended. Container homes can integrate multiple containers connected together to achieve a desired size and shape. The containers are also substantially modified to make room for windows and doors, to partition the space inside, and lay plumbing and wiring.

Some container homes are designed to be fixed on site. They can be mounted on a foundation with bolts and will remain fixed in place as permanent structures. Other container homes are portable. Several designers have developed structures for use as temporary housing in settings ranging from refugee camps to music festivals. Flexible, mobile housing can be useful for situations where people need to be able to rapidly establish and configure housing while also leaving a minimal footprint. Each container home can be self-contained with use of water tanks, solar panels, and similar measures, allowing structures to be moved to accommodate needs.

Shipping containers, usually made of corregated steel sides, top and bottom for strength, can be repainted, covered in new siding, insulated, and modified in other ways. In some container homes, the structural core is almost invisible after a conversion, while in others, the shipping container may be left more visible. There are aesthetic considerations involved and some designers may want to stress the use of recycled materials by making those construction materials readily evident and visible.

Containers suitable for home conversion can be found in many ports around the world. While shipping containers are usually shipped back and forth on a regular basis with loads of varying items, when trade deficits develop, it is not uncommon for unused containers to pile up. These containers can be purchased at low cost and trucked to a final destination. Costs for conversion vary, depending on the project. An architect or contractor with experience can provide estimates to help people price out a container home conversion.

Examples of shipping container homes are shown on the next page.

11.4- Preparing the Shed Structures for Solar Rooftops

This topic is addressed in detail in previous Chapters 9 and 10. Suffice it to say, that the solar rooftop can be installed back at the factory at the time of fabrication of a manufactured home or shipping container home. If the shed is hand built by a DIY owner, best economy is achieved by installing the solar rooftop at the time that the shed is fabricated, whether on site or other locaton.

If a solar rooftop is to be added, but not EMP protected until a later date, at a modest additional cost, add a 30 OPI screen over the shingles or tiles before the solar panels are put in place. This allows for subsequent EMP shielding of solar rooftop at significant cost reduction. Details are in Chapters 8-10.

11.5- Sources and References

Manufactured Homes (some cover the entire Continental USA)

• Jacabson Homes, Tel: 1-727-726-1138, 600 Packard Court, Safety Harbor, FL 34695

• Palm Harbor Homes. Tel: 1-888-466-3718, 15301 Spectrum Drive, Ste. 500, Addison, TX 75001

• Schult Homes, http://www.schulthomes.com/our_homes.cfm 8671 South Frontage Road, Yuma, AZ 85366

Amish-Built Cottage Sheds

Route 51 - Pittsburgh / Whitehall

3290 Saw Mill Run Blvd., Pittsburgh, PA 15227
(1 Mile South from the intersection of Rt. 88 & Rt. 51)
Phone: 412-943-7163

Second location: Route 19 - Canonsburg / Peters
2641 Washington Road, Canonsburg, PA 15317
(Right Across the street from King's Family Restaurant)
Phone: 724-746-0100

Call Us Toll Free: 1-855-AMISH-YD

Shipping Container Homes

- MODS International Shipping Container Homes and Buildings, Tel: 1-800-869-1277, 5523 Integrity Way, Appleton, WI 54913

- Contractors:http://www.bing.com/images/search? q=Container+Home+Contractors&FORM=RESTAB

- Kits:http://www.bing.com/images/search? q=Shipping+Container+Homes+Kits&Form=IQFRDR

For EMP protected, escape-cottage developments on the outskirts of towns and small cities, manufactured homes are the most cost-effective. EMP protected solar rooftops are added and the entire structure tested in the factory for EMP susceptibility compliance. Quality control is also optimized.

Chapter 12
Farms & Real Estate, Cottage-Shed Communities

Chapter Overview

This chapter builds on the recognition that larger groups of neighboring families represent greater post-EMP security, but their location in the form of a small escape dwelling may have to move to a farm or other, not-to-distant location.

This is also predicated on the cost consideration that an EMP protected 150 to 400 sq ft, cottage shed with solar rooftop, can be built at a fraction of the cost to shield a 2,500 sq. ft., home with solar rooftop. When this is built around a pond or small lake, it can be an enjoyable vacation get-away location.

In recent times a new community emphasizing solar rooftops has independently come to pass. They are called *Community Solar Projects* or simply *Community Solar Gardens*. Because of their total EMP vulnerability these folks should become informed about opportunities for later EMP protection by using a single layer of roof screening described herein.

12.1- A Nearby Supporting EMP Protection Farm & Birth of Real Estate EMP Protection Developers

EMP Survivalists recognize seven items needed for survival:

- Water (and tools and methods for purifying water)
- Food, especially freeze-dried, 25-year food
- Prescribed medications and first aid supplies
- Bartering items (since money is worthless)
- Guns and Ammo for self protection against starving neighbors breaking in.
- An escape place or hut in the country away from starving neighbors and other uninvited intruders who pose a bit security threat.

Much has been written in the preppers and survivalist communities about the use of bicycles, bicycles pulling carts, or all-terrain vehicles, as means for getting to urgent destinations. These are helpful because after an EMP attack there will be EMP-damaged vehicles blocking roads and bicycles and all-terrain vehicles can better navigate around obstructions.

12.1.1- EMP Protected Shed in Survivalists Backyard.

At first blush, having the survival cottage shed in the backyard of the house may seem like the most practical location for a family. The main problem is the shed could become the target of starving outsiders willing to kill for a meal. So, the survivalist will benefit if there are several or many of his ilk close by! A group or community can employ the strategy of "circling the wagons" as U.S. West-bound pioneers did in the 1830-1850s when they ran into American Indians on the warpath. There is then, additional safety when people work together and are willing to act together to build security and repel hostile people.

An extension of the above concept exists when a homeowners

association, has built a defensive perimeter around the housing complex. This would likely involve a six foot fence with barb wire topping (or electronic topping) and a loud perimeter intrusion alarm. In this case members share 24/7 grounds surveillance. Each family can continue to have its own EMP protected back yard cottage shed, and/or to share a larger structure with bigger and more expensive EMP protected items. The problem here is that a back yard cottage shed may not be permitted by property covenants. Thus, alternatives must be considered.

12.2- Birth of Real Estate, EMP Protection Developments

As EMP survivalists learn they can live better and more secure with enhanced lifestyle in larger EMP protected communities, they may form such communities. There are 62 million members of homeowners associations in the U.S. They tend to have a tighter cohesion among their members.

As the EMP threat becomes clearer, homeowner associations' members may develop a community of cottage-sheds within, perhaps, 50 miles to their main residence. This gives rise to new real estate development prospects.

12.1- Small Real Estate Development of EMP Protected Cottage Sheds with Solar Rooftops and Accommodation Center

3 1 or 2 sheds this lot permitted	4	Appx 1/4 acre 5	6	7	8	9	10	11	12 1 or 2 sheds this lot permitted
	Development 22-ft Property Access Roadway								
2	13	14	15	16	17	18	19	20	21
1									22
Exit Guard Shack Entrance	190 ft x 480 ft. pond = 2 acres for relaxation and source of drinking Well-replaced, water supply			120 ft boardwalk Gazebo Seats 40		Organization Open Beach	Organization Entertainment & Replenishment Center		23
44									
43	32	31	30	29	28	27	26	25	24
	Development 22-ft Property Access Roadway							© copyright, 2014, EMP Solutions LLC	
42 1 or 2 sheds this lot permitted	41	40	39	38	37	36	35 Appx 1/4 acre	34	33 1 or 2 sheds this lot permitted

Small, Early EMP Protected Development of Cottage-Sheds for Sale or Rental
See other "Circle-the-wagons" development layouts

One of scores of examples is shown in Fig.12.1 for a 44-unit, 1/4 acre parcels developed around a two-acre pond used for both entertainment for weekend escapees, and for a water supply that can be accessed and purified for drinking water if needed.

Illustrated, is a group of about 44, 1/4-acre lots (could be as low as 1/10 acre) surrounding a two-acre pond – both for relaxation/ aesthetics, as well as a water source for enhanced survival along with one or more deep submersal wells. The compound is partly protected from outside invasion by a high wall with proximity alarms surrounding the facility. The right side contains an owners' common area for entertainment and/or vitals storage and replenishment. There is added a beach for those not having a property front on the pond. A community gazebo seats up to 40 with 120-ft. boardwalk access.

Deed restrictions permit larger corner lots to have two small sheds ranging in size from 126 sq ft, as in the previous example to about 400 sq. ft. Additionally, each lot owner may build a second cottage-shed for another family member, neighbor, friend or the like within the confines of the deed restrictions.

The above concept invites other real estate entrepreneurs to create their own development with completely EMP protected facilities. These may be sold or rented or both. The beauty is that a typical size 200 sq.ft. EMP protected cottage hut with solar rooftop discussed in Chapter 9 can be had for about $50,000 as discussed in Chapter 16.

12.3- Community Solar Projects & Community Gardens

The folllowing page and a half has been abstracted from *Wikipedia Encyclopedia*

12.3.1- A Community Solar Garden

A CSP is a solar power installation that accepts capital from and provides output credit and tax benefits to individual and other investors. In some systems you buy individual solar panels which are installed in the farm after your purchase. In others you purchase kW capacity or kWh of production. The farm's power output is credited to investors in proportion to their investment, with adjustments to reflect ongoing changes in capacity, technology, costs and electricity rates. Companies, cooperatives, governments or non-profits operate the farms.[1]

Centralizing the location of solar systems has advantages over residential installation that include:

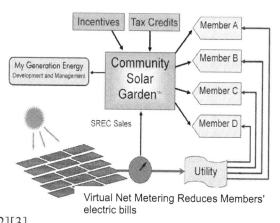

Virtual Net Metering Reduces Members' electric bills

• Trees, roof size and/ or configuration, adjacent buildings, the immediate microclimate and/or other factors which may reduce power output.[2][3]

• Building codes, zoning restrictions, homeowner association rules and aesthetic concerns.[4]

• Lack of skills and commitment to install and maintain solar systems.[2]

• Expanding participation to include renters and others who are not residential property owners. The Solar Gardens Institute maintains a national directory of community solar projects and organizations. As of 2011, farms encompassed both photovoltaic and concentrating solar power technologies.

An estimated 85 percent (?) of US residents can neither own nor lease systems because their roofs are physically unsuitable for solar or because they live in multi-family housing. (Author's Note: this is believed to be a substantial over-estimate percentage. At least 52 projects are under development in at least 17 states, and at least 10 states encourage their development through policy and programs.

Federal and other tax policies are necessary to finance community solar farms. U.S. Senator Mark Udall introduced the SUN Act (Solar Uniting Neighborhoods) to extend the existing 30% tax credit to community solar farms in 2010 and 2011.

The bill would enable groups of individuals or homeowner

associations to develop utility-scale solar power facilities in collaboration with local utilities that would distribute the power and credit owners based on their percentage of investment in the solar farm, extending the tax credits accordingly.[9]

"These projects have the potential to drastically increase the adoption of clean energy nationwide, but the tax code hasn't kept up," Udall said. "You can get a 30-percent tax credit for putting a solar panel on your house, but not for investing in a solar farm."[9]

Author's Note: It is sad to say that the EMP threat is all but unknown in these Community Solar Projects. At the very least provisions should be made to lay down a foil or screen shield under the solar installations so that they can be EMP protected at a later date (see Fig 10.1 and the text explaining it.)

EMP-protecting a building is "old hat" to those with clearance who have done this for decades at classified government sites. Since the authors have no current security clearance, and nothing appears on the Internet, we re-engineer expectations so the rest of the civil community can benefit.

Chapter 13
EMP Protecting Existing Facilities

Chapter Overview

This chapter is perhaps the most difficult of all chapters to implement - the EMP protection of existing houses, buildings and related structures and their associated unprotected solar rooftops. The problem is that a home or building shield cover on the outside cannot be carried around the foundation that is buried underground. Simply shielding the inside of all underground foundations will not work because the outside-to-inside wall thickness (ranging from 5" to 12" (13 to 30 cm) around the periphery represents an enormous shielding leakage gap. Thus. some major "band-aid engineering" must be used at both a significant cost increase and it produces uncertain EMP protection without test measurements.

The problem has to do with how to electrically connect (bond) a building's outside facade shield to the below underground building's inside shield. As explained herein, three things serve to help improve shielding performance in this big gap area: (1) The attenuation offered by concrete or dirt surrounding the foundation, (2) rebars and distance between adjacent rebars connected to both overlapped outside and inside foundation locations, and (3) blown-in radiation absorptive material between outside and inside walls assuming air fills the walls and not insulating materials. Other approaches are also discussed.

Until a significant database is developed, the final "EMP protected" structure will have to be EMP tested out in the open in order to develop empirical shielding models, as the several discontinuity variables constitute too large a problem to permit math modeling.

As discussed herein, partial lower price "EMP protection" is available where only one or a few rooms need to be protected in a larger home or building structure. Building an empirical database of the above structures shielding effectiveness is the first order of business.

13.1- EMP Protecting an Existing Home, Building & Infrastructure

As remarked in the overview, there are two big problem areas where shielding the sides, top and bottom of an *existing* home or building faces problems: (1) the shield on the building outside can't be bonded to the foundation shielding on the inside, and (2) shielding the solar rooftop can't be enclosed if one is already installed. Each will now be addressed.

13.1.1- Shielding the Foundation-side Interfaces

Figure 13.1, previously shown in Chapter 8 on shielding the foundations for *new buildings,* focuses on the lower left area for *existing buildings.* Again, the heavy black vertical and horizontal lines are the corresponding shields of the sides and foundation added to an *existing building.* Notice the huge gap in the shielding process where the two shields come closest, separated by the thickness of the vertical wall.

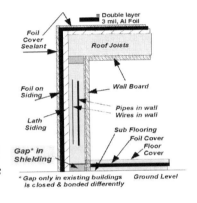

New structures do not have this problem as the foundation is made first and extended beyond where the added wall will be constructed later. So, how are the vertical and horizontal shields to meet and be bonded for *existing structures*?

Before answering this question, what is the conductivity of concrete, earth and wood around or next to the foundation to act as a partial shield? Answer: a tiny fraction of that of metal making it insignificant to help reduce the missing shielding gap.

Suppose that the foundation shield were to be extended at the corner to turn up the inside wall a few inches, and a conductive rod inserted from the inside shield to the outer side shield after drilling a hole through the frame, inserting the rod and bonding the rod to the shields via conductive caulking. Then, the two shields are bonded together at the horizontal separate rod-bonding distance. This will improve the overall shielding as shown in Fig, 13.2. Note, that columns A and B are a repeat of Table 2.1 in Chapter 2 showing the shielding effectiveness that is needed. By inserting the conductive bonding rods, the new shielding effectiveness needed is reduced to those shown in col. C and E.

Fig. 13.2 – SE Effectiveness Needed,Transfer Rod Performance & dB Shortfall

Colum	A	B	C	D	E	F
		Shielding Effectiveness	Distance Between 3 feet (91cm)		Distance Between 1 foot (30 cm)	
Row	Frequency	Needed	Result	Short	Result	Short
1	100 kHz	80 dB	70 dB	10 dB	60 dB	0 dB
2	1 MHz	80 dB	50 dB	30 dB	40 dB	20 dB
3	3 MHz	77 dB	41 dB	*36 dB*	31 dB	*26 dB*
4	10 MHz	65 dB	30 dB	35 dB	20 dB	25 dB
5	30 MHz	52 dB	21 dB	31 dB	11 dB	21 dB
6	100 MHz	30 dB	10 dB	20 dB	0 dB	10 dB
7	300 MHz	10 dB	1 dB	9 dB	0 dB	0 dB
8	1 GHz	0 dB	0 dB	0 dB	0 dB	0 dB
	A	B	C	D	E	F

Note: Wavelength in meters = 300/Frequency in MHz
Wave attenuation between Screen-blocking conductor distances, D in meters = 20*Log[300/(D*Fmhz)] dB

They help increase shielding effectiveness but show their deficiency in shielding needed in column D and F. These could possibly be made up by the absorption of the surrounding packed earth, but only confirmed by field testing, an expensive process.

The above clearly demonstrates that shielding an existing structure can become a difficult and expensive process. Furthermore, if the foundation has an underground basement, the process becomes even more complex although the absorptivity of more earth will reduce the magnitude of shield-bonding problems. The type of earth and moisture content add to the variability and complexity and lack of quality control. Further discussion is discontinued here as the entire problem needs examination, constructing and field

203

testing - beyond the objectives of this book.

Conclusion: The above problem needs to be quantified. This can be assigned to a DoD or DOE field laboratory to build a small village and establish an EMP open air testing procedure. Then, similar buildings can be EMP protected including those under construction as well as those already built. The test results will become an invaluable database to help optimize decisions and guide future work.

13.2- Adding Solar Rooftop to be Protected

The previous section, as well as elsewhere in this book, addressed the EMP protection of already built structures vs, those under construction, A somewhat parallel problem exists with the nearly 1,000,000 solar rooftop homes and buildings already existing *without* EMP protection. The missing link is that shielding under the racking of the solar panel was not emplaced immediately before the solar paneling was placed into position. A single rooftop shield under the solar paneling, whether or not future EMP protection will be done, is paramount for an insurance cost of less than $1,000. This point has already been addressed in Chapters 9 and 10.

13.3- Addressing Community Solar Projects & Gardens

These community solar projects (CSP) have been increasing rapidly in recent years and have already been discussed in section 12.3. The bottom line is that all CSP project candidates or prospects should be advised about the low-cost insurance option of less that $850 (for most houses) to add a rooftop screen shield before solar installation, whether or not EMP protection will ever be added. The purpose is to avoid a cost of roughly 10 times this until solar panel manufacturers build this into their off-the-shelf solar panels, expected to become available as an option in 2016-2017. Of course this applies to all installers in USA – not just those involved in CSPs.

13.4- EMP Protection Test Compliance & Certification

No home, building or other infrastructure to have a solar rooftop should be built and installed without having a simulated EMP protection test and certification. Otherwise, there is absolutely no assurance that the Table 2.1 EMP protection and certification exists.

13.4.1- An Overview of Site Simulated EMP Tests

Nothing having an electronic control or protection of a vital human survival item or system should be permitted to be advertised for sale unless some remark has been made that it has been tested for EMP protection or not. One of many examples is the heart pacemaker with over 10 million human installations in USA. One well-known manufacturer told the author that they don't know (test method, RS-105) or report the potential susceptibility of their heart pacemakers. (author's note: this will change in time as AMA, FDA or other agency will insist).

In a like manner, any electromagnetic shield, bond, surge suppressor or filter must have its EMP protection performance tested and reported. This is especially necessary for a cottage, home, commercial or industrial building, and vehicle that has EMP protection. Otherwise, its true radiated susceptibility is unknown and scam artists or other dishonest people will plague the market and deceive the population.

Fortunately there are several EMP test houses. Using the seven test frequencies from the time-domain Fourier Transforms (Chap. 3), employing an EMP field test, confirmation and certification of any suitably protected building structure can be done by the test services.

13.4.2- Basic EMP Test Procedures

Once an EMP protected installation is declared to be finished, it is time to verify its EMP protection compliance by on-site testing. A small van or pickup truck is located at the left in Fig.13.3. It contains an RF scanning oscillator or sweeper which feeds a power amplifier that drives radiating test antennas pointing at the building to the right. Inside the building is a tracking receiver driven by matching pickup antennas.

The test configuration is first calibrated to form a reference with both transmitter and receiver configurations located on the outside (step 1, Fig. 13.3). Tests are made at the seven test frequencies (1 MHz – 1 GHz) in Table 2.1, Chapter 2. (obtained from the Fourier Transform of the EMP pulse

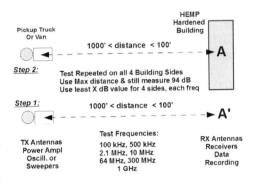

Fig. 13.3 - Test setup for determining on site shielding performance

waveform threat), and the RF attenuator settings recorded. Then, maintaining the same distance between transmitter and receiver, both are moved as shown in step 2 with the receiver configuration moved to the middle of the building and attenuator settings again recorded to get the same received levels. The difference between the attenuator settings in step 1 and step 2 constitutes the building RF shielding effectiveness in dB for the test frequency.

The tests are repeated for the other remaining three sides of the building, recording the shielding effectiveness of each side for all seven test frequencies. Then, for each of the seven frequencies, the corresponding four side shielding effectiveness are compared and the smallest value (least shielding) is selected. These results constitute the building EMP shielding effectiveness. They are compared with 80 dB (or other, per Fig 2.2) to determine EMP test compliance.

There is a more automated procedure than just explained. Also, if the building is large (several floors or acres in size), the transmitter may have to be located

Tab. 2.1 Shielding Effectiveness

Frequency	SE Needed
≤100 kHz	80 dB
1 MHz	80 dB
3 MHz	77 dB
10 MHz	65 dB
30 MHz	52 dB
100 MHz	30 dB
300 MHz	10 dB
≥ 1 GHz	0 dB

206

in a helicopter or blimp.

Contractually, it is necessary in performance tests to demonstrate compliance with the shielding requirements over the designated Table 2.1 frequency spectrum.

While the building EMP and Solar EMP compliance tests can be done simultaneously, in the early stages it may be best to do each separately. This will facilitate diagnostics-and-fix. The building compliance test must be done first. Test procedural details are well beyond the level of this handbook and will not be discussed here.

In addition to the procedure, a few selected potential inside victims are chosen to be placed in a recording operational mode. Examples include one or more computers, peripherals, cell phones and HVAC temperature monitors for the building and solar developed AC voltage wave forms. *These and maybe others will be monitored only to see if any disturbance is detected.* This will confirm the adequacy of the 80-dB (Table 2.1) shielding requirement in case any potential victim had not already complied with the applicable 10 V/m radiated susceptibility requirement of Section 2.1. The contractually accepted EMP compliance simulation is not based on these other potential victims, whose role is to confirm the adequacy of the 80-dB during early stages (first year) of EMP hardening implementation.

13.4.3- Some Further Test Considerations & Refinements

 In practice the EMP compliance tests of checking each test frequency for all four sides may not be possible or sufficient. For example, some building sides may be blocked by other buildings or a wooded region. Maybe one or two building sides are surrounded by water, requiring that tests be done from a boat. Or, the only viable test access may be from a helicopter or blimp. Also, there are the questions of how many measurements per building side to take and of the movement of the receiver antenna around seeking the highest value (least shielding). Since there is much to be said here, use the following as a starting EMP shielding effectiveness test compliance criteria:

• Use the seven test frequencies from 100 kHz to 1 GHz as mentioned above. Perform the test on all four sides. If one or two sides only are available, double the test locations below.

• At each frequency for each side: move the receiving antenna around (always pointing at the transmitting antenna) within a distance [from start of 10 ft (3 m)] seeking the highest reading (poorest shielding effectiveness) and lowest reading (best shielding effectiveness). Then determine and record the two shielding effectiveness at that frequency and side. Also record the geometric mean of the two readings as: dB_{median} = sq. root $(dB_{high} \times dB_{low})$.

• EMP Test Compliance Conditions:

Use Table 2.1 for 10 V/m victim susceptibility. If any victim to be protected has a known lower susceptibility rating, add to the Table 2.1 value: $dB_{adjusted}$ = $20 * log_{10}(10/victim_{suscept-value})$

For the seven frequencies x four sides = 28 subset:
• all 28 dB_{median} values must be above Table 2.1
• not more than three dB_{low} conditions below Table 2.1 are permitted. Passing Score = B, Acceptable.
   If all dB_{low} > Table 2.1, Score A, Best
   If more than three dB_{low} > Table 2.1, Score is Fail.

The above recommended starting test compliance, Pass-Fail criteria and measurement specifics will need to be analyzed and discussed in detail since the reliance and legal consequences and costs are significant.

13.5 Reference Test Laboratories

EMP Test Organizations:

Dayton T Brown, Inc., Tel: 631-589-6300, Fax: 631-589-3648,

www.dtbtest.com, 1175 Church Street, Bohemia, NY 11716-5031

ETS – Lindgren, Tel: 512-531-6400, Fax: 512-531-6500, www.ets-lindgren.com, 1301 Arrow Point Drive, Cedar Park, TX 78613..

Protection Technology Group, Tel: 208-772-8515; 800-882-9110, Fax: 208-762-6133, www.protectiongroup.com/home, 10701 North Airport Road, Hayden, ID 83835

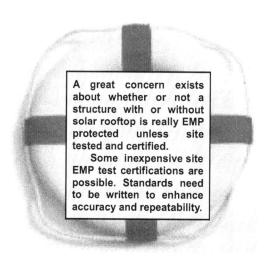

A great concern exists about whether or not a structure with or without solar rooftop is really EMP protected unless site tested and certified.
Some inexpensive site EMP test certifications are possible. Standards need to be written to enhance accuracy and repeatability.

Chapter 14
Communications Protection

Chapter Overview

Communications is the spine of global lifestyle. Without it, no one knows what is going on. Thus, communications is the exchange between two or more sources and receptors of thoughts, messages, or information, in either analog or digital in real or delayed time.

The end elements involved in communications include humans, devices, systems and vehicles. The media include speech/voice, countenance, telephone, facsimile, Internet, writings, books, magazines, newspapers, video, radio and TV talk shows, satellites, pods, pads, ad infinitum.

Communications necessitates that electronics be involved at both (or all) ends and that the transceivers include at least one of: radio. TV, microphone, speakers, ground wiring, fiber optics, wireless, via submersibles, earth based or satellite platforms.

EMP susceptibility and protection of electrical and electronic parts and systems are emphasized. Since the subject is so vast, specifics are limited.

14.1- Broad Picture of Communications

Below are two of hundreds of images on communications seen on the Internet: Many more portray communications from the perspective of a CEO, a non-profit organization, a government agency, from an employee, etc). Since we were not able to find one with EMP protection in mind, we generated one on the next page. Meanwhile, spend a few minutes to examine the two images below. In Fig. 14.1

Fig. 14.1 – Two images from Google search engine on Communications:

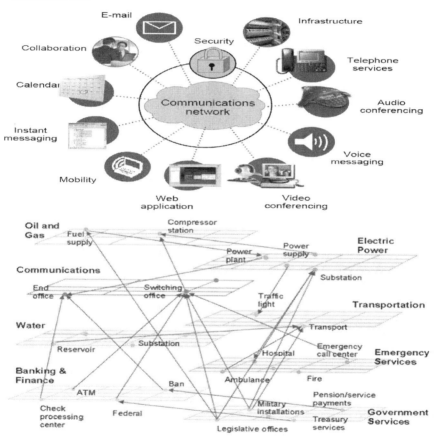

14.2- Example of Early EMP Impact on Consumer Communications

From the previous figure and from Fig. 14.2 shown two pages later, and in studying the communications meaning, missions, goals and problems, it becomes evident there exist literally millions of communications parts and subparts to accomplish many objectives. Here, the book focuses on the more frequent requirements and use. The broader subject is reserved for a dedicated book in this EMP protection subject at a later date.

One of the first reactions by many people when suddenly the electric power goes off is something like , "Damn Sam, here we go again - electric power interruption. I'll check our neighbor, first." Or, if night, look out the window to see if all is dark or all is normal and if the immediate area lost power, too. "Then I'll call Bill to see if he lost power too." Or, "I'll call the Zebra Power Company to hear what they say". "Oh, my gosh. The telephone is also dead". And, "My cell or iphone is dead also." Then, in only a few moments, it begins to get real scary.... as the radio and TV, of course, are also dead.

However, if you are one of the roughly 1% of the Americans called Preppers or, especially, the fewer EMP Survivalists, you go to your oversize, aluminum, foil-lined shoe box containing a battery operated (and AC power) short-wave radio tunable to the prepared list of designated stations, written on the box cover. The stations provide weather and emergency information. Presumably, you will learn in minutes that you have had the first EMP event.

By trying other stations and listening to the reports, it doesn't take long to quantify the effective regional area or distance of the EMP blackout (presumable several hundred miles, The distance away to non-EMP impacted areas is important to know because this involves potential replenishments of food, water, medications and other survivals especially since the roadways are cluttered with scattered motionless vehicles and closed gasoline stations.

Before proceeding, review lessons learned from the above scenario (representing perhaps 99% of unprepared Americans and 95% uninformed or unaware Americans of what just happened). The first lesson is to have a battery operated, short-wave radio stored in an EMP protected box, lined with household aluminum foil, like Reynolds Wrap, by ALCOA. Also, know how to operate it (tuned to listed designated stations) and estimate the distance to unaffected areas for replenishment distances, since this can enormously impact your options and length of survival.

14.3- Broad Impact of EMP on Communications

Return to Fig. 14.2 on EMP communications organization chart below. Note that it is divided into nine communications topics. There is a substantial redundancy within the chart as different missions or applications may share one or more common media or sub-topic media.

Each of the nine topics of Fig. 14.2 is numbered to quickly find the right box in discussion. Each, also has up to seven subtopics of concern in a pre and post-EMP event. The just discussed short-wave radio is now shown as box 6 in Fig. 14.2.

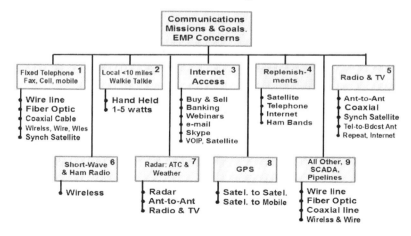

Boxes 1 to 3 are the communications items up front that the EMP event person would expect to use. However, unless separately protected from an EMP event, telephone, fax, and the Internet become dysfunctional as well. Exception is if these and related electronic devices are already located in an EMP protected cottage shed, house or building. So, there is no protection unless the smaller devices are stored in foil-lined envelopes or boxes.

Box 4, Replenishments, is extremely important to the unprotected majority as that represents human protection from starvation, and death. Of course, the town or nearby county must have a 4,000 ft mat-covered dirt runway so that a Globemaster III, cargo aircraft, can periodically bring in 70 tons of replenishments. All this must be coordinated by planned communications between the town and the sources supplying emergency aid. Here, communications can be by a number of sources excluding telephone, fax, Internet which are burned out. Satellite relay is possible if the arrangements were made in advance.

Box 8, GPS (Global Positioning System) for vehicles may still be functional for the satellite transmitters, but the vehicle's receivers are dysfunctional unless the vehicle was parked in a shielded building at the time of an EMP event.

Adding it all up, individual families may not survive for long. However, coordinated groups of many families like Communities who have planned for EMP protection, survival and lifestyle increases up to the size of towns and small cities or large developments, where EMP protection safety and survival load are shared by many families as discussed in Chap 3.

14.4- Example of Early EMP Impact to SCADA-Related Communications

Box 9 of Fig 14.2 shows a few modes of interconnecting SCADA (Supervisory Control and Data Acquisition) systems. SCADA examples include circuit and network sensors of controlled systems communicating results on display screens or causing other actions to happen, such as, on a gas or oil pipeline, where pump stations may be located every 50 miles. If one station sensor fails due to electromagnetic interference (EMI) receptions or EMP, the entire pipeline may shut down.

A specific SCADA system may be interconnected over distances of only a few feet up to hundreds of miles. EMP protection of an entire system may be extremely problematic and/or expensive to effect. Such EMI/EMP protection may involve double-shielded cable in parts, surge suppression and filtering and system grounding. So, it is seen that myriads of SCADA parts may lead to a system nearly impossible to EMP protect unless that system is spread over a short distance like inside an EMP protected building or operations control room.

Further EMI/EMP complexity results from long interconnected SCADA lengths. For example part of the communications may be by satellite; part by fiber-optics; and parts by coaxial cable. Even fiber-optics links can be EMI/EMP susceptible because they have at each end, an electronics-to-fiber interface and the electronics portion will fail while the fiber part is immune.

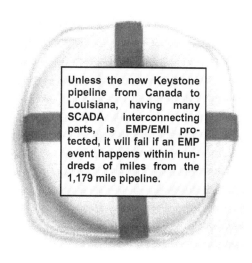

Unless the new Keystone pipeline from Canada to Louisiana, having many SCADA interconnecting parts, is EMP/EMI protected, it will fail if an EMP event happens within hundreds of miles from the 1,179 mile pipeline.

Chapter 15
Vehicle Protection

Chapter Overview

While not as devastating as losing electric power, that operates most things to maintain lifestyle in the 21st century, vehicle loss is perhaps second in importance, Some though will argue it is communications because we want to know what is happening so we can adjust our planning and actions.

Vehicles are defined here as devices which move people or materials and things. This includes motor scooters, wagons, bicycles, motor bikes, motorcycles, golf carts, cars or autos, trucks, trailers, aircraft, helicopters, train engines, rolling stock, subways, boats, ships and submarines. A few are super vital to our existence, especially after an EMP incident which can have a radius of 500 miles. Vital replenishment is paramount to a post-EMP era with some degree of lifestyle.

In general, the best EMP protection for smaller vehicles, say a car or truck or smaller, is to park the vehicle in an EMP enclosure at home and at work, which protects the vehicle over 90% of the time not in use.

Vehicle manufacturers can greatly help by ending the 90-year old practice of grounding the negative battery return to the vehicle frame. Instead, use a shielded, twisted-wire pair to replace old wire and frame return. This low cost additive will reduce radiation pickup in the octupus-like, wiring antenna system by more than 40 dB.

The golf cart may be the best compromise of a vehicle to own, as it needs only one battery for up yo 100 miles of use between charging. Charging can be done at home or elsewhere where there is a solar panel(s) at home, work place or the 200,000 to be built and ubiquitously located stations around the country in the next 10 years by the electric utilities in their new "side"mission described herein.

About 150 inexpensive mat-dirt, 4,000-ft runways will be build around the country. This permits one every 250 miles to allow local replenishment by Globemasters III with a 70 ton load.

Railroad sidings will be added to hundreds of locations reachable by rail, using steam engines kept in reserve.

Hundreds of marinas on both coasts, larger rivers and the great lakes will be dredged deeper to enhance replenishment egress and access.

15.1- EMP Susceptibility and Protection of Vehicles

The word, "vehicles" means any form of transportation. such as motor scooter, bicycle, motor bike, motorcycle, car, truck, bus, aircraft, helicopter, railroad, subway, boat or ship. However, this discussion here covers only automobiles (autos or cars) and trucks when speaking of vehicles. Other vehicles are addressed later in this chapter.

Unlike EMP shielding a component, such as a cell phone, ipad or computer, EMP protecting a vehicle requires complex shielding because of (1) the vast number of variables, (2) no inter-vehicle connected wiring and (3) partial shielding already offered by vehicle metal skin, metal frame, cables, and other nearby metal parts, not already plastic. Thus, without simulated EMP testing, forecasting EMP susceptibility is difficult because of the variables, such as the 26 shown in the chart below. The different combination of variables can result in a range in excess of 100 times (40 dB) In vehicle-system susceptibility. Therefore, the Hollywood myth that all EMP unprotected moving vehicles will stop, following an EMP event is untrue and misleading.

Summary of Findings and Comments:

• Vehicles after about 1982 started to use microprocessor (low voltage, wide band) controls of engine, breaking, air-bags, and other operations. Thus, later vintage gasoline-engine and diesel vehicles are more susceptible to malfunction than those made before before 1982. And, more recent microprocessors are even more susceptible because of still more circuits operating on lower voltages. One manufacturer claims to have 60 microprocessors in its new 2015 vehicles.

• From reported USA EMP Commission test results and from simulated radiation tests performed at White Sands Missile Test Facility, some vehicles exhibit only active engine turnoff, but can be restarted. Others evidence comparable susceptibilities whether or not the engine is running. A few vehicles had to be rebooted by disconnecting and reconnecting the battery first before starting. Tests, vehicles and test results were too limited to profile accurate susceptibility statistics.

• Based on similar EMP test results on trucks by the EMP Commission, few effects were observed below about 12 kV/m. At higher field-strength levels, 70% or more of the trucks on the road will manifest some anomalous response following EMP exposure. Roughly 15% or more of the trucks will experience engine stall, sometimes with permanent damage that the driver cannot correct.

In summary, it is seen that the results mentioned above are far from conclusive and suggest that some vehicles will not fail an EMP exposure in contrast to earlier perceptions and reports to the contrary. However, since many of the tests were performed below 50kV/m, and since almost no diesel-engines were involved, conclusions and recommendations are difficult to make.

BTW, the reader is referred to website: http://www.futurescience.com/emp.html which has more information on EMP vehicle vulnerability.

15.1.1- Recommendations for Vehicle Mfgs.

• Design and test selected vehicles to meet MIL-STD-188-125 field strength 50 kV/m EMP limits. (the k = 1,000 multiplier)

• Provide a retrofit kit and services to reduce vehicle radiated susceptibility. Some measure of the safety margin must be reported along with its meaning by the manufacturer.

• Provide vehicle owners with an EMP manual of vehicle use and parking recommendations (see below).

• The greater the vehicular sheet metal vs. plastic skin overage of engine and cab the lesser is susceptibility. Cover or coat microprocessors with metal foil or metal paint or deposition.

218

• Protect cable entry and exit with surge suppressors. Selected cables should be shielded. Cables should have ferrite clamps at both ends. Keep cables close to metal vehicle frame.

• Since air gaps in metal parts break down at 3 kV/mm potential difference, insulation of some wiring and especially motors, generators, starter relays, and ignition coils are vulnerable. Increased EMI protection is needed.

• The 80 year old practice of grounding the negative terminal of the battery to the vehicle frame and use of the frame as the return in circuits should be ended. The reason is that the circuit loop area is somewhere between 100 to 10,000 times (60-100 dB) greater than a replaced twisted wire pair. This means that all the potential EMI (electromagnetic interference) picked up from coupled transmitter radiations, local and distant, from radar and especially from EMP will be reduced accordingly. For less than $100 in wiring increase plus labor, the EMP hardening impact will be many times rewarded. (Remember you heard this here first).

15.1.2- Recommendations for vehicle owners:

• Until the vehicle EMP susceptibility data base becomes far greater, the following will not eliminate EMP susceptibility; but will help reduce it.

• Park your vehicle in a sheet metal shed or steel building to further mitigate susceptibility. Further improvement would result from sheet metal placed over the floor. (acts as a HF/VHF capacitor to short the induced EMI/EMP)

• Temporary storage of vehicle: Ten mil sheet metal floor. Cover vehicle with some 18" - 24" overlapped. 1-3 mils (household aluminum foil). Secure overlap with duct tape and connect foil to mat flooring with widths of foil bonded to each with duct tape. (This is a crude tempo shield).

219

• In the northern latitudes above roughly 38 degrees, engine oil warmers are plugged into AC outlets to make starting the vehicle easier in cold winter in the following morning. Use cable surge suppressors and ferrite absorbers at the cable auto entrance points.

• Do not count on any significant susceptibility reduction if vehicle is parked in your resident garage, since walls are radiation unprotected. Also, all house wiring enters at the breaker panel that feeds an octopus-like antenna house circuit wiring. This, then, conductively couples EMP to whatever appliances or equipment is connected to their circuit duplex outlets.

• The more vehicular sheet or foil or deposited metal vs. plastic skin overage of engine and cab, the lesser is susceptibility. Are microprocessors metal foil or metalized covered and protected with surge suppressors? Is the cabling shielded and clamped to the metal frame?

• The problem with the above suggestions is that that there appears to exist no sound quantitative documentation on vehicle EMP susceptibility. This is especially puzzling as USA is a litigious society. Thus, perhaps the AMA might nudge its members to do this by (1) establishing test set-up conditions and test procedure standards, and sharing costs and results. Meanwhile, some of the above EMP vehicle recommendations may represent an EMC overkill; and some are still inadequate for EMP protection. Quien sabe? This is an unthinkable and unprofessional situation; the year is not 1933.

15.2- Shielded Enclosure for multi-hour parking

Two kinds of parking enclosures are addressed: (1) location associated with a home and (2) at place of work. If each of these were EMP protected. a car or truck would be EMP protected more than 90% of each day.

15.2.1- Parking Shielded enclosure at home

This topic has already been addressed in Chapter 11, but is re-shown here for an EMP protected 20 ft x 20 ft cottage shed with solar rooftop and includes enclosure for auto and golf cart. This is one of the least expensive, complete EMP protected small living and storage

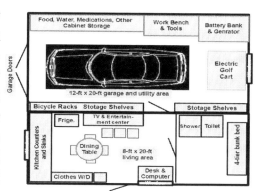

20-ft x 20-ft Cottage Shed with Utility Garage
Full roof area for solar panels = 5 kW max.
Probable roof area for solar panels = 2-3 kW

facilities at less than $50k for everything including shed building, solar, et al.

15.2.2- Parking Shielded Enclosure at Place of Work

This is another application of Chapters 6 and 11 on building EMP protection with a solar rooftop. Basically, the parking garage photo on the right is modified to replace roof parking with the solar rooftop instal-

lation. The sides are covered with heavy duty 20 opi screen and the floor is covered with either 30 opi screen or 10-mil aluminum foil with a protective coating.

The big change is to have a 2-3 car length vestibule in which cars are admitted with large doors at one side open and the others are closed. Then the reverse to let the vehicles out. This way. The entire inside is always completely shielded. This is the vehicle version of the shielded people entrance of Fig. 8.17.

15.2.3- Parking Shielded enclosure at transportation locations

This is basically an extension of the proceeding section at airports, train terminals and boat cruises where the participant parks his car for a day, week or extended period.

15.3- EMP Protection of Vehicles

15.3.1- Golf Carts

Golf carts are light weight, four-wheeled vehicles for two people, (can haul up to six) used for local transportation, that can be licensed for limited-use, road travel. They are motor driven from a single, 12-volt battery. Their range for one full charged battery is

about 50 miles. If they have a solar rooftop and the day is not overcast, range can be extended to about 100 miles.

Golf carts use expensive deep-cycle batteries ranging from 12 volt to 48 volt depending on system and manufacturer.

No EMP susceptibility measurement data are reported on the Internet for golf carts. Here are our comments:

- Few, if any, micro-processors are used vs autos and trucks. So, golf carts are less susceptible to an EMP radiation. This does not mean that they are not susceptible.

- Since there are head and tail lights, there are interconnecting

222

wires, which also act as a pick-up antenna and go to the battery which also goes to the motor. *Unless EMP surge suppressed, the large transient voltage on the wires* (perhaps, in excess of 10 kV) may instantly cause insulation breakdown (>3kV/mm) on the drive motor windings which destroys its performance.

15.4- EMP Test Facilities in USA

• White Sands Missile Test Range, New Mexico. In addition to military testing, the EMP test simulation facility is rented to automotive manufacturers.

• Naval Air System Command has an EMP test simulation facility in Pax River, Maryland.

• Oak Ridge National Laboratory, Tennessee

• Naval Weapons Center China Lake, Ridgecrest, CA

• Sandia Labs, Albuquerque, NM has a bounded wave simulator (4x11x5 m).

• Air Force Weapons Lab at Albuquerque, NM has an HPD and a VPD. The largest open-air, EMP simulator in the world.

• Edwards AFB, CA Also a site at Palmdale HPD for unique aircraft EMP testing

• Army at Ft. Monmouth, NJ. It may have moved its EMP facility to Aberdeen Proving Ground, Aberdeen, MD.

• More limited EMP testing can be done at: Dayton T. Brown,- Engineering & Test Division - 1175 Church Street - Bohemia, NY 11716. Email: test@dtbtest.com - Phone: 800.837.8456 - Fax: 631.589.3648

• Most of the EMI test houses that perform MIL-STD-461E or later testing, also perform RS105 and CS-115 testing. Some of the labs have large chambers to be able to test vehicles for the Army.

Until the auto manufac-
turers via AAA or the
Feds have a vehicle test
database, we do not
know the EMP suscepti-
bility profile. Thus,
billions of dollars of EMP
protection planning are
uncertain. Profile data-
basing is paramount.

Chapter 16
National Vitals Replenishment Programs

Chapter Overview

Once the EMP unprepared family, group, community, village, town or small city has witnessed the first day or two after the EMP event shock, the thought of how long their water, food, medications and other vitals will last, suddenly becomes a major concern. Not only were all the food chains, WalMarts, raided with stripped food shelves and fist fights early on, realization of the absence of replenishments is shocking.

Remember, the EMP event is not like a hurricane, tornado, Noreaster, earthquake, volcano, or tsunami, where damage replacement is only 5-20 miles away. Rather, the EMP event distance to replacements or replenishments may range from a few hundred miles (400 km) to over 1,000 miles (1,600 km). There are no functional gasoline or diesel stations in between. In fact, except for some infrequent exceptions, there is no road traffic, although, the streets and highways may exhibit scattered dysfunctional vehicles. Then, what are the solutions?

Again, the boy scout motto comes into play. "Be prepared". Four options come to the rescue although only two apply to where you live: (1) have a 4,000-ft. mat-dirt runway or airport within 100 miles of where you live, (2) have railroad access and extra sidings within 150 miles, (3) have extra-dredged marinas for coastal locations, and (4) become part of a large group or Community who has prepared for an EMP which includes some Community storage of vitals with each family, home and solar rooftop EMP ready.

16.1- The Replenishment Challenge & Preparation

Let's begin with a short story about Hurricane Charley in August 2005 in Port Charlotte, SW Florida. We were vacationing at Hendersonville, North Carolina, listening to the evening news. Hurricane Charley was featured and expected to hit inland at Tampa Bay, FL about 150 miles from where we lived. The news reported a huge traffic jam as 250,000 vehicles headed inland - out of the expected hurricane path.

The next morning we awakened early and turned on the radio to get a hurricane update. Oh, mon dieu! ("OMG") Hurricane Charlie unexpectedly turned East into Charlotte Bay and the Peace River, where our home is located. We quickly ended our vacation and headed South for home about 700 miles away. We slept the first night at a motel on the GA-FL boarder.

We got up early Saturday morning and headed for the nearest Home Depot/Lowes to buy a generator. A big sign in front of Lowes said, "Sorry we are sold out of generators", but another sign in front of Home Depot, about two miles away said, "Yes we have Generators". We bought a 5,500 watt generator and quickly headed south.

As we arrived about five miles from our home we saw much damage, a few roofs blown off and much lumber, billboards and signs scattered everywhere including the streets and roads. The neighbor's roof was half blown off, but ours was intact. As it developed all stores were closed and we were without power for 13 days. The telephones and cells were not working. All non-battery electrical and electronics devices and equipments were dead. Our cell phone was acting dead because the nearby relay tower lost its power.

We quickly learned to make a daily pilgrimage to North Port eight miles to the north for replenishments. The cell phone there worked because the tower never lost its power. There were long gasoline lines; but the food stores were stocked with food and other essentials we got at Ace Hardware.

As mentioned above, Charlotte County and others were without power for 13 days. Our generator serviced two refrigerators (spare in the garage) which stored some neighbors perishables as well.

Now comes the big point of the story. Suppose our replenishments at Northport, eight miles away, had been 500 miles away, like in an EMP event. For this, there are no gasoline stations pumping gasoline as there was no electricity there either. In fact, the roads had scattered vehicles that became dysfunctional with many accidents as vehicles tried to avoid crashing into each other. Local and other stores were closed because no electricity and the whole area became the dark ages of the 1870s. Yes, Hurricane Charlie was a sobering reminder of what an astronomical event an EMP incident can become with no replenishments – no food, medications ad infinitum, A bed of starvation and disease. For more detail read our one and only novel, "Contrasting EMP Survivals – A Tale of two Towns".

16.2- Dirt Runways and Globemaster Cargo Aircraft

The idea here to have prearranged (or can be updated after an EMP event) points of contact between the county representative or his designee having the dirt runway and specific points of distant contact to be initiated following an EMP event. Modes of contact are phone to satellite relay to designations. This presumes, of course, that the phone, wiring to its antenna are EMP protected. A second backup communications is wise.

A Globemaster III (could be another cargo aircraft) has a 70-ton payload, capable of taking off for noload return from a county 4,000 foot mat-covered dirt runway. The purpose of the steel metal mat cover is to eliminate dirt erosion for all weather conditions over the years and last for more than 10 years with little or no maintenance. The runway supports local redistribution to designated WalMarts, storehouses and/ or other targets. The cargo contents have been prepared by the county administrator 's assignee and updated annually.

16.3- Railroad Sidings and Steam Engines

Those counties having an active rail line connected to a distant location (TBD over 500 miles) can generate a few or several rail spurs. These are of multiple box-car length going to industrial or other centers capable of easy freight car unloading and redistribution to local distribution centers.

Some of these rail lines can be added to US East and West coast deep-water ports handling major imports from other countries for internal distribution centers described in the previous paragraph.

Railroad engines are either electric or diesel-electric for diesel fuel source. Since they would likely become dysfunctional following an EMP event (they must be EMP tested to determine their susceptibility), some yesteryear steam engines with no microprocessors or protected electronics are used for rail propulsion.

16.4- Dredged Marinas and Electric Boats

There are about 22 deep-water ports in US coastal cities: five on the West Coast, 13 on the East Coast and five in the Gulf of Mexico. All of these have good railroad access to serve the interior. However, about 15 north central and central states are more than 1,000 miles away from a coastal port.

Some TBD ports in between, perhaps 20-30 more, may be identified for less deep water access. In fact, some large marinas can be selected for some dredging, if necessary, to increase the size of the ships that can access them. Options exist to increase the number of smaller ships and boats that can serve US exports and and foreign goods imports, as necessary. To be useful, each should have a rail access within 50 miles to serve the hinterland and some cargo aircraft as mentioned above.

16.5- The Home and Builders Communities.

Earlier chapters addressed in some lengths farm and real estate community developments of waterfront cottage-shed EMP protected homes with solar rooftops and larger ones serving the suburban-rural regions of larger cities. These can work especially well in the above north-central states located more than 1,000 miles from coastal port access.

Recognize that 2% of the American farm population – farmers - service 100% of the normal domestic food needs. However, an EMP event may dysfunction more than 50% of the farm tractors. This resulting food shortage can be alleviated by introducing community food-garden partners in each of the real-estate cottage and small home developments and Community Solar Gardens that are modified to become EMP protected. These will be somewhat bigger than the "Victory Gardens" food and vegetable plots that tens of millions of Americans had during WWII to help in the war.

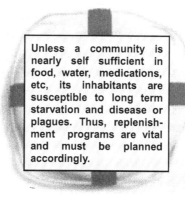

Unless a community is nearly self sufficient in food, water, medications, etc, its inhabitants are susceptible to long term starvation and disease or plagues. Thus, replenishment programs are vital and must be planned accordingly.

Chapter 17
Epilogue and What the Future Portends

Chapter Overview

This an epilog for the previous 16 chapters. The mission for this book remains as follows:

(1) Since an EMP is so devastating and the literature is so sparse regarding how to EMP protect a pantry, garage, cottage shed, house, commercial office and industrial buildings with solar rooftops, and other infrastructure, this book, our fifth in the series, attempts to Wake up America. But, America, you are still asleep. This is more than rocket science, and America is negligent – asleep at the switch.

Hope that Prime Minister Netanyahu doesn't do his thing to Iran any time soon. In response to Ahmadinejad Iran's statement before the United Nations, that Iran will wipe Israel off the face of the earth, Netanyahu later replied that if Iran achieves an 80% uranium enrichment, Israel will preempt. A nuclear bomb capability is assumed to be meant, with an EMP being "a humane approach." This may trigger the beginnings of WWIII.

(2) There are so many facets to EMP protection, why does the Department of Homeland Security appear to many to be in a coma? We need a lot of work to be done as our adversaries have calibrated our Achilles heels. If you don't know what to do, contact, your senator or congressman, or the Department of Defense. If you are still perplexed, contact the IEEE, EMC Society. If all else fails, call me, Don White, at 941-743-8100. I'll give you straight answers with supporting rationale (Remember, I have not had access to classified information for over 20 years).

We take a peek at the future, since it is apparent what will happen. Some specifics are forecast. But, we must first wake up, get started and catch up. Then, my future disclosures will make sense. So, the immediate motive is to generate new products and services as outlined herein, put them to work on Phase I and Phase II of *"National EMP Protection Options"*. As explained herein the prototypes and templates will generate over 43 million job-years over the next decade. After catch up, we can surge ahead and pay down some of our $18 trillion national debt.

17.1- Strengths and Weaknesses in this book

The strength of this book is the creation of a large number of fixes or preventions ranging from (1) optimizing the type and OPI (openings per inch) of solar panel shields to (2) EMP protecting a home with solar rooftop to (3) EMP protecting an entire community including its infrastructure. Most of these creation details do not yet appear in the Internet as some may be classified, not yet developed, or not yet created in writings. They are in the mind and writings of the author over the past 35 years who has been very active in the sister (EMP) disciplines of the EMC (Electromagnetic Compatibility) Community.

The principal weakness of this book is in the identified suppliers of the EMP protection materials and techniques. They are mostly hidden within the EMC Community which is dedicated to solving Electromagnetic interference problems. Several were (and some still are) contracted to the Department of Defense and related agencies. As contractors to the government, they are prevented by agreement from advertising and promoting their EMP skills and products because of their original security classification. Fortunately, the author has written many unclassified books on EMC related subjects and has not had a security clearance in the past twenty years. So his mission is to present this knowledge along with many newly created and updated EMP protection products, services and ways and means. Hopefully, his books and planned 2015 seminars, webinars and bi-monthly journal will remove many of the above lack-of-access short comings.

17.2- Fixing the Solar Panel Protective Shield

Leading the needs is having a few off-the-shelf suppliers of suitable screen shields to cover the solar panels at an economically viable price. Currently, China and Germany seem to be the only suppliers at prices that should be a fraction of presently quoted screens.

Along with the above is to have a few off-the-shelf suppliers of solar panels with the above screening built in, both for quality control and quantity price reduction. This is expected to happen by 2017, when the number of solar rooftops in USA goes beyond one million installations. During the interim, the options for solar panel shielding (externally) will follow the discussion in Chapter 10.

17.3- Quantify Susceptibilities of Vehicles; then Fix

As remarked earlier in this book, the EMP tests done at US Army, White Sands Proving Ground, were inconclusive and had too many qualitative remarks when quantitative data are necessary. Thus, this needs to be updated and done correctly with new vehicles using approved test plan from AAA (American Automobile Association) and endorsed by IEEE/EMC Society and other TBD sources.

The goals of these tests using the radiated susceptibility spectral profile of Fig. 2.2, repeated here as Fig. 17.1 for convenience of discussion, are:

(1)- Determine the vehicle stop - restart susceptibility profile vs. simulated EMP level.

(2)- Determine the EMP level of vehicle microprocessor failure, both separately and insitu. Their difference in dB is the vehicle shielding effectiveness.

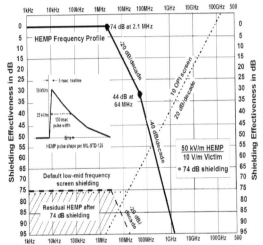

(3)- Prioritize the critical devices and corresponding susceptibility levels. Select the 10% (TBD) worst cases, and shield-surge suppress fixes.

(4)- Install X% (TBD) fixes for worst cases on production vehicles and

Fig. 17.1- Shielding effectiveness requirements used for calculating EMP protection

offer additional EMP protection models at extra cost.

A Few More Details

The early testing will be for the purpose of determining radiated susceptibilities of the most popular domestic and foreign cars and trucks. The first series of tests will be of a more general nature, For example, after a TBD EMP test burst at a defined level, starting at 10 kV/m, the vehicle will be monitored for stop-re start only, with restart testing to see if TBD actions still work.

From the results of the first series of tests, depending on the data, a second more elaborate test takes place. For each such vehicle, a radiated level will be run corresponding to levels (TBD) of 10 kV/m up to 100 kV/m in 3-dB steps (increase of 1.41 times) will be run while identifying where failures occurred. This means identifying the applicable microprocessor controlled device not responding at the identified level.

It is understood that one manufacturer disclosed that it uses 60 microprocessor-controlled actions in its 2015 vehicles. If this is the case, expect vehicle failures at lower EMP levels.

Remember, it was disclosed in Chapter 15, that the single biggest change vehicle manufacturers can make is to change the 90-year old practice of grounding the neutral (or positive battery terminal) to the frame to save up to 50% of the circuit wiring. Reduce the radiated susceptibility of this antenna-octopus area pickup by replacing this obsolete practice with shielded, twisted-wire pair, for an estimated 40+ dB improvement. This single practice will result in a susceptibility reduction at the lowest cost.

17.4- The Future of Electric Vehicles

Chapter 15 also briefly addressed electric vehicles and some future expectations, especially for electric charging, by ubiquitously located charge stations provided by the electric utilities. Such vehicles however, are presently slower to catch on in popularity, especially with gasoline in USA having fallen in price from $3.65/gallon in Fall 2014 to $2.00/ gallon in January 2015 (a 45% reduction). However, battery prices are also expected to fall as more homes go the solar rooftop way.

Electric vehicles are great as golf carts as discussed in Section 2.2.3 with a maximum range of about 100 miles (160 km), but of no value for longer ranges unless the number of batteries exceeds one. If a vehicle has a maximum of six, 200 watt solar panel roof tops (1.2kW), this will extend the golf cart range by only 4 miles – not enough to be meaningful.

17.5- EMP Protection Countermeasures

Section 2.5 addressed Anti-missile lasers (AML) as being a nearly instantaneous destruction countermeasure for a terrorist or rogue nation launched EMP missile. However, it was remarked (unclassified) that the DoD was not funded to mass produce these devices for land mounted, aircraft or shipborne platforms - already tested and proven. Thus, the author is not aware of the degree of protection to USA as this information is apparently classified.

It is understood that the highest altitude a gas filled balloon can reach is about 75,000 feet (15 miles or 24 km). Of course with an EMP bomb mounted as a payload, the altitude is greatly reduced, and an EMP may not be produced at a much lower altitude. Also, the balloon may be detected by a ground radar..

Other countermeasures are classified and not reported here.

17.6- EMP Protection Agency, New Gov. Agency

Considering the magnitude of the undertaking and the cataclysmic impact when an EMP event strikes, a Government Agency is long needed since the Commission of 2007 met and concluded that EMP is "Not if, but when".

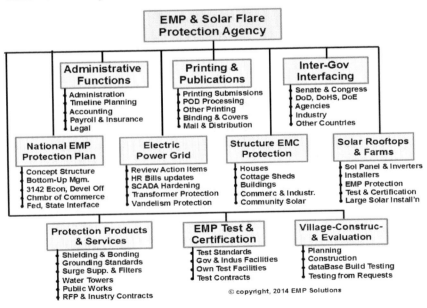

234

The above org chart for EPA (EMP Protection Agency or another possible name = EDA for EMP Defense Agency) should not really be developed as it includes many of DHS missions and goals needing timely attention and action. A more pragmatic approach may be to form a skeleton version of Fig. 17.2, as a "watch dog and expeditor" group. Therein, a group of about 50 professionals including support staff, have face contact with relevant government agencies, their contractors and applicable congressional committees.

Their mission is at a higher level to spot delays, duplications and voids, bottlenecks or distracting sideisms and discretely report these to their applicable managers with recommended corrections and supporting rationale. No fault-finding; only result-oriented goals. This might also reduce the need for some congressional hearings as the problems were corrected earlier-on.

17.7- Reversing America Gone Wrong

While this topic of **Reversing America Gone Wrong** is beyond the mission and goals of this book, this topic impacts the effort, mission, goals and achievement of EMP protection. Thus, a few words are offered on the topic – which is also the next of my books being written.

Abstract

Reversing America Gone Wrong highlights the sinking American morality, damaging greed and corruption, loss of leadership and loss of national and global respect. The book (1) identifies 47 major problem topics, (2) finding or creating corrective options with supporting rationale, and (3) ways and means. The book mission is to act as a catalyst to help make corrective things happen in a timely fashion; however, some may take years. A few will require Amendments to the Constitution.

The presentation will also demonstrate how the wasteful parts of socialism can be gainfully reduced or eliminated and the resulting savings used to improve lifestyle, increase economic productivity and create many new jobs.

If only 40% of the wastes from topics discussed herein were

235

stopped, savings would approximate $1 trillion per year corresponding to 6% of the USA Gross Domestic Product or 10 million jobs.

Since the biggest part of getting started is getting started, the book presents the 47 topics needing correction. Fix options for each are presented and for many, how to measure and score their success.

This book should be completed and published by fall, 2015.

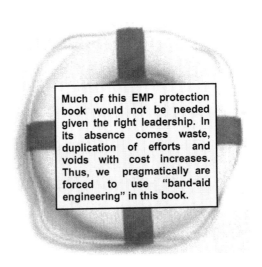

Much of this EMP protection book would not be needed given the right leadership. In its absence comes waste, duplication of efforts and voids with cost increases. Thus, we pragmatically are forced to use "band-aid engineering" in this book.

Index

A

C

237

D

E

F

G

H

I

J-K

L

T

U-V

W-Z

X-Y-Z

Curriculum Vita of the Author

Don White, registered professional engineer, ret'd., holds BSEE and MSEE degrees from the University of Maryland. He is past CEO of three Electromagnetic Interference and Compatibility companies in Metro Washington, D.C., one of which traded on the NASDAQ.

Don has written and published 14 technical books over a span of 30 years, which became well known and used worldwide in electronics circles. His last book was "The EMC, Telecom and Computer Encyclopedia Handbook", an 800-page compendium. Don taught over 14,000 engineers via seminars in 29 countries.

At Don White Consultants, he published a bimonthly trade journal called *EMC Technology* magazine circulated over four continents. In addition to being technical editor, he wrote many of the tutorial articles.

Don received the IEEE award for development of automatic spectrum scanning, recording and analysis intercept systems. A 2nd award for contributions to the EMC education and publishing arena. He is a senior member of the former Institute of Radio Engineers and life-time senior member of IEEE. He is past president of IEEE, EMC Society.

Other books by Don White aka Donald R.J. White

- **Nuclear EMP Threats – What Next?,** REC Press, 2012, 162 pages,
- **Save, Survive and Prosper in an Economy in Crisis**. Dougherty and White, 132 pages, 2008, D-W Press
- **Handbook of Electromagnetic Compatibility,** White and Violette, 2002, Van Nostrand Reinhold
- **The EMF Controversy and Reducing Exposure from Magnetic Fields,** White, Barge, George and Riley, 201 pages, the EEC Press
- **The EMC, Telecom and Computer Encyclopedia, Third Edition,** 800 pages, 1999, *emf-emi control Press*
- **12-Volume Handbook Series,** 1988, The EMC Press:
  - **Vol. 2, Grounding and Bonding,** 487 pages
  - **Vol. 4, Electromagnetic Shielding,** 615, pages
  - **Vol. 6, EMI Test Methodology and Procedures,** 675 pages
  - **Vol. 8, EMI Control Methodology and Procedure,** 544 pages
- **Shielding Design Methodology and Procedures,** 1987, DWCI Press
- **EMI control in the design of printed circuit boards and backplanes** 1981, DWCI Press
- **A handbook on electromagnetic shielding materials & performance** 1975, DWCI Press
- **Five-Volume handbook Series on Electromagnetic Interference and Compatibility,** 1972, DWCI Press
- **Glossary of Acronyms, Abbreviations & Symbols,** 1971, DWCI, Press
- **Methods and Procedures for Automating RFI/EMI Measurement,** 1966, WEI Press
- **Electrical Filters – Synthesis, Design & Applications,** 295 pages, WEI Press

Appendix A

Lightning and Grounding
(emphasis on Solar-PV rooftops)

(Parts of this appendix are courtesy of NOAA)

Lightning is the number one cause of catastrophic failures in solar electric systems and components. The principal reason is that many solar-PV systems are poorly protected including poor grounding.

First to be discussed are facts and myths about lightning.

The purpose of lightning protection is **not** to stop the lightning from striking. That can not be done. Lightning protection controls the **path** of the lightning after it hits by diversion. It's not lightning that causes the damage, it's lightning going through damageable places containing susceptible components or systems.

At any instant, there are more than 2,000 thunderstorms taking place throughout the world. These storms combine to produce about 100 lightning flashes per second, many with a potential of up to a billion volts, currents ranging up to 200,000 amperes and temperatures of over 54,000 degrees Fahrenheit.

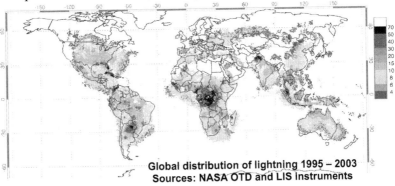

**Global distribution of lightning 1995 – 2003
Sources: NASA OTD and LIS instruments**

The first illustration is the lightning density for the world and the second is the flash density for the United States. Florida is seen to be about 100 times greater than most western regions. The state has an average flash density of about 5,100 strikes per day or a town of 100 sq. mi would have seven per day. This map does not show the relative intensity, so it can be a little misleading.

Although the Southwest does not rate that high in the total number of strikes, some of the largest strikes ever recorded are from that area due to the sometimes violent updrafts from the super heated desert floor.

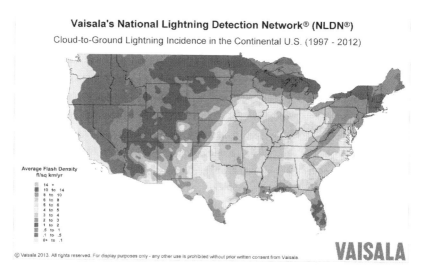

Vaisala's National Lightning Detection Network® (NLDN®)
Cloud-to-Ground Lightning Incidence in the Continental U.S. (1997 - 2012)

Lightning travels at about half the speed of light or 100,000 times faster than sound and therein the lies the reason that thunder is heard after the flash at about one mile per five seconds.

According to NASA Lightning strikes 90 percent over land. Almost nothing can offer 100% protection damage - but it can be reduced 95% or more with relatively simple precautions and relatively inexpensive installation methods.

Myths

There are a lot of myths about lightning. Some have persisted for centuries.

Myth 1: A lightning rod or grounded tower or high structure makes it more likely that lightning will strike:

Wrong - It will have little or no effect on how likely it is that it will strike in the immediate area. The important thing is it will be conducted directly to ground, without having to go through a solar rooftop inverter or a computer first. It does make it more likely to strike where it is directed. There is some evidence that a few strikes can be prevented with the use of special sharp-pointed "air streamer" lightning rods, which bleed off some of the accumulated charge. However, that has been a controversy for at least 50 years.

Myth 2: Lightning always strikes the tallest object:

Wrong - It can strike anyplace - although it is most likely to hit the highest object, there is no guarantee. It is also more likely to strike something with a good conductive path to ground, such as a steel tower. Sometimes, even if it strikes the highest object, you can get side flashes if the object it hits is not well grounded. For example, the lightning current from a stricken lightning rod on a roof is heading down a conductor to a poor ground. As the current heads south on the outside conductor, it may side flash through the building siding to an inside wall water pipe, finding a lower path to ground. The damage can cause water leaks or in the extreme, set the building on fire.

Myth 3: You should not touch metal objects if lightning is in the area.

Wrong - yet the myth has even been perpetuated on some of the National Weather Service web pages. Note how birds safely stand on overhead power distribution lines as there impedance between their legs is perhaps a million times higher than an inch (few cm) of bird leg-spacing between wires. On the other hand, don't stand under a tree during a lightning storm (like dead cattle did for "protection") as a lightning struck tree, exits thousands of amperes into the earth and the voltage difference between your wet feet may run into the thousands, electrocuting you.

Where Lightning can Strike

Lightning originates around 15,000 to 25,000 feet (5 km to 8 km) above sea level when raindrops are carried upward until some of them convert to ice. For reasons that are not widely agreed upon, a cloud-to-ground lightning flash originates in this mixed water and ice region. The charge then moves downward in 50-yard sections called step leaders. It keeps moving toward the ground in these steps and produces a channel along which charge is deposited. Eventually, it encounters something on the ground that is a good connection. The circuit is complete at that time, and the charge is lowered from cloud to ground. The flow of charge (current) produces a luminosity that is very much brighter than the part that came down. This entire event usually takes less than half a second.

What Kind of Damage can Lightning Cause?

Most electrical and electronic damage in both grid-tie and off-grid solar electric systems is **not** due to a direct hit. In fact, direct hits are rare. Most damage occurs from nearby hits, usually within a few hundred feet (100 meters). A near-strike can induce thousands of volts onto the house and PV array wiring if not protected. In a ground hit, it can also spread out and travel into buried conductors, such as pipes and buried cables. Contrary to popular assumption, the panels themselves are not the biggest victim - inverters and controllers are. The frames and mounts on panels are usually grounded (sometimes more by accident than design), and that often diverts the lightning directly to ground, saving the panels. Also, the battery banks on most off-grid PV systems acts as a fairly good surge arrestor if you have good connections and a good ground - but it may take out the controller on it's way. If the battery bank is not grounded, damage can be much more severe - it may then leap around all over trying to find a path to ground.

Cloud-to-ground lightning can kill or injure people by direct or indirect means. The lightning current can branch off to a person from a tree, fence, pole, or other tall object. In addition, flashes may conduct their current through the ground to a person after the flash strikes a nearby tree, antenna, or other tall object. The current also may travel through power or telephone lines, or plumbing pipes to a person who is in contact with an electric appliance, telephone, or plumbing fixture.

Similarly, objects can be directly struck and this impact may result in an explosion, burn, or total destruction. Or, the damage may be indirect when the current passes through or near it. Sometimes, current may enter a building and transfer through wires or plumbing and damage everything in its path. Similarly, in urban

247

areas, it may strike a pole or tree and the current then travels to several nearby houses and other structures and enter them through wiring or plumbing. In some cases lightning can strike the ground and travel up buried power lines for hundreds of yards (meters).

It is important to note that lightning does NOT have to hit directly to cause damage. In fact, because of the EMP (electromagnetic pulse) associated with large strikes, the static and electric fields that occur actually cause most of the damage in unprotected electrical and electronic equipment. In a nearby strike, the wiring in a house or photovoltaic system acts like an antenna, and if unprotected and/or ungrounded can feed thousands of volts back into your inverter and other equipment.

Step One - Proper Grounding

First, the *National Electric Code (NEC)* , Article 780 (NFPA) codes for lightning protection, may not be totally adequate for off-grid installations. In fact, in some cases, the recommended practices can actually make it MORE dangerous. Unfortunately, some local inspectors assume that the National Electrical Code book is a bible and will not allow any deviations. For example, Zones of protection, including cones and rolling balls, lack warnings about lightning's unpredictable nature. These geometric abstractions are presented as factual, rather than statistical levels of protection. This is not to say that you should not follow the NEC recommendations in most cases - but you should be aware that recent research shows that there might be considerable variations from the average. Further steps may be needed for PV systems. NEC grounding is primarily concerned with electrical safety, not lightning protection, and the two may not always be compatible. For lightning protection you may need to take steps beyond the code minimum requirements.

The Purpose of Grounding: Equipment: Panel frames and mounts are grounded in order to provide the easiest (low impedance) path for lightning to get to ground. You would much rather have it go down the mounting pole or your ground rod than down your wiring to your controller or inverter or new wide screen TV. Without proper grounding, lightning can do some really strange things, and can jump around all over while trying to get to earth. If your inverter happens to be in the way, you will probably be buying a new one. You cannot stop lightning, but you can usually direct where you want it to go.

Fuses and Breakers offer NO protection: Fuses and circuit breakers offer no protection at all to lightning strikes. That is not their purpose. Lighting usually lasts for several microseconds - much faster than any fuse or breaker can blow. It's pretty unlikely that a one-inch fuse gap is going to offer much protection from a bolt that just cut through two miles of open air. Yet the myth persists that a fuse will offer lighting protection. It will not.

Single-Point Grounds: The importance of a single-point protection ground cannot be stressed enough. All equipment should normally be bonded to one single good earth ground. If you have some equipment connected to one ground, and other equipment ton another ground, it is quite likely that in a nearby strike that there will be a large voltage difference between the two grounds. This means that the equipment will be at different voltages, sometimes high enough to get arcing from one to another. There is an exception to this: If you have a panel array that is more than 50 to 75 feet (16-24meters) from the rest of the system, it should have it's own frame/mount ground (not electrical ground).

A Single Ground Rod is Seldom Enough: Tests done over the past few years show that in most cases, a single 6 or 8 foot (2-2.6 meters) ground rod is NOT enough, even when the ground is salted to improve conductivity. The problem is, in arid climates with dry soil, it could take as many as a dozen rods to get it down to the 10 ohms ground resistance that is usually accepted as the optimum (25 ohms is the NEC minimum). To get down to the 25 ohm NEC minimum, you may have to use 2-3 10-foot (3.2-meter) rods, all bonded together with #6 AWG wire and copper wire clamps. However, if you cannot do this, something is better than nothing. In some cases you may have to go so far as to bury lengths of bare copper wire or copper pipe in trenches. Or, mix bauxite material in the ground.

Grounding and NEC Requirements

The National Electric Code requires that all exposed metal surfaces be grounded regardless of the nominal system voltage. Systems with PV open-circuit voltages below 50 Volts are not required to have one of the current-carrying conductors grounded. This is because 50 volts approximates the threshold of feeling a shock trickle. Any system with AC voltages at 120 volts must have the neutral grounded. Some inverters do not isolate the AC and DC sides; grounding the AC neutral will also ground the DC negative. Other inverters have the case (which must be grounded) connected to the negative input which grounds the negative current-carrying conductor.

The NEC requirement can be extended. A separate conductor (as large as possible, but not less than number 10 AWG) should be fastened to each metallic module frame with a grounding lug or other approved method. The other end of these conductors should be connected to a single point on the array frame or rack again with another self-threading, stainless-steel screw or with a stainless-steel bolt in a drilled and tapped hole. From this point, number 4-6 AWG or larger copper conductor should be run directly to the nearest earth where it is connected to the longest, deepest ground rod that can be afforded. Eight feet is the minimum length recommended. Use a UL-listed clamp to make the connection. If a steel well casing is available, drill and tap the casing and use this as the ground rod.

In dry areas, several ground rods spaced 20-50 feet apart in a radial configuration, all bonded to the central rod can be effective. Buried copper water pipe can also improve the grounding system. Pipe or copper wire can be buried in trenches 12-18 inches deep in a radial grid. All grounding members should be connected or bonded to the central ground rod with heavy, bare conductors buried under ground. Direct-burial, UL-listed grounding clamps or welding should be used for all connections. Soldering should never be used for underground connections - it can corrode underground due to the different metals.

There is no such thing as a "perfect" ground unless you spend huge moneys on buried copper cables. However, a good ground is possible to get in most areas and need not be expensive. In dry and/or rocky locations, it may be more of a "challenge". If you can't get it perfect, anything is better than nothing at all. If you have bedrock at 3 feet (1 meter) try driving in 3 to 6 short ground rods and tie them all together with at least #4 AWG wire and good clamps. - not perfect, but far better than nothing. Another way is to bury heavy wire or (usually cheaper) lengths of copper pipe in ditches. Keeping the ground wet and/or salting the nearby area will also help.

The negative side of the battery bank should be grounded to the same point as all other ground wires. Batteries usually have a very low internal resistance, and can help act like a large surge arrestor on all but a direct hit. This may stop a hit near your panels from jumping around to your inverter and other equipment. The ground wire should be at least #8, and #6 or #4 AWG is recommended.

Surge Arrestors

Surge arrestors act like "clamps" in most cases. They go across the live wires with another wire going to ground. Normally they just sit there, but if the voltage goes above a certain level, they start to conduct, shorting the higher voltage to ground. In lighting prone areas you should also install a surge capacitor - this is not really an arrestor, but acts extremely fast, and will catch those high voltage spikes on the AC line that are too fast for a surge arrestor. For most systems to get the best protection, you should have a DC surge arrestor, such as the LA302DC on the side coming from the array - this should go on the INPUT to the charge controller. It should be as near the charge controller as possible. On the AC side (and this applies to BOTH the inverter AC input and AC output (for generator and/or grid tie systems) you should have both an AC surge arrestor and a surge capacitor.

Most inverter damage is caused by surges on the AC side coming in through house or generator wiring. In many systems with a backup generator, the generator is located outside, some distance from the inverter, and is a common hit point for lightning strikes. The Delta LA302R AC surge arrestor and the CA302 surge capacitor should be used on the AC portions. The benefits of also putting arrestors at the generator end are not all that great, and if installed you will probably need a separate ground rod system. For most mid size and larger systems the *Midnite Solar surge arrestors* are recommended or the *Outback Power* types. For smaller systems, or for general household AC protection the *Delta* brand will offer some lesser protection but are quite a bit cheaper.

The Delta arrestors are not perfect, but they work a lot better than nothing. Better arrestors are available, but the problem is price - complete system protection using the *Polyphaser* units could easily cost over $1000. The biggest problem with the Delta arrestors is that they may not always trigger on "low "level" spikes, but if you also have a surge capacitor installed, that will catch most of those.
It may seem a bit high to spend over $200 on surge arrestors, but the typical repair bill for large sine wave inverter that has been lightning hit can run well over $1000.

Installing Delta Arrestors

Most of the Delta surge arrestors have three wires (a few, for pumps, have 4). In all cases, the GREEN wire is ground, the black and white wires are wired across the AC or the DC power side. Even though the white in most AC systems is neutral, and is supposedly grounded, don't count on it - make sure you have both sides protected. In DC systems, such as PV arrays, it really does not matter much which of the two wires go to what,
but again both sides of the input to the charge controller or whatever the panels are feeding should have one wire from the arrestor attached.

To protect a 3-phase submersible pump motor, connect the black wires to the line terminals and the white and/or green wire to the casing ground. Most of the arrestors have a separate green ground wire - this wire should always be attached to a good ground.

Appendix B
Terms and Definitions

The following lists some of the most often appearing terms in EMP and Solar installations and their protection.

Alternating Current (AC): The flow of electricity that constantly changes direction between positive and negative sides. Almost all power produced by electric utilities in the United States moves in current that shifts direction at a rate of 60 times per second.

Alternative Energy: Another name for renewable energy – alternative to fossil fuel (oil, gas and coal).

Ambient Temperature: The temperature of the surrounding area.

Amorphous Silicon: A thin-film, silicon photovoltaic cell having no crystalline structure. Manufactured by depositing layers of doped silicon on a substrate. See also single-crystal silicon an polycrystalline silicon.

Ampere (Amp): The unit of measure that indicates how much electricity flows through a conductor. It is like using cubic feet per second to measure the flow of water. For example, a 1,200-watt, 120-volt hair dryer pulls 10 amperes of electric current (amps = watts/volts).

Ampere-Hour (Ah/AH): A measure of the flow of current (in amperes) over one hour; used to measure battery capacity.

Annual Solar Savings: The annual solar savings of a solar building is the energy savings attributable to a solar feature relative to the energy requirements of a non-solar building.

Average Demand: The energy demand for a given location over a period of time. For example, the number of kilowatt-hours used in a 24-hour period, divided by 24 hours, tells the average demand for that location in that time.

Avoided Cost: The amount of money an electric utility would need to spend for the next increment of electric generation to produce or purchase.

Azimuth Angle: The angle between true south and the point on the horizon directly below the sun.

Battery: Batteries are often sold with a solar electric system. The primary purpose is to store the electricity not immediately used, which could be used at some later time.

Billion: $= 1,000,000,000 = 10^9 = 1,000$ million

Biomass: a renewable energy source, biological material derived from living, or recently living, organisms, such as wood, waste, and alcohol fuels. Biomass is commonly plant matter grown to generate electricity or produce heat.

BIPV (Building-Integrated Photovoltaics): A term for the design and integration of photovoltaic (PV) technology into the building envelope, typically replacing conventional building materials. This integration may be in vertical facades, replacing view glass, spandrel glass, or other facade material; into semitransparent skylight systems; into roofing systems, replacing traditional roofing materials; into shading "eye-brows" over windows; or other building envelope systems.

BTU (British Thermal Unit): The amount of heat required to raise the temperature of one pound of water one degree Fahrenheit; equal to 252 calories.

Cap and Trade: A central authority (usually a government) sets a limit or cap on the amount of a pollutant that can be emitted. Companies or other groups are issued emission permits and are required to hold an equivalent number of allowances (or credits) which represent the right to emit a specific amount. The total amount of allowances and credits cannot exceed the cap, limiting total emissions to that level.

Companies that need to increase their emission allowance must buy credits from those who pollute less. The transfer of allowances is referred to as a trade. In effect, the buyer is paying a charge for polluting, while the seller is being rewarded for having reduced emissions by more than was needed. So, in theory, those who can easily reduce emissions (such as renewable energy producers) most cheaply will do so, achieving the pollution reduction at the lowest possible cost to society. The "Cap and Trade" is believed by many to create more damage than good.

Capacity Factor: The ratio of the average load on (or power output of) an electricity generating unit or system to the capacity rating of the unit or system over a specified period of time.

CIGS = copper, indium, gallium, and selenium, thin film, solar semiconductor used for 2nd generation solar panels

Circuit: One or more conductors through which electricity flows.

: A CSG is a solar power installation that accepts capital from and provides output credit and tax benefits to individual and other investors. In some systems you buy individual solar panels which are installed in the farm after your purchase. In others you purchase kW capacity or kWh of production. The farm's power output is credited to investors in proportion to their investment, with adjustments to reflect ongoing changes in capacity, technology, costs and electricity rates. Companies, cooperatives, governments or non-profits operate the farms.

Concentrator: A photovoltaic module, which includes optical components such as lenses (Fresnel lens) to direct and concentrate sunlight onto a solar cell of smaller area. Most arrays must directly face or track the sun. They can increase the power flux of sunlight hundreds of times.

Converter: An electrical apparatus that changes the quantity or quality of electrical energy.

Cottage Shed (EMP Protected): A small compressed, livable shed, with solar rooftop specially designed for an EMP escape community living. Some accommodate a vehicle and a golf cart for transportation. They are clustered for community vitals storage and week-end entertainment. They range in size from 8 ft x 16 ft up to 16 ft x 30 ft. and most cost less than $100/ sq. ft. including solar rooftop all EMP protected when built in a development.

Crystalline: Photovoltaic cells made from a slice of single-crystal silicon or polycrystalline silicon.

CSP (concentrating solar power): is focused sunlight. CSP plants generate electric power by using mirrors to concentrate (focus) the sun's energy and convert it into high-temperature heat (or steam). That heat is then channeled through a conventional generator. The plants consist of two parts: one that collects solar energy and converts it to heat, and another that converts the heat energy to electricity. Within the United States, over 350 MW of CSP capacity exists and these plants have been operating reliably for more than 15 years.

Customer Load: The amount of power your site uses. Load may be expressed in kilowatts (capacity) or kilowatt-hours (energy). A site's peak kilowatts generally refers to when electric demand requirements are highest.

Demand: The level at which electricity is delivered to end-users at a given point in time. Electric demand in measured in kilowatts.

Direct Charges: Those charges directly attributable to a contract or job. They do not include operational expenses, such as overhead, G&A and taxes.

Direct Current (DC): The flow of electricity that flows continuously in one direction. Frequency - The number of cycles through which an alternating current moves in each second. Standard electric utility frequency in the United States is 60 cycles per second, or 60 Hertz (Hz).

Due Diligence: to a potential acquirer, due diligence means "making sure you get what you think you are paying for." This means doing your homework or examination on the offer or situation.

DUNS: Data Universal Numbering System.

Earnings/Share: The after-tax profit of a company divided by the issued and outstanding number of shares.

EBIDTA: Earnings Before Interest, Depreciation, Taxes, and Amortization.

Economic Development Office: In USA, A county government office, with the responsibility for increasing county revenue from manufacturing, tourism, retirement and related business operations. There exists 3,140 such offices in the 50 USA states.

EE: Energy Efficiency: Improving efficiency by cutting energy use, improving quality, reducing downtime, and reducing waste streams.

EFD = Energy Finance District is a special district created by local government to raise funds to finance the installation of renewable energy systems and permanent energy-efficiency improvements.

Funding for the improvements would be raised from public and/or private sources and loaned to the property owner. The loan would be repaid over a term of 15 to 20 years as an addition to ad valorem tax bill. If the property were to be sold, the new owner would assume repayment of the loan. Participation is voluntary.

Electric Grid: the electricity transmission and distribution system that links power plants to customers through high-power transmission line service.

A power transmission network is referred to as a "grid". Multiple redundant lines between points on the network are provided so that power can be routed from any power plant to any load center, through a variety of routes, based on the economics of the transmission path and the cost of power.

Electromagnetic Environmental Effects (EEE): a broad term meant to include all electromagnetic interference or disturbance – unintentional or intentional, including, but not limited to EMI, EMP, HEMP, HPM, jamming,

Electromagnetic Pulse (EMP): an electromagnetic radiation from an upper atmospheric nuclear explosion that couples into all manner of cables and metallic objects. To test for compliance a field strength is developed at 50 kV/m having a rise time of 5 nanoseconds and a pulse duration of 150 nanoseconds.

Energy - The ability to do work; different forms of energy can be converted to other forms, but the total amount of energy remains the same.

Energy Audit: A survey that shows how much energy used in a home, which helps find ways to use less energy.

EIA: Energy Information Administration: The U.S. EIA collects, analyzes, and disseminates independent and impartial energy information to promote sound policy making, efficient markets, and public understanding of energy and its interaction with the economy and the environment.

Energy Information Administration
1000 Independence Ave, SW
Washington, DC 20585

National Energy Information Center
(general energy information)
(202) 586-8800
infoctr@eia.gov

Technical Information
(202) 586-8959
wmaster@eia.gov

Factory-Built (or manufactured) Homes: Inexpensive houses manufactured in plants in single wide (8 feet), double wide (16 ft) and triple wide (24 ft) widths from 10 ft. up to 70 ft. These can become the basis for the smaller sizes used for EMP protection with solar rooftops.

Fixed Tilt Array: A photovoltaic array set in at a fixed angle with respect to horizontal.

Geothermal Energy: energy derived from the warmer (or colder) temperature below the surface of the earth than the inside of the infrastructure being heated (or cooled).

GigaWatt = 1 GW = 1,000,000,000 Watts = 10^9 watts.

Global Warming: See greenhouse effect.

Greenhouse Effect: The carbon pollutants dumped in the air act like a carbon dioxide layer to trap the gases like a greenhouse, thereby warming the earth.

Grid: see electric grid

Grid-Connected System: A solar electric or photovoltaic (PV) system in which the PV array acts like a central generating plant, supplying power to the grid.

Gross Profit: Profit developed from sales in which only the direct charges are applied. This excludes operational expenses (overhead and G&A) and taxes.

HEMP: A High altitude Electromagnetic Pulse generated from an upper atmospheric nuclear explosion. In military terminology, HEMP results from is a nuclear warhead detonated hundreds of kilometers above the Earth's surface. Effects of a HEMP device depend on a large number of factors, including the altitude of the detonation, energy yield, gamma-ray output, interactions with the earth's magnetic field, and electromagnetic shielding and protection of targets.

HEMP is usually described in terms of three components defined by the International Electrotechnical Commission, called E1, E2, and E3:

The **E1** pulse is the very fast component of nuclear EMP. It is a brief but intense electromagnetic field that can quickly induce very high voltages in electrical conductors. The **E1** component causes most of its damage by causing electrical breakdown voltages to be exceeded. **E1** is the component that can destroy computers and communications equipment and it changes too quickly for ordinary lightning protectors to provide effective protection.

The **E2** component is generated by scattered gamma rays and inelastic gammas produced by weapon neutrons. This E2 component is an "intermediate time" pulse that lasts from about 1 microsecond to 1 second after the beginning of the electromagnetic pulse. The E2 component of the pulse has many similarities to the EMP produced by lightning, although the electromagnetic pulse induced by a nearby lightning strike may be considerably larger than the E2 component of a nuclear EMP. Because of the similarities to lightning-caused pulses and the widespread use of lightning protection technology, the E2 pulse is generally considered to be the easiest to protect against.

The **E3** component is very different from the other two major components of nuclear EMP. The E3 is a slow pulse, lasting tens to hundreds of seconds, that is caused by the nuclear detonation heaving the Earth's magnetic field out of the way, followed by the restoration of the magnetic field to its natural place. The E3 component has similarities to a geo-magnetic stormflare. Like a geo-magnetic storm, E3 can produce geo-magnetically induced currents in long electrical conductors, which can then damage components such as power line transformers.

Because of the similarity between solar-induced geomagnetic storms and nuclear E3, it has become common to refer to solar-induced geomagnetic storms as "solar EMP." At ground level, however, "solar EMP" is not known to produce an E1 or E2 component.

Hertz: The unit of electromagnetic frequency that is equal to one cycle per second.

Hydroelectric: Electric power generated by turbines driven from the fall, passage or head of water.

Insulation: The solar power density incident on a surface of stated area and orientation. It is commonly expressed as average irradiance in watts per square meter (W/m^2) or kilowatt-hours per square meter per day ($kWh/(m^2/day)$) (or hours/day). In the case of photovoltaics it is commonly measured as kWh/(kWy) (kilowatt hours per kilowatt year, peak rating)

Interconnection: The linkage of transmission lines between two utilities, or between a utility and an end-user, enabling power to be moved in either direction.

Inverters: Electrical devices used to convert low DC voltage from solar-PV cells or panels to higher AC voltages for direct use in homes and non-residential buildings.

IPO: Initial Public Offering: The first time that a private company has gone public by selling its registered securities.

Irradiance: The direct, diffuse, and reflected solar radiation that strikes a surface. Usually expressed in kilowatts per square meter.

Isolate: An acronym for **Sol**ar bright days, Site **Lat**itude, and electric utility rates. Isolate scores applied to each US state will give a first, quick-look, rough measure of the viability of a proposed or existing solar rooftop installation performance, yet independent of the installation specifics. There are three main parts contributing to overall solar system installation performance:

- (1) Location = site latitude, % bright solar days, and electric utility rates

- (2) Solar technology, mounting and roof configuration
  Financial, prices, costs, subsidies, break even, P&L, cash flow and ROI.

- Isolate score is a rough measure of the state site location in producing affordable solar energy. Its viability score is defined as:

$$\textbf{Isolate} = \textbf{Sol} \times e \times \cos(\textbf{lat}) \times N \qquad (3)$$

where, N is a normalizing/scaling constant and cosine of the latitude, rather than latitude, per SE, is used because that is the way the physics of the math model works.

ITC = Investment Tax Credit: The Fed Gov. offers an ITC to companies and homeowners who install Renewable Energy devices to increase affordability by effectively lower the price.

kilowatt (kW): 1,000 watts. A unit of measure of the amount of electricity needed to operate given equipment. For example, a one kW system is enough power to illuminate 10 light bulbs at 100 watts each. (volts x amps = watts). Or, a one kW system, if operating at full capacity for 5 hours will produce (or use) 5 kWh of electricity.

kWh = kilowatt hour, an energy term = 1 kW of electric power for one hour or X kW for 1/X hours, or any combination of power and time, yielding 1 kWh.

Mat-dirt Runway A low-cost. packed dirt runway covered with steel matting for endurance and erosion control. It is usually 4,000 ft, in length, enough to accommodate a 70-ton payload, Globemaster III cargo aircraft. It is primarily used in a post-EMP era for vitals replenishment.

Maximum Power Point (MPP): The point on the current-voltage (I-V) curve of a module under illumination, where the product of current and voltage is maximum. For a typical silicon cell, this is at about 0.45 volts.

MegaWatt = 1 MW = 1,000,000 Watts = 10^6 watts.

Meter: A device that measures levels and volumes of customer's electricity use.

Million = 1,000,000 = 10^6

Moore's Law: A law of electronics technology made famous in an article in Electronics magazine in 1965 by Gordon L. Moore, who would later become the co-founder of Intel. Moore's law states that the number of transistors on an integrated circuit will double in less than 24 months, with corresponding decreases in the cost of electronics technology.

Mounting Equipment: Equipment/apparatus used to fasten solar (PV) modules to the roof.

Multicrystalline: A semiconductor (photovoltaic) material composed of variously oriented, small, individual crystals. Sometimes referred to as polycrystalline or semicrystalline.

NAIC: North American Industry Classification System.

National Electrical Code (NEC): Contains guidelines for all types of electrical installations. The 1984 and later editions of the NEC contain Article 690, "Solar Photovoltaic Systems" which should be followed when installing a PV system.

Net Metering: "Net Metering" is the metering of electricity consumed from the electric utility grid and conversely, exported to the grid (the meter runs backward when excess solar electricity is fed back) by a home or business (office building)

One-Axis Tracking: A system capable of rotating about one axis used to track the sun's daily path in the sky.

Orientation: Placement with respect to the cardinal directions, North, South, East, West. Azimuth is the measure of orientation from north.

Peak Load - The highest electrical demand within a particular period of time.

Peak Sun Hours: The equivalent number of hours per day when solar irradiance averages 1,000 w/m^2. For example, six peak sun hours means that the energy received during total daylight hours equals the energy that would have been received had the irradiance for six hours been 1,000 w/m^2.

Photovoltaic Cell or Module or Panel: (PV) - A device that produces an electric reaction to light, thereby producing electricity.

Photovoltaic (PV) Array: An interconnected system of PV modules that function as a single electricity-producing unit. The modules are assembled as a discrete structure, with common support or mounting. In smaller systems, an array can consist of a single module.

Photovoltaic (PV) Conversion Efficiency: The ratio of the electric power produced by a photovoltaic device to the power of the sunlight incident on the device.

Polycrystalline Silicon A material used to make photovoltaic cells, which consist of many crystals unlike single-crystal silicon.

Power Factor of an AC electric power system is the ratio of the real power flowing to the load to the apparent power (assuming voltage and current are in phase), and is a number between 0 and 1, expressed as a percentage. When PF < 1, the electric utility must send more apparent power, thus, charging more than consumed. Hence, correct the power factor to appx. 100% to save money.

Rainwater Harvesting: Collecting and storing rain from structure roofs or other collectors for reuse other than processed for drinking.

Renewable Energy: Energy derived from that which will never run out, such as from wind, sun, rain, rivers, waterways, and heat from the earth, trees and vegetation.

Revenue Streams: From product manufacturers and/ or service companies, on-going regular or periodic (e.g: monthly) sources and amounts of sales revenues.
Examples:

- From carbon credits, such in "Cap and Trade" legislation
- From making business deals with utility companies, clients, & banks
- Continuing local, national international seminars
- Introducing new Trade publication(s) with paid ads.
- From/for municipality clients
- Maintenance and post expiration guarantee services
- Special EMP-mitigation hardware protects clients from catastrophic vulnerability of national electric grid.

ROI = Return on Investment: Net moneys received above an invested sum. ROI = (total present value – original investment)/ (original investment).

Sector Identification: level of renewable energy installation ranging from an individual home or small commercial-office building to municipalities.

SGEMP = System Generated EMP: When gamma and x-rays from a high altitude detonation encounter a satellite in space they excite and release electrons as they penetrate the interior of the system. This phenomena is referred to as system generated electromagnetic pulse (SGEMP) because the accelerated electrons create electromagnetic transients. Systems must be configured with special cables, aperture protection, grounding, and insulating materials in order to survive these transients.

SGEMP impacts space system electronics in three ways. First, x-rays arriving at the spacecraft skin cause an accumulation of electrons there. The electron charge, which is not uniformly distributed on the skin, causes current to flow on the outside of the system. These currents can penetrate into the interior through various apertures, as well as into and through the solar cell power transmission system. Secondly, x-rays can also penetrate the skin to produce electrons on the interior walls of the various compartments. The resulting interior electron currents generate cavity electromagnetic fields that induce voltages on the associated electronics which produce spurious currents that can cause upset or burnout of these systems. Finally, x-rays can produce electrons that find their way directly into signal and power cables to cause extraneous cable currents. These currents are also propagated through the satellite wiring harness.

Shell Company: a public corporation which has discontinued its business but holds cash in its treasury hoping to be acquired by an attractive, growing private company in order to go public.

Shipping Container Homes: Used and otherwise large (8 ft w. x 8.5 ft h. x 10, 20, 24, and 40 ft. long containers left over from unloaded shipping cargo. Some manufacturers have converted them into storage sheds and livable houses.

SID, See Sudden Ionospheric Disturbance

Smart Grid: Electric grid stake-holders have identified the following characteristics or performance features of a smart grid:

- Self-healing from power disturbance events (except EMP)
- Enabling active participation by consumers in demand response
- Operating resiliently against physical and cyber-attack (Questionable)
- Providing power quality for 21st century needs (Questionable)
- Accommodating all generation and storage options

- Enabling new products, services, and markets
- Optimizing assets and operating efficiently (Questionable)

Solar: Energy from the sun shining on collectors whose elevated temperature is used to heat water for pools, hot-water heaters, and other applications..

Solar-Earth Seasons: Since the earth is tilted on an 23.5° axis as it rotates around the sun in a year, four seasons are developed which greatly impact the efficiencies of solar installations. The seasons begin:

- Vernal Equinox, 21 March = day and night of equal length.
Sunrise = location latitude

- Summer Solstice, 21 June = longest daylight of the year.
Sunrise = location latitude + 23.5°

- Autumnal Equinox, 21 Sept. = day and night of equal length
Sunrise = location latitude

- Winter Solstice, 21 December = shortest daylight of the year.
Sunrise = location latitude - 23.5°

Solar Energy: Heat and light radiated from the sun.

Solar Flares: the eruption from active sunspots which produce excess radiation during the solar 11-year sun-spot cycle. Among other disturbances, they impact ionospheric propagation which can disrupt communications, especially in the HF-VHF (3 MHz – 300 MHz) spectrum.

A solar flare is a sudden brightening observed over the Sun's surface or the solar limb, which is interpreted as a large energy release They are often followed by a colossal coronal mass ejection also known as a Corona Mass Ejections (CME). The flare ejects clouds of electrons, ions, and atoms through the corona into space. These clouds typically reach Earth a day or two after the event.

Solar flares affect all layers of the solar atmosphere (photosphere, chromo-sphere, and), when the medium plasma is heated to tens of millions of corona and electrons, protons, and heavier ionisphsare accelerated to near the speed of light. They produce radiation across the electromagnetic spectrumat all wavelengths, from radio waves to gamma rays, although most of the energy exists at frequencies outside the visual range. For this reason the majority of the flares are not visible to the naked eye and must be observed with special instruments.

The frequency of occurrence of solar flares varies, from several per day when the Sun is particularly "active" to less than one every week when the Sun is "quiet", following the 11-year solar cycle. Large flares are less frequent than smaller ones.

Strong solar flares can happen at any time, but are more common during the peak half of the 11-year sunspot cycle, can cause wide regional blackouts to the electric grid. Since they are a very low frequency phenomena, long high-voltage, electric power lines act as pick-up antennas resulting in the possible burnout of transformers at substations since transformers are not designed to handle the very low frequency (nearly DC) currents induced in the windings.

Solar, First Generation: Crystalline Silicon solar represents the most popular with about 85% of the solar installations as of 2010. It is the most expensive and about 20% efficient in converting sunlight into electricity. It is the oldest of the technologies and, typically, has a 25 year guarantee and a 40+ year life expectancy.

Solar Panel: Devices that collect energy from the sun (solar energy). This is usually solar photovoltaic (PV) modules that use solar cells to convert light from the sun into electricity, or solar thermal (heat) collectors that use the sun's energy to heat water or another fluid such as oil or antifreeze.

Solar-P: Energy from the sun shining on cells converted to DC electricity by photovoltaic action. Through inverters, this is then converted to AC electricity for driving electrical loads.

Solar Resource: The amount of solar insulation a site receives, usually measured in $kWh/m^2/day$, which is equivalent to the number of peak sun hours.

Solar, Second Generation, Thin-Film solar is made from amorphous silicon (the least favorable) or popular cadmium tellurium (CdTe) or CIGS in thickness less than a human hair, but mostly formed into rigid, glass-covered panels. Efficiencies are about 11%, but reader beware as this is not the correct measure of better performance (see below).

Solar, Third Generation, Inks and Dyes: mostly in experimental stages and a few to several years away from practical, competitive installations.

Solar Thermal: The process of concentrating sunlight to create high temperatures that are needed to heat fluids, like water (solar hot water) or to vaporize fluid to drive a turbine for electric power generation.

Solar Water Heating: Using the sun's rays to heat an absorber material which transfers the increased temperature to buried pipes carrying water.

Every solar water-heating system features a solar collector that faces the sun to absorb the sun's heat energy. This collector can either heat water directly or heat a "working fluid" that's then used to heat the water. In active solar water-heating systems, a pumping mechanism moves heated water through the building. In passive solar water-heating systems, the water moves by natural convection. In almost all cases, solar water-heating systems work in tandem with conventional gas or electric water-heating systems; the conventional systems operate as needed (night or overcast days) to ensure a reliable supply of heated water.

Stand-Alone System: An autonomous or hybrid photovoltaic system not connected to a grid. May or may not have storage, but most stand-alone systems require batteries or some other form of storage.

Storage: Storage refers to saving surplus electricity produced by a photovoltaic (PV) system. Generally, batteries are used as storage devices.

String: A number of photovoltaic modules or panels interconnected electrically in series to produce the operating voltage required by the load.

Sudden ionospheric disturbance (SID): an abnormally high ionization/plasma density in the D region of the iososphere caused by a solar flare. The SID results in a sudden increase in radio-wave absorption that is most severe in the upper medium frequency (MF) and lower high frequency(HF) ranges, and as a result often interrupts or interferes with telecommunications systems.

When a solar flare occurs on the sun, a blast of intense ultraviolet and x-ray radiation hits the dayside of the Earth after a propagation time of about 8 minutes. This high energy radiation is absorbed by atmospheric particles, raising them to excited states and knocking electrons free in the process of photo-ionization. The low altitude ionospheric layers (D Region and E region) immediately increase in density over the entire dayside. The ionospheric disturbance enhances VLF radio propagation. Scientists on the ground can use this enhancement to detect solar flares; by monitoring the signal strength of a distant VLF transmitter, sudden ionospheric disturbances (SIDs) are recorded and indicate when solar flares have taken place.

Short wave radio waves (in the HF range) are absorbed by the increased particles in the low altitude ionosphere causing a complete blackout of radio communications. This is called a short-wave fading. These fadeouts last for a few minutes to a few hours and are most severe in the equatorial regions where the Sun is most directly overhead. The ionospheric disturbance enhances long wave (VLF) radio propagation. SIDs are observed and recorded by monitoring the signal strength of a distant VLF transmitter.

Equipment: Structure that houses PV modules and that can automatically follow the sun across the sky throughout the day to maximize output.

Utility: The interconnection of electricity generation plants through the transmission and distribution lines to customers. The grid also refers to the interconnection of utilities through the electric transmission and distribution systems.

Volt (V): The amount of force required to drive a steady current of one ampere through a resistance of one ohm. Electrical systems of most homes and offices use 120 volts. (volts - watts/amps) (volts = amperes x resistance)

Watt (W): Electric measurement of power at one point in time, as capacity or demand. For example, light bulbs are classified by wattage. (1,000 watts = 1 kilowatt).

Waveguide beyond cutoff: A condition in waveguides (or any other metal tube including air vents), when a frequency from a potential interfering source, $f_{EMI,}$ somewhat below that corresponding to a half wavelength (of the waveguide or tube), propagates with significant, but predictable attenuation.

A first approximation of the attenuation is, $A_{db} = 30\ l/d$, where l = tube length and d = tube diameter or width. To assure 80 dB shield attenuation, used several places in this book, make l/w greater than 3.

(for details and exact equation, see, *The EMC, Telecom and Computer Encyclopedia Handbook*, third edition, by Don White, emf-emi control, 1999.)

Wind Turbine: is a rotating machine which converts the kinetic energy in wind into mechanical energy. This is then converted to electricity via a turbine or generator.

Appendix C

Ten Tips to Reduce Cost of Electricity up to 60%

Some solar experts say, "For every dollar you put into energy conservation, you can save $3-$5 in the cost of producing your own power."

While going solar is not going to make one wealthy, it is good as an anti-pollutant for the environment, will increase the value of your home, makes us less susceptible to the increasing costs of energy, and not hold USA hostage to foreign oil. As you use our solar calculator, we ask that you think about all the benefits, and not just the bottom line cost and break even. So, it is important in the decision process to identify what you are *trying to optimize* in the first place.

Ten Tips to Reduce Your Electric Bill

First, see remarks on Insulation and "The 3-minute rule," (Part 1). Then, come the 10 tips (Part 2).

Part 1- Insulation

The home insulation status is the largest single factor con-attributing to your electric bill. Fig. 1 shows the five principal areas that must be examined for adequate insulation.

If the house is already built, the options for saving are less. Start by focusing on the heat loss in the attic. Attic fans and extra insulation blown-in or flat fiberglass insulation on the

Fig. 1 House showing the five areas of primary heat and cooling loss.

attic floor to attain an R-30± rating is the first step. For basements used in the Northern latitudes in USA, use a 1-2" solid foam between the concrete blocks and the wall-board or knotty pine or other decorative finish to an R-12 rating. Some new insulating paints are available with an R-4 rating.

Leakage at outside door-to frame regions rank second in loss. Change or modify their insulation. Replace any single-pane windows with at least double pane types. Since this latter expense is usually, at least schedule their replacement over a specified time.

Figure 1 also shows other areas which can then be addressed for insulation upgrading.

The Three-Minute Rule

With one exception, this conservation rule requires some discipline and involves no additives. The rule states.

"If you are the only person in a room, watching TV, using electric lights, operating an electric device, and the like, turn off all items if you will be gone for more than three minutes. Exceptions may be a computer under certain conditions (put in a sleep mode instead) or something which may require a reset time or re-operative conditions. If only for a "few minutes", do not turn off and on, as there is some life-expectancy stress in surge, unless a surge suppressor is used in the power line.

The benefits from *the three-minutes rule* may result in your electric bill savings from 8% to 22% (maybe more), if you do nothing else. Thus, in a typical $150/month electric bill, you may save $240±/year.

Part 2 – 10 Tips for Electric Power Conservation

Electrical power is measured in watts and kW; 1 kilowatt = 1,000 watts. Cumulative power over time is measured in units of energy or kW-hours = kiloWatts x hours.

1. Hot-Water Heater (HWH).

The HWH consumes about 10% of your electric load. Reduce its thermostat to about 110° from a typical 125° setting to save wasted money. Search around the house for old blankets and towels to wrap around the heater tank and secure for improved insulation. Or, buy a preformed blanket made specifically for this purpose.

Keep the HWH circuit breaker "off" until 30± minutes before you need hot water for the clothes washer, dishwasher or for personal showering. When you are finished, switch off the breaker.

2. Air Conditioning and Heating Savings

Set the AC to 78° F or somewhat higher in the summer to save electricity. Turn it a bit higher at night or more (say 82°) when away for ½ day or longer. Setting the AC much higher to save more electricity is not advised because of the danger of mold buildup in the Southern coastal states.

When heat pumps are used for winter home heating (even for oil, gas or coal furnaces), set the daytime room temperature to 68°-72°. During the night, upon going to bed, reset the thermostat to 65°. Actually, most new homes in the past 10-15 years have a programmable thermostat. Thus, the different settings can be done to cover a month or a season. Honeywell seems to be the leader in this sector, and they are carried at both Home Depot and Lowes.

3. Washer and Dryer

The Washer–Dryer represents a large electrical load. The washer costs about $0.04 per load for electricity and about $0.12/load for water. For hot water, the cost is $0.16 + about $0.30 for heated water = roughly $0.40/load. EPA says the average family uses 7.6 loads/wk ($13/month). The big saving is to use fewer loads and at cooler (or cold) water temperature. Have you ever tested to see how well clothes get cleaned using cold water? You may be surprised.

The dryer is the big electrical load. The average drying load consumes roughly about $0.34 in electricity For the average EPA loads of 392/year, the dryer cost $133/year to run. Here, consider some air drying like on wood racks or close lines if no home deed restrictions.

In summary the washer-dryer combination costs about $0.75/load or $295/yr. Cutting down the number of loads, using cold water washing, and drying on racks will save much, if not most, of this cost.

4. Dishwasher

Most of the savings here is not to run the dishwasher unless it is fully loaded with dirty dishes. Small loads, or dishes needed again soon, can be hand washed and placed in a drainage rack to dry. The cost will also be reduced if the hot-water heater was set to 110° F instead of 125° as mentioned above.

5. Pool and Irrigation Pump Motors

Sprinkler or lawn irrigation systems use 1-1.5 horse-power motors and pool pumps also use about 1-1.5 HP motors. A pool heater, when applicable, should use roof solar or butane gas heat) since an electrical heater is very expensive to operate and could double your electric bill (depending on your latitude).

One horsepower in a motor or pump rating corresponds to 746 watts. If you made the mistake of buying a heat pump for your pool, sell it and replace it with a rooftop solar heating or gas heater with the proceeds of the electric heater. You will save big time and use the pool longer as most users quickly learn how expensive it is to electrically-heat a pool.

Many owners will run a pool pump for 4-6 hours in the summer (to combat algae), and 2-3 hours in the winter if in the South (zero in the North as the pool was winterized. If these numbers are reduced to 3 hours in the summer and one in the winter, approximately 60 kWh will be saved in the summer and 45 kWh in the winter. This approximates 630 hours/year, or 950 kWh for a 1.5 HP motor. At an average cost of 13 cents/kWh, the owner in the South will save about $122/year. The Savings in the Northern latitudes is far less.

6. Incandescent Light Bulbs

Traditional incandescent light-bulb filaments are subjected to inrush stress current thereby limiting their life expectancy. Incandescent bulbs from 25 watts to 100 watts can be replaced by the same size fluorescent bulbs which produce comparable light intensity for 25% of the electricity consumption. Fluorescent bulbs also have 10 times longer life expectancy. This is a very compelling reason to replace many if not all incandescent bulbs in the house.

For example, suppose the family room and other areas collectively use eight incandescent bulbs totaling 600 watts for six hours a day. The cost is 600 watts x 6 hrs x $0.13/kW x .001 (kW/watt) = $0.47/day. If you used fluorescent bulbs, the cost savings would be 0.75 x $0.47 = $0.35/day = $10.53/month = $126/year.

The average cost of an incandescent bulb approximates $0.35 and the cost for its fluorescent mate is roughly $1.50 or four times more. However, the life expectancy of the incandescent bulb is less than 1,000 hours, while that of the fluorescent exceeds 5,000 hours. Thus, their replacement costs per lifetimes are somewhat better for fluorescence. Meanwhile the user enjoys one fourth the electricity consumption. (Ed. Note: I have observed about eight fluorescent bulb burn outs in a four period. Thus the life expectancy is questioned).

7. High Duty-Cycle Appliances

Duty cycle means the percentage of the time in use. If the house has two refrigerators, such as one in the garage or for outside patio use, consider disconnecting the outside one as it is expensive to use in the summer (it is also much hotter outside than in the house). Set the kitchen refrigerator to warmer temperatures if it is at or near the coldest setting, which is not needed.

The heating and A/C system duty cycle is also high in the summer and winter, but low in the spring and fall. It was addressed in Subsection 2 above.

8. Low Duty-Cycle Appliances

If the oven and burners are electrical, not much can be done to reduce the electric bill, other than to turn them off when finished using. These are the big kitchen loads, so don't heat up until you are ready to use. The microwave oven shuts off when a selected period for cooking is over. So when the MW can do the lighter cooking, us it in favor of the oven and burners. Remember, don't turn on the MW oven with no load placed therein as damage may result or keystroke life shortened.

Turn off the coffee maker after use or put it on a timer. Some people let it run for hours; then, turn it off.

A ceiling fan takes about 100 watts or about 2-5% of an A/C load. Run one or more it at low speed, if needed. This can reduce some of the A/C duty cycle. This also keeps hot food from cooling on the counters.

9. Den and Office

Most computers today are laptops (15-45 watts; desk-tops consume 60-250 watts) and consume about four times the power of a desktop computer. The LCD screen in a laptop consumes most of the power, typically about 30 watts.

Many laptop computer owners add a 19-23 inch LCD external screen as it is easier to read than smaller print. The power consumption is correspondingly more (roughly 50 watts). Modern computers have internal "sleep" modes when not in use for a while (they power down to 3-5 watts), which time is internally settable. Thus, when leaving a computer for a half hour or longer, place it in the sleep mode. Turn it off during the night when not in use.

Supporting printers, copiers, scanners and the like should be turned off when not in use. Some standby modes waste power.

10. Outside Lighting

Nearly all outdoor lighting should be put on timers which cost less than $10 each. With the new fluorescent light bulbs, where appropriate (flame shaped decorative incandescent bulbs do not yet have a fluorescent counterpart), the cost to operate outside lighting be-comes 25% of the older incandescent bulbs.

Finally, solar outdoor lights tend to become a waste of money as the batteries have to be replaced each year at $2 apiece or $4 per lamp. Low-voltage AC lighting is more cost effective since the bulbs last much longer than the battery life of solar outdoor lighting.

The Bottom Line:

Of course, if you are already doing many of the above electricity-saving conservation steps, your options to save will be considerably less. Otherwise, when all the dollar savings above are added up for the typical $150/month electric bill, they approximate $65-$80/month or $850±/year. This is equal to 47±% savings. Note: this is also roughly equal to about what you would save if you invested in a solar rooftop electric system saving equal to 50% of your electric bill. And, except for the insulation cost mentioned above, it costs you nothing except, possibly, a change in yourself discipline attitude about conservation.

Made in the USA
Lexington, KY
13 April 2015